THE ART OF

D0355487

THE ART OF STILLNESS

·

THE THEATRE PRACTICE OF TADASHI SUZUKI

Paul Allain

First published 2003 by PALGRAVE MACMILLAN™
175 Fifth Avenue, New York, N.Y. 10010 and
Houndmills, Basingstoke, Hampshire, England RG21 6XS.
Companies and representatives throughout the world.

PALGRAVE MACMILLAN is the global academic imprint of the Palgrave Macmillan division of St. Martin's Press, LLC and of Palgrave Macmillan Ltd. Macmillan® is a registered trademark in the United States, United Kingdom and other countries. Palgrave is a registered trademark in the European Union and other countries.

ISBN 1-4039-6170-0

Library of Congress Cataloguing-in-Publication Data available from the Library of Congress.

First published in the United Kingdom in 2002 by Methuen Publishing Limited.

First PALGRAVE MACMILLAN paperback edition: May 2003.

10 9 8 7 6 5 4 3 2 1

Printed in the United States of America.

For the memory of Don, for Augustine and for Jo

CONTENTS

•

ACKNOWLEDGEMENTS

•

I would like to thank the Arts and Humanities Research Board, Goldsmiths College and the University of Kent at Canterbury for generously allowing me the time and opportunity to write this book. I would also like to thank the Japan Foundation for their grant to Methuen to assist with publication costs and the Sasakawa Foundation for funding a research trip to Japan.

The following have all assisted me, either in thinking through the content or by offering their time or other resources and skills: Peter Bailie; Fran Barbe; Jon Brokering (for the best sort of informal collaboration); Antje Diedrich; all at Methuen, but especially Michael Earley who was the original commissioning editor, Eleanor Knight, and Eugenie Boyd for her enthusiasm, insight and curiosity; Robert Gordon; Jen Harvie; Peter Hulton; Mamoru Iriguchi; Joanna Labon; Dick McCaw; Katie Mitchell; Patrick Morris for his incisive mind and the benefit of his rich experience; Ichiro Nakayama; Sophie Nield; John Nobbs and Jacqui Carroll of Frank for their warm help in Toga, their interviews, copious material including photographs, their enthusiasm, and fruitful discussions; Ikuko Saito for thoughtful and essential assistance with my second trip to Toga; Yoshiko Sakai; Richard Schechner; Simon Shepherd, and Wlodzimierz Staniewski for first taking me up the mountains to Toga. I would also like to thank Ellen Lauren for patiently giving me her precious time for interviews, for her generous contribution to some of the ideas in this book and for allowing me to observe her teaching. Kelly Maurer also kindly let me watch her teach and I am immensely grateful to her and to Will Bond, Patrick Morris, Tom Nelis and Kameron Steele for interviews which were conducted in New York and in Derry in 1996.

Chapter Three is based loosely on my article 'Suzuki Training' published in the *Drama Review*, Vol. 42, No. 1, T157, Spring 1998, copyright New York University and the Massachusetts Institute of Technology. I would like to thank Kath Ratcliff for modelling the 'Suzuki method' photographs.

NOTE

It is a hotly debated subject, but Japanese names are given here in a Western order with surnames last, rather than the system native to Japan – e.g. Tadashi Suzuki and not Suzuki Tadashi. The Western order has predominated in previous studies of Suzuki's work (including his own book *The Way of Acting*) and is therefore more widely known and recognised, which explains my hesitant preference for this book. Awareness of the implications of this ordering is growing (e.g. *Drama Review*, Spring 2000, follows the Japanese system). Some sources cited adopt the Japanese model so inconsistencies might occur in a few references. Similarly, I use the spelling *noh* throughout, though there are several ways of writing this, creating further inconsistencies. I give *kabuki* a lower-case 'k' and place it in italics throughout, but there are, of course, different ways of writing this word.

ONE

•

INTRODUCING SUZUKI

Tadashi Suzuki has played multiple roles for over forty years, including that of director of a large number of performances, many of which have attracted acclaim around the world. His creation and theorisation of his training system – the Suzuki method – has transformed comprehension of the performer's vocation and the processes of preparation. He continues to gather international plaudits, which he first received in the early 1970s, the decade after he began his theatrical explorations as a student. Such recognition has even resulted, to name one illuminating example, in his receipt in 1994 of the Order of Art and Cultural Merit of France. Since his beginnings in Tokyo, he has developed his practice in various urban, rural and semi-rural sites throughout Japan, including the remote mountain village of Toga which he has called his and his group's home. Throughout his career Suzuki has integrated Eastern and Western sources, the urban and the rural, as well as the contemporary and the traditional. His life and work are full of such doublings. This opening chapter will introduce some of the characters and influences encountered on his long and varied journey. It will also establish how Suzuki arrived where he is today.

Phrases like 'the Suzuki method', 'the Suzuki Company' and the title of this book all endorse the singular accomplishments of one man, but Suzuki's practice is inevitably the result of several collaborations. The playwright Minoru Betsuyaku worked with him throughout the 1960s, before Suzuki started to generate his own *mises-en-scène* and dramaturgy. This was also before Betsuyaku pursued a more solitary career and became one of Japan's most successful playwrights, with over sixty plays to his name. Ikuko Saito has collaborated since the 1960s, first as actress and then as administrator, being Managing Director of SCOT (the Suzuki Company of Toga) and General Secretary of JPAC (the Japan Performing Arts Centre), SCOT's sister organisation. Suzuki has worked with the world-renowned architect Arata Isozaki for over twenty years in order to realise his vision of appropriate sites for his theatre events. Actor Tsutamori Kosuke has performed with Suzuki since the days of the Waseda Little Theatre in the late 1960s and is just one of many company members who have played out the director's dreams, several of them over decades rather than years. The actress Kayoko Shiraishi was the most celebrated of these. Initially untrained, Suzuki shaped her as much as she formulated and put into practice his vision. Even the mayor of Toga has been an accomplice for decades. He has underpinned the large-scale international festivals and Suzuki's material expansion in the tiny village with financial and infrastructural support. Suzuki does not hide the contribution each of these has made. I also hope to do them justice, even if I consider their achievements only in Suzuki's terms rather than in their own right. After all, it is Suzuki who has amalgamated their and his resources with such substantial consequences for contemporary theatre. But what are the ramifications of these collaborations?

Suzuki's vision has entered discourses and practices world-wide. His most recognised contribution has been his insight into how and for what end the actor might be trained. His rigorous approach to exercising the performer's body–mind* uses fixed positions and deceptively simple locomotive movements. This physicality is extended into the voice by linking action to the breath and the text. For some, it is an answer to the vagaries of psychologically dominated acting and the constraints of realism. For others, it provides a daily routine which hones mental abilities – concentration, rhythmic sensitivity and spatial awareness – as much as it coaches muscles. Many find it refreshingly challenging regarding the vexed issues of discipline, individualism and creativity in training, and the role of the teacher or trainer. It certainly demands an authoritative teaching

---

* By body–mind I mean the body's integrated psycho-physical infrastructure which many training methods explore, most recognisably the approaches of Konstantin Stanislavski and Jerzy Grotowski.

manner. Whatever the attractions or detractions, Suzuki training has spread around the world and continues to be influential and challenging. These issues will be examined in passing in the next chapter and in detail in Chapter Four.

Suzuki is also recognised for the emphasis he has placed on the need for companies to create a home for their theatre activities. He has followed this process through somewhat extravagantly, resulting in the building of several theatres of differing dimensions and styles in locations throughout Japan. He is an extremely successful entrepreneur, who operates on a large scale with multimillion-pound budgets. Yet this business acumen is strongly rooted in cultural rather than commercial priorities and a socially committed artistic vision. His longest standing and most recognised material achievement is the transformation of the small village of Toga-mura (*mura* means village in Japanese) into an international theatre centre. This is in Toyama prefecture (a prefecture is the rough equivalent of a British county) on the opposite side of Honshu island from Tokyo. There he has hosted annual festivals with performances from the likes of Robert Wilson and Tadeusz Kantor. Without being sentimental, his participation in the village's cultural life has transformed and possibly saved this small community from extinction. The establishment of SCOT's residence has not, however, prevented him from pursuing projects further afield, and he has also developed extensive arts complexes closer to Tokyo, in Mito City and Shizuoka, as demonstrated in Chapter Three. All these sites have fed his aspiration to decentralise artistic activity in Japan, which historically has been concentrated in larger urban centres and in Tokyo.

The global influence of the constructions themselves is inevitably partly limited by the fixity of architecture and the specificity of their use. Several of Isozaki's larger-scale overseas projects, such as the Team Disney building in Florida (1990), are widely recognised as challenging postmodern paradigms. But Suzuki's collaboration with Isozaki has made a compelling contribution to the perplexed issue of space in contemporary performance. Their theatre buildings attempt to be 'open' and 'sacred' and foster a sense of a company home, concepts that Suzuki has articulated in his book *The Way of Acting*. Isozaki has designed and built both intimate and epic spaces within the same arts complexes and unified these by technical devices and linking concepts. These are demonstrably and overtly public, and yet singularly tailored for Suzuki's needs and wishes. The combined accessibility and flexibility of staging that Suzuki also prioritises are fundamental for any theatre director today. Chapter Three reveals how such principles have been put into practice.

Aesthetically, Suzuki and Isozaki have tried to integrate traditional Japanese spatial values with European ones, in particular those found in ancient Greek and Shakespearean theatres. They blend up-to-date technologies with lessons from the past, when theatres were located outdoors or were open to the elements. Through a symbiotic relationship between theatre and the natural environment, they have sought to revitalise the spectator's way of perceiving the event itself. Suzuki's desire to create 'sacred' spaces and raise theatre above mundanity has been enhanced by siting buildings in out-of-the-way and rural surroundings. Yet, as the example of Mito shows, he can also adapt some of these ideals to an industrial city.

Japan's main religions of Shinto and Buddhism possess intrinsic links to nature, recalling that this was an agricultural nation until modernisation in the twentieth century. Suzuki may be drawing on this, but more concretely he is remembering the premodern* roots of theatre and in particular *noh*, the classical Japanese dance-theatre form that originated in the fourteenth century. He wants to bring 'the gods' (*kami*) back into Japanese theatre culture, even if in a reconstructed and more personal form. These spirits were displaced by the rational and political slant and the realism of *shingeki*,† on which I elaborate later in this chapter. David Goodman has described this erstwhile break from the spiritual in his *Japanese Drama and Culture in the 1960s: The Return of the Gods*. Suzuki was part of the 1960s counterculture against this rupture, as Goodman points out.

A key concept in Suzuki's theatre is 'animal energy'. In broad terms, he wishes to conjure in performance the equivalent of the gods of *kabuki* and *noh*, but he uses this more 'pagan' notion to

---

* Premodern means pre-1868 and the Meiji reformation, when Japan opened up to the influences of Westernisation and modernisation.

† 'New theatre' is a direct translation of *shingeki* which denotes a Japanese theatre style imitative of Western European naturalism. I discuss this in more detail later in the chapter.

describe his re-rooting. His 'gods' are not culturally specific or anthropologically modelled, but energetic and physiological. The performer has a sense of speaking through the gods on stage, but the deities' nature is not prescribed. The audience perceives this as an altered mood, a precise external focus and a physical intensity. Suzuki's chosen mode of performing is energised, forward-facing and combative. The performer is exposed and vulnerable on stage in this highly charged state. Rather than attempting to suppress these qualities or mask or eradicate them with relaxation techniques, Suzuki proposes that they should be cultivated and harnessed. The training helps the performer come to recognise and control this process. Specific use of the space enhances animal energy, revealing the individuals rather than hiding them behind scenery or props, showing them metaphorically in 'dialogue' with the gods.

The concept of animal energy recognises an essential characteristic of performing – the need for the performer to survive on stage rather than 'die'. This is, of course, the recognised term for someone who fails to hold an audience's attention, familiar even in Shakespeare's day. Encouraging animalistic sensitivity shifts the performance away from being an aesthetic entertainment and towards a transgressive interactive event. As self-appointed representatives, the performers play out human concerns and fears. They become partners with the audience in a social ritual in a shared 'sacred' space, where the presence of the gods is acknowledged by both parties, however individually these gods are perceived. This is similar to Jerzy Grotowski's 'total act' of public sacrifice which the audience witnesses.* The spectators almost actively 'participate' in the event through the vitality of their

---

* Suzuki has been labelled the 'Japanese Grotowski', which in part shows the esteem in which he is held. In 1971 he had reviewed *Towards a Poor Theatre* for a Japanese journal and there are obvious correlations in their focus on the physical actions of the performer. But this designation reveals a narrow Western perspective that he has continually tried to challenge and such comparisons are finally misleading. Suzuki was more interested than Grotowski in textual adaptation and culturally diverse referencing. Their contact in the 1970s, in Western Europe, Poland and when Grotowski briefly visited the WLT in Japan in 1973, came at a time when Grotowski was abandoning the spectator–actor relationship to focus on the work of the performer. Suzuki, however, has continued his investigations into the public theatre event itself.

physical responses, which affect the performer's impulses in a continuously interactive cycle.

With such values, Suzuki's performances have created ripples around the world at various festivals, particularly in the 1970s and 1980s. *The Trojan Women,* starring Shiraishi, was the most celebrated of these. It shocked audiences with its brutality and anguish, contained and channelled by the rigorous discipline of the Waseda Little Theatre's actors, as SCOT was then known. Shiraishi was considered to have embodied Suzuki's vision, much as Ryszard Cieslak exemplified Grotowski's. For this and her charged stage presence, she was applauded internationally.

These performances led to Suzuki's invitations to teach at several American universities. Many Western performers also trekked to the remote mountains of Japan to train during WLT/SCOT's extensive international workshops from 1983 onwards. This followed on from the WLT's own daily training programme, which they maintained during their annual two-month visits to the mountains from 1976 to 1980. Opening up the training in Toga, combined with the overseas touring of Suzuki's idiosyncratic but affecting interpretations of Greek dramas, led to major collaborative projects in America and Australia. The most prominent of these were *The Bacchae* (1981), *The Tale of Lear* (1988) and *The Chronicle of Macbeth* (1992), the first two mixing Japanese and American casts. These synthesised a range of source texts that included contemporary and ancient material, Eastern and Western influences and sometimes two languages.

Such juxtapositions and intermingling were initially contained by a 'collage' style that exploited irony and quotation, detailed in Chapter Five. Suzuki is often described as a consummate postmodern artist, in spite of the complex problematics of this labelling. The questionable genealogy of postmodernism in Japan is epitomised by two Japanese theorists' symbolic 'boast' to Jacques Derrida that 'there is no need for deconstruction as there has never been a construct in Japan'.[1] In Suzuki's performances, high culture is undermined by scatological or functional moments of action. One character recites classical poetry as another slurps noodles. Sentimental pop songs are played with a sense of sophisticated irony. We should not approach Suzuki's adaptations of classics with too much reverence. He playfully and constantly reiterates human materiality and mundanity, however sacred the context. Suzuki's emphasis on the feet reminds us that we all need the ground to stand on and that we all turn eventually to dust.

In a similar vein, Suzuki occasionally reveals an almost self-denigrating, or at least diffident, relationship to his performances. He often jumped on to the outdoor amphitheatre stage in Toga with microphone in hand to chat to the audience as soon as a piece had finished. (This can be seen at the end of a video recording of *Clytemnestra*, which shows scant time for the spectator to absorb the production's impact.) This book does not give any insights into Suzuki's personality other than what is revealed through passing analysis of such behaviour, together with his theories, practices and writing (which also show the great seriousness with which he takes his chosen *métier*). Neither does it attempt an investigation of Suzuki's character, though this would certainly divulge intriguing traits.

The Way of Acting is perhaps the best key to Suzuki's personality. It may disclose how his mind works but reveals almost nothing about his performances. It collates five essays, extracts from an unpublished diary and the text of *Clytemnestra*. The whole ranges from a humorous discussion of white radishes (a 'ham' actor is called a 'radish' actor in Japan) to sociological concerns about the survival of both theatre and other communities, peppered with illuminating but transitory insights into his processes. The social function of theatre permeates the book. Suzuki's concerns lie beyond the purely personal or artistic: 'Where I want to go with theatre is to approach and deal with problems or issues which cannot be solved by individuals in their daily lives.'[2] In his writing, Suzuki's humanity fuses appealingly with his demanding rigour.

Suzuki's capacity and desire to explicate his work and theories has meant that principles of his theatre practice have reached a wider audience beyond spectators alone. Few may have seen his performances, yet central tenets of his vision, such as animal energy, have gained widespread recognition. He has published twelve books in Japan and central sections of his major writings have been published and republished in English. His writing style is direct, clear and light-hearted, opening up Japanese performance culture to Western readers in the way that Eugenio Barba has elucidated Asian performance techniques through his International School of Theatre Anthropology (ISTA).* Suzuki is less methodical and more personal in his tone than Barba. Barba's theories (defined broadly as Theatre Anthropology) are intentionally acultural and asocial, focusing on pre-expressivity† and the extra-daily, or those movements and behaviour that lie outside a daily register. Suzuki, on the other hand, has carefully considered the cultural implications of his practical investigations, which draw on daily and extra-daily movements. This focus is perhaps inevitable, given his aspiration to probe his own native sources, in particular the performance traditions of *noh* and *kabuki* with their long and complex histories.

Suzuki's questioning has been compounded by ongoing uncertainty about the survival of such forms in the face of competition from sophisticated technologies and mediated modes of human interaction such as the Internet provides. Japan is clearly a nation of extensive innovation, and premodern forms like *noh* sit awkwardly alongside these. Suzuki's intracultural‡ introspection is skewed through the prism of cross-cultural casting and international collaboration, propagated by the diversity of performance texts with which he engages. His practical and theoretical sources and reference points are eclectic and accessible, but rooted precisely in Japanese traditions and conditions.

---

* There are other connections between the two. In *The Paper Canoe*, Barba repeatedly cites the Kanze brothers, master exponents of *noh* theatre, who have collaborated with Suzuki. Hisao Kanze, who worked the most with Suzuki, was reputedly the best post-Second Word War *noh* actor and was designated an Important Intangible Cultural Asset. This is the highest status an artist can achieve and is an honour endowed by the state. Suzuki directed Hideo in a *noh* piece, *Uto*, for the Theatre Olympics in Shizuoka in 1999.

† Eugenio Barba's almost biological emphasis endorses performance analysis that focuses on what is happening before (but also at the same time as) a performer expresses themselves. How they stand, the space the body occupies and even involuntary physical processes such as the pulse rate all affect the performer's communication, in spite of what they intend to show. This is the pre-expressive.

‡ 'Intracultural' is how the Asian theatre expert James Brandon has identified cultural introspection like Suzuki's that feeds on an artist's own indigenous sources. See his 'Contemporary Japanese Theatre: Intraculturalism and Interculturalism' in *The Dramatic Touch of Difference*, Erika Fischer-Lichte, Josephine Riley and Michael Gissenwehrer (eds), Gunter Narr Verlag, Tubingen, 1990.

Suzuki's writing and practice have made an invaluable contribution to one central theoretical field of late twentieth-century performance – interculturalism. Interculturalism grew out of the ideological, social and racial aspirations of multiculturalism in the 1970s which filtered into artistic practices. The search for parity and harmony was epitomised (albeit questionably) in multiracial, multicultural groups, such as Peter Brook's troupe in France and productions like his *Mahabharata* (1985). This then led to the more realistic aspirations and negotiations of interculturalism.

Interculturalism accepts separate voices and distinct cultural positions without demanding integration or harmony. Instead, it prioritises disjunction, fragmentation and contestation, having affinity with postmodernism. Performance struggles to adhere strictly to ideological positions for it must often pursue the pragmatism of what works within given constraints, be they economic, social or artistic. Interculturalism has been useful for several reasons: for encouraging and exposing such gaps and inconsistencies; for informing theoretical debates on the ethics of practical engagements; and for elucidating a heritage of borrowing and cross-cultural inspiration. This ran throughout the twentieth century and is clearly identifiable from as early as the 1920s in artists like Antonin Artaud and W. B. Yeats. Such a movement continues in this century with Suzuki. All these artists still generate intercultural debates.

Interculturalism has only a generalised meaning that embraces diverse practices and artists. It represents a way of thinking that might, but only might, be overt in performance. Some practitioners, like Mexican-American Guillermo Gomez-Pena, consciously and artfully play with and exploit racial stereotyping and cultural assumptions, as Suzuki has also done. Others approach interculturalism less wittingly. What is certain is that the redefinition of terms such as multiculturalism, fusion, intraculturalism and interculturalism, by the likes of Richard Schechner and Patrice Pavis, has meant that theatre artists can no longer work in ignorance of post-colonial and global perspectives. They must acknowledge questions posed by the cultural complexity and intermingling which the move towards globalisation has produced, even if they do not specifically intend to answer these in practice. In his writings and collaborations as well as in his productions, Suzuki has contributed cogently to such issues.

Another crucial advancement in the attempt to define the theoretical parameters of intercultural practice has been the devalorisation of Eurocentric and Western positions and the promotion of alternative viewpoints. Rather than responding purely from within our own cultural position, we should attempt to operate transculturally and assess how something works or is depicted within its own terms and field. Reception of performance is always essentially an act of translation, but the anthropological notion emic* is useful for guiding analyses of practice, reminding us not to theorise from a narrow or fixed cultural position. We should be able to move between interior and exterior perspectives, without either one dominating. The necessity of attempting to get inside theatre practices (rather than standing aloof as an observer/spectator) is central to this book.

The interrelationship between emic and etic perspectives are blurred by Suzuki's deliberately eclectic practice. His *œuvre* and theoretical stance are provocative and challenging when viewed from the Western perspective which this book inevitably takes. As an Asian artist drawing on European traditions and contemporary materials, he reverses familiar positions and debates derived from Western outlooks. His views have circulated widely in Western academic and professional theatre spheres, not just through his tangible practical influence (which this book will focus on) but also through the questions posited by his intercultural theorising. However much he began as a Japanese 'underground' theatre director, Suzuki appears today as neither definitively Western nor Asian, operating on multiple levels in multiple spaces.

Although Suzuki has realised few of the achievements outlined alone (except perhaps his writing, though his publications in English depend, of course, on diligent translation), he must take the credit for masterminding all operations. Collaboration is arguably harder

---

* James Brandon has utilised the anthropological terms 'emic' and 'etic' to help define positions of engagement with other, perhaps foreign, cultures. Etic means drawing on a vocabulary and perspective which we bring with us from the outside, while emic means using that which arises from inside a particular culture.

than solitary flight. Suzuki is a master juggler of projects and people, knowing how to channel the energies of his partners. Where did he gain such abilities? I will briefly investigate the primary factors that shaped Suzuki's artistic practice and outline the context in which he has operated in order to attempt to answer this question.

Inspirational Sources

Tadashi Suzuki was born in 1939. He grew up in a country that was adjusting to the humiliation of defeat after the Second World War and was negotiating the tension between sustaining valued traditions and coping with modernisation and Westernisation. After over two centuries of closure, Japan's openness to the West began in the Meiji period at the end of the nineteenth century, but the American occupation after the Second World War saw a much more rapid transformation. Initially, this accelerated transition period led to intense financial struggle, with many suffering hardship after the devastation witnessed in cities like Nagasaki and Hiroshima where the atom bombs were dropped. Characters in Suzuki's productions, such as tramps, 'broken' old people and economic victims like the Little Match Girl of Betsuyaku's play of that name, personified this reality. Suzuki's vision that theatre should portray human struggle and 'wretchedness' was rooted in *actual* poverty and suffering. This outlook incongruously lasted throughout the economic dynamism and prosperity that later followed. It still governs his work today.

Suzuki's use of framing devices that surround and recontextualise the texts within his productions may have originated in his observation of the rapid conversion that Japan underwent from post-war poverty to Asian 'tiger' and one of the world's most prosperous nations. Change and duality were also evident in the co-existence and shifts between Eastern and Western in Japan. These positions were contested most fervently during Suzuki's late youth and in the early years of his practice as a director during his studies at Waseda University between 1958 and 1964. Thomas Havens has observed that 'Japanese artists during the past quarter-century have grappled ingeniously with the question of national identity in the most international age in Japanese history [. . .] remarkable public preoccupation, especially in the 1960s and 1970s, with what it means to be Japanese'.[3] This trend even led to the coining of a new term, *Nihonjinron.** Such troubled introspective self-analysis might explain Suzuki's recurring metaphor of all the world as a hospital, with nurses attending to sick characters in crisis (like Lear in *The Tale of Lear*) and wheelchair-bound patients. Suzuki frames and adapts because his reality was itself undergoing a process of transformation and continual self-examination.

It is impossible to pinpoint such connections precisely, but this social complexity must have stimulated Suzuki's fascination with the investigative nature of drama. Rapid transformations such as internationalisation encourage self-consciousness, as nations interrogate their past identity and forge new ones. The Western media have revelled in the spectacle of Japan's imitative youth groups, such as 'rockers' jiving in Tokyo's parks, as they seek respite from constraining uniformity. Playful framing devices, multi-referencing and metatheatrical techniques followed the intensive influx of Western playtexts and philosophies into Japanese culture in the 1960s. This coalesced with a widely felt sense of the fossilisation of native traditional forms and *shingeki*. The 'gods' might have been present once in *noh*, but for Suzuki, as for *noh* performer Hisao Kanze, they were then being sacrificed on the altars of expediency and commercialism. The melting pot of new inspiration and the re-evaluation of the old propelled artists like Suzuki to reinterpret and recontextualise accepted values. Drama's transformative potential yielded space to explore Japanese history, traditions and identity (or *Nihonjinron*).

Yasunari Takahashi has written informatively about the early period of Suzuki's evolution as a theatre director in a succinct overview in *Alternative Japanese Drama*. He stresses that the most significant developments in Japanese theatre happened towards the second half of the 1960s, as they did in Europe, with which he makes comparisons. He describes the specifically local stimuli that precipitated the formation of new ideologies and artistic concerns in Japan. These include the demonstrations and riots against renewal of the US–Japan Mutual Security Treaty (Ampo) in 1960, when the

* This translates loosely as 'theories of Japaneseness' and defines a national obsession with cultural self-definition and exploration.

progressives and conservatives came to loggerheads. The original treaty had been signed in 1951. Left-wing groups, including students, artists and workers, fought to prevent the renewal in order to further Japan's democratisation and independence from America. Japan's Hobson's Choice fell broadly along the lines of either cultivating their alliance with America (and consequently continuing to accept US military bases and, potentially, nuclear weapons on Japanese soil) or the building of allegiances with the Soviet Union. Many students and younger activists advocated non-alignment outside these Cold War polarities. There followed the huge mobilisation of a mostly dissenting public on a scale akin to America's anti-Vietnam protests later in the 1960s. Widespread disruption to campus life became a feature of this decade.

Takahashi locates Suzuki at the centre of these developments. He lists the dynamic appearance of several 'talents' and companies in 1966 and 1967, including the Waseda Little Theatre, the Free Theatre, the Gallery, the Situation Theatre and, in 1969, the Modern Man's Theatre (co-founded by Yukio Ninagawa). As with Suzuki, some of these groups had been in existence for a while, but in the late 1960s there was a clear sense of the emergence of a powerful new movement. At the same time, *butoh* became more established. Initially led by dancer/choreographer Tatsumi Hijikata, it began as a critique of contemporary culture's politics and excesses in the 1950s and 1960s. These dances turned attention back on to the simplicity of the stripped-bare, almost animal body and the dark recesses of the Japanese psyche. *Butoh*'s white figures recalled the ghosts of *noh* and brought the gods back into the theatre, much as *angura** did. In 1972, the standing of *butoh* was reinforced by the foundation of the

---

* *Angura* is the Japanese term for underground theatre, which was predominant in the 1960s and 1970s. In his doctoral dissertation on Suzuki's work, 'Suzuki Tadashi: Innovator of Japanese Theatre', Yukihiro Goto points out that *angura* is a pejorative term coined as a way of delegitimising and marginalising the alternative movement by calling it underground. The term 'underground' is more familiar in an East European context where, under Communism, it implied broad popular support and was used positively to contrast with official culture which was considered partisan and moribund. See David Goodman's *Japanese Drama and Culture in the 1960s: The Return of the Gods* for an account of how Japanese experimental theatre came to focus once again on potential spiritual dimensions within performance.

first *butoh* group, Dairakudakan, led by Maro Akaji, who had worked with The Situation Theatre. Challenges to the orthodoxy occurred on an artistic as much as a political level.

Takahashi states that these emerging practitioners (labelled the 'first generation' of innovators) subscribed to 'a "revolution of theatre" that would be total and far-reaching, aiming at no less than a revolution of the consciousness of the audience'.[4] These groups became recognised as part of the *angura* movement, known later as 'little theatre' because of the small and non-commercial scale on which they operated. While the state was building large structures to contain and support the traditional forms of *kabuki* and *bunraku* (the National Theatre for the Performing Arts opened in 1966 in Tokyo), other groups were moving out of confinement into liminal spaces, some with portable tent structures. The most notable of these were Centre 68/69 (known more familiarly as the Black Tent Group/*Kuro* or *Kokushoku Tento*, whose chief operator was Sato Makoto) and the Situation Theatre with their red tent, led by Juro Kara.

The loss of the left wing's cause created a crisis of confidence. The Ampo conflict had become a symbolic as well as actual battle, representing distinctly polarised values, much as the fall of the Berlin Wall in 1989 symbolised for many the end of a system of beliefs and the embrace of capitalism. For theatre artists, it meant a breach with the *shingeki* movement. In its direct lifting of socialist realist principles from the Russian context, *shingeki* had always been associated with left-wing politics which had now proved wanting. The younger artists sought alternatives because the 'new theatre' seemed old – redundant, ideologically outmoded and ineffective.

Shingeki was founded at the beginning of the twentieth century partly as a reaction against the stylisation of *kabuki*, even if it was initially dependent on actors from the *kabuki* theatres. Its principal theorist was Kaoru Osanai, who in 1926 stated that 'We must destroy *kabuki patterns.* By divorcing ourselves from *tradition* and ignoring *kabuki patterns,* we must create completely separately *our own theatre art,* new and free.'[5] Osanai visited the Moscow Art Theatre and religiously took notes on production processes in order to recreate them at home. Realism became the new orthodoxy. Western playwrights (particularly Henrik Ibsen) initially provided appropriate material until Japanese writers like Kunio Kishida were schooled in the imported techniques.

There are two strands identifiable within *shingeki* – psychological realism and socialist realism. Benito Ortolani notes that a 1909 production of Ibsen's *John Gabriel Borkman* by the Liberal Theatre (representative of the former strand) is generally considered to be the first *shingeki* performance. This is a moment that is hard to pinpoint precisely, as Takahashi's 'Suzuki's work in the Context of Japanese Theater'[6] demonstrates. In this he accentuates *shingeki's* origins in earlier productions of Shakespeare. After the Second World War, *shingeki* diversified further in its material and modes of presentation beyond these two schools. But it remained largely dependent on bodies like the Workers' Theatre Council (affiliated to the Japanese Communist Party) to build its audiences, for it was a comparatively new form and struggled to gain public support.[7]

Shingeki's politics also meant that it could not rely on business sponsorship. Most actors from *shingeki* therefore always depended on financial sources outside theatre work. In the latter half of the twentieth century they increasingly relied on the commercial areas of film and television as well as popular performance, not only to survive personally but also to keep the *shingeki* companies afloat. Fees from such projects were ploughed back into rehearsals. *Shingeki* diversified but still struggled for a wide support base. It has now moved well beyond the initial artistic parameters set by realism and its founders' political intentions and affiliations, but this has led to suggestions that it has lost its sense of direction and purpose. Such internal conflicts and a history rooted in left-wing politics alienated young artists in the 1960s, who perceived *shingeki's* response to the crisis surrounding the Security Treaty renewal as inadequate and entrenched. Once revolutionary, *shingeki* was now a catalyst for the growth of *angura* groups, as they sought to find their own artistic criteria and political positions outside what was increasingly proving itself to be the passive mainstream.

Numerous commentators on Japanese culture, such as David Goodman, have described the inertia and feelings of hopelessness endemic to this decade. The suffering that followed the widespread destruction of the Second World War and the atom bombs had initially given the nation a sense of purpose and struggle. Twenty years on, this had faded. It appeared that 'nothing had changed', as Suzuki stated in 1966: 'True enough, the riots over the treaty were a factor, and situations were shifting; yet in one sense, we believed that nothing had changed. We thought to put on plays because of the sad lot of humankind.'[8] This indicates the timbre of Suzuki's work prior to 1966, which also permeated the Waseda Little Theatre's projects (the WLT was founded in 1966). Suzuki was not alone in his disaffection with political struggle, that bred a bleak world view:

> The one thing that I learned from the activities of my student days is that no matter how you may struggle to make it otherwise, nothing can ever happen beyond a human scale. To put this another way, the only way you can achieve anything at all is by constantly confronting yourself with a sense of poverty and wretchedness. I suppose that my initial impetus to enter theatre came from a struggle with the problem of how to maintain this sense of human wretchedness'.[9]

Ironically, Suzuki's stance coexisted with greater prosperity and material comfort as the country dragged itself up from post-war poverty and devastation. In 1967, Japan's Gross National Product was the second highest in the world. Yet there was a concomitant loss of identity and sense of direction with the adoption of foreign values and altered circumstances. Influenced by the existentialist thought that was inspiring Japanese intellectuals at that time, Suzuki stressed the necessity of remembering the fundamental condition of man's struggle and his ephemerality in the midst of economic recovery and forward progression.

Suzuki has been called 'apolitical',[10] but in such a context this seems less a consciously constructed position and more an inevitability, reflecting the neutrality craved by anti-Ampo demonstrators and general disillusionment with politics. In a strongly polarised climate, an apolitical stance can also take on ideological implications. But the political imperative of Takahashi's 'revolution of the theatre' should not be overstated. Although there were many shades of political ideology in avant-garde performance at this time, artists like Suzuki were primarily concerned with reviving and restructuring relations within the theatre – among artists, and between them and their audience. Suzuki's fundamental aim was creative rejuvenation, as indicated by his leadership of the Waseda Free Stage (WFS) while at university, when he attempted to move the focus away from internecine political wrangling towards artistic issues. Like the Workers' Theatre Council, the WFS was associated with the Japanese Communist Party, which clearly circumscribed its artistic and ideological parameters.

The 'revolution' necessitated the abandonment of former values synchronous with the search for new frameworks, be they less hierarchical company structures or another actor–writer relationship. With the actor's role more central and the author in the wings, the director could resurface centrestage. Often, as with Suzuki, this was as director and writer. Outdoor and non-theatre spaces were also ripe for exploration. Goodman has described the potential that a tent, for example, gave Japanese artists to go beyond the restrictions of the proscenium arch and to meet unfamiliar audiences.

Shingeki was an approach in which he and his peers had been inculcated, but Suzuki was not alone in challenging its emphasis on the written text. Drawing directly on Stanislavski's hypotheses, *shingeki* posited the actor's role as an interpretative one. Suzuki also positioned the actor in relation to given playtexts, but from the very start he tipped the balance in the actor's favour: 'The actor is not an instrument of the play. He creates his own "stage language" [*butai gengo*] by confronting the totality of his personal history and background with the play.'' For Suzuki, the actor rather than the playwright and his characters held the key to the theatre. Suzuki began to define the performer more in relation to the spectator than the writer.

The work of absurdist writers like Samuel Beckett was central to this rejection of realism. Senda has noted the impact of *Waiting for Godot* (premiered in Paris in 1953 and first performed in Japan by the Literary Theatre troupe in May 1960) on playwrights like Betsuyaku. The year 1960 was a watershed, when young writers, directors and companies began to renounce the restrictions of *shingeki*, both formal and cultural. *Shingeki* was imitative, rational and literary, consciously departing from premodern Japanese poetic aesthetics (ambiguity, spirituality and the supernatural), embodied in *noh* theatre in particular. Beckett was a Western influence, but ironically he gave the young Japanese artists more room to experiment than did realism (or at least the Japanese version of Western realism). The absurd worlds that writers like Beckett created and the minimalism with which they did so gave artists like Suzuki access to their own stylised, presentational and symbolic performance traditions of *noh* and *kabuki*, while still holding on to the notion of a playtext. This did not happen overnight, but one can trace the resurrection of interest by contemporary artists in premodern forms to the very beginning of the 1960s.

With the influence of writers like Beckett, the existential philosophies of Jean-Paul Sartre and Maurice Merleau-Ponty arrived in Japan and were taken up avidly by students in the 1960s. In *The Way of Acting* Suzuki is explicit about his attraction to Sartre. Less obvious is the inspiration he drew from Merleau-Ponty and especially his book *Phenomenology of Perception.* This text accorded with Suzuki's theatrical impulses and with his later attempt to locate perception in the self-reflexive corporeal body, be it of the performer or spectator. Briefly, in a complex work, Merleau-Ponty attempts to obviate the divisions and categorisation that analysis entails. He explores self-perception as a sensory process centred on our physical being, as contrasted with Sartre's subject–object dualism which implies the significance of how the other (object) sees us. Merleau-Ponty's views provided credibility for the 'world as the field of experience' in which we find ourselves, an experiential emphasis that has dominated Suzuki's thinking and practice ever since. More directly, it furthered notions of performance as self-encounter and self-revelation before others.

Suzuki has also acknowledged the formative influence of surrealism at this time, which arrived again in Japan in the wake of existentialism and on the back of the Theatre of the Absurd. Surrealism had had its Japanese proponents in the 1920s, but now it was embedded in playtexts as well as more experimental performance. Surrealism advocated that identity is shaped by subconscious as well as conscious impulses, and prioritised the former. As an artistic genre, it also proffered structural devices which could be applied directly in performance, such as collage, dislocation and absurdity. These could be used both as rehearsal tools and in production to provoke the performer's self-realisation. Before Suzuki had fully reaped the fruits of Shiraishi's potential and developed a training method to reveal her and other actors' creative and emotional vitality, he deployed stylistic and philosophical devices from surrealism to open actors up both to themselves and to the audience. Existentialism, surrealism and phenomenology led Suzuki to focus more on the performer and their experience than on the writer, who inevitably mediates reality and in this mediation puts some distance (however small) between the performer and the spectator.

The foregrounding of the performer led to Suzuki's break with Betsuyaku in August 1969. He had become increasingly redundant as Suzuki transformed into the company 'writer', as Akihiko Senda called him.[12] This description is a little misleading, but it does indicate a marked shift in Suzuki's authority and role within the performance process. But what could these post-*shingeki* performers be, and what were their practices, relieved now from *shingeki* models and the onus of interpreting the text?

The acting techniques of *noh* and *kabuki* and other such forms were one obvious starting-point. Suzuki expressed his overarching concern of the 1970s in an interview: 'There must be some method to make traditional consciousness compatible with modern habits.'[13] This reflected Japan's general aspiration to embrace the new while still valorising the old. Rapid social transformation meant that these two worlds coexisted in Japan (most notably in the rural–urban divide) even if such differences were becoming increasingly less discernible. James Brandon has remarked that 'Suzuki explains that his work and *kabuki* both draw on the physicality of Japanese peasants (feet planted, knees flexed, stamping the earth)'.[14] The rural context that Suzuki sought in Toga did not just allow different organisational, economic and spatial values. The villagers' physicality, that was disappearing, provided a tangible connection to the actors' own practices.

As the demonstrating students read Beckett and Sartre, Suzuki also returned to the works of one of the founders of *noh*, Motokiyo Zeami. Zeami (1363–1443) documented his own insights and practices and those of his father Kiyotsugu Kanami (1333–1384) in treatises that have had a profound influence on European artists, such as Eugenio Barba and Jerzy Grotowski, as much as on Japanese theatre practitioners. Zeami categorised principles like Grace (*yugen*) and the Flower (*hana* – this is the spiritual quality and presence a performer can acquire with maturity, insight and practice) as well as more pragmatic notions like 'reading the audience'. His work offers not only invaluable historical information but vital instructions to the contemporary actor. Zeami's writings and *noh* (which is also known simply as 'the art of walking') gave Suzuki concrete technical and artistic alternatives to help him move away from *shingeki*.

Kabuki and *noh* led Suzuki to his formulation of an actor's 'grammar of the feet', the Suzuki method, drawing on historic, artistic and, to a lesser extent, archaic and living anthropological sources. In *The Way of Acting* Suzuki describes the possible roots of the stamping, a central component of the training. Stamping was believed to pacify the souls of the dead in the ancient rituals of *kagura* or early Shinto dances and music, in which Japan's traditional performing arts originated. Such symbolic physicalities, found also in *noh* and *kabuki* as well as the work of the mountain peasants, were condensed in Suzuki's training. He skilfully managed to integrate 'traditional consciousness' into modern sensibilities, continuing and reinventing historic traces. In Suzuki's practice, Beckett metaphorically dances with the Shinto goddess Ame Uzume no Kami on her overturned tub, a typically postmodern conjunction.*

The outcome of such combinations is examined in the chapter on training and in the analysis of Suzuki's performances. These show how Suzuki synthesised the new and the old, the rural and the urban, as well as Eastern and Western practices and modes of thinking in his exercises and productions. Suzuki's vision manifests the artistic vibrancy, social turmoil and questioning of national identity in Japan during the 1960s and 1970s.

Festivals and Theatre Communities

As the situation in which artists were operating became more stable and internationalisation became more established, Suzuki decided to

---

* A creation myth describes how Uzume danced to bring the sun goddess out from her cave to restore light to the world, while exposing her genitals. This combined action is seen as the origin of theatre and dance in Japan and points to the regenerative, reproductive mythical origins of performance. See also Benito Ortolani's *The Japanese Theatre: From Shamanistic Ritual to Contemporary Pluralism*, Princeton University Press, New Jersey, 1995.

completely change his local environment and working context. In some ways the decision was out of his hands. After fifteen years of working in Tokyo (examined briefly in Chapter Five), the relocation to Toga was determined mostly by economic constraints and the difficulty of sustaining unsubsidised experimental practice there. Companies like WLT and SCOT have had to manage with extremely limited financial resources. As with *shingeki*, groups like SCOT relied on the benevolence of individuals and the personal sacrifices of group members. Ongoing central state support for experimental work such as Suzuki's is, and has consistently been, almost non-existent in Japan, with highly selective corporation backing being the most familiar model of patronage.

Only two (non-traditional) theatre groups in Japan can pay a salary to their members all year round. SCOT is one and the other is the Shiki theatre, a semi-commercial *shingeki* company, known for their youth-oriented budget musical versions of *Phantom of the Opera* and *Cats*. Shiki is lucky to receive sponsorship in the form of a central Tokyo venue from Nissei (the Japan Life Insurance Company), one of whose top executives is the theatre company founder's son. SCOT is not so fortunate. Among other sources, their funding comes from performance fees, occasional government project grants, and tours or activities abroad, frequently funded by overseas charities promoting international understanding such as the Japan United States Friendship Commission. Suzuki's international success and collaborations have ensured his survival with good artistic conditions, though this took years of relatively unsupported work to establish. Beneficent well-wishers funded Suzuki's performances during his first five years in Toga. Any strategy that reduces overheads or encourages local subsidy, like the move to the mountains, is helpful if not essential. Prefectures (be it Shizuoka or Toyama) as well as local bodies such as Art Tower Mito, Toga village authority or SPAC (the Shizuoka Performing Arts Centre – founded in 1995 to run the arts complex and activities in Shizuoka) have helped with building and running costs. The mixture of groups Suzuki has simultaneously managed broadens the pool of potential funders, though it inevitably spreads costs. Funding issues have no doubt constrained Suzuki's repertoire, necessitating the commercial productions that he has occasionally directed.

Obstacles are not only financial, but also pertain to public support and standing. Thomas Havens has researched the hurdles facing Japanese theatre artists and he observed in 1980 that 'Although many avant-garde or underground productions are of the highest artistic significance in the Japanese theater world, the combined attendance at all such performances probably does not exceed 100,000 per year.'[15] This is a tiny proportion of a population of approximately 123 million (1998 census). While the constructive tension between Eastern and Western influences and the rich resources of the past might have stimulated experimentation in Japanese theatre, there has been little popular or governmental sanction for such practices. Havens noted that 'between 1955 and 1975 the combined number of actors, actresses, and dancers increased by two-thirds to 37,400 – even though live drama lost 40 percent of its audience'.[16] Such contradictions are not uniquely Japanese, but they heighten the significance of what Suzuki has implemented. The little activity there is has always been centred in the major cities, despite a governmental push to distribute the arts to the regions in the early 1970s. Unfortunately, this focused far too much on prestige-seeking building programmes that could host urban productions, rather than on fostering and maintaining local talent. Health cannot be measured by statistics alone, but they are a useful indicator.

One way of subsidising and promoting your own work is to present it within an international or festival context, attracting audiences for longer periods than the single night of a performance. Suzuki began the Toga International Festival in 1982, which soon acquired world-wide acclaim and helped build local and national support. This ran in a comparable format up until 1999. It was Japan's first international theatre festival and, lacking precedents, was deliberately small-scale. (European festivals like the Théâtre des Nations in Nancy, which Suzuki had visited in the 1970s, often hosted over sixty groups, well beyond Toga's resources). Suzuki invited 'friends and people with a common interest' to his 'home'. As might be expected in a remote site like Toga, the festival stemmed from his curiosity and desire to network rather than from commercial aims. It could also enable the kind of collaborations which have cropped up throughout Suzuki's career. In 1984, for example, Lithuanian director Jonas

Jurasas was invited to direct SCOT in Chekhov's *Three Sisters* for the festival.

Many of these 'friends' happened to be eminent international artists and companies. Poland's Gardzienice Theatre Association, Russia's Anatoly Vassiliev Company and Britain's Welfare State International are just three who have performed in Toga. Alongside foreign groups and individuals, Suzuki hosted Japanese artists, including choreographer–dancer Saburo Teshigawara, director Shuji Terayama, and the Kodo drummers, whose pounding reverberated around Toga's river valley. The festival was also multi-disciplinary, including dance, music and folk culture, though centred predominantly on theatre. The list is impressive, particularly for such a small, out-of-the-way place. Artists were attracted not only because of Suzuki's reputation, but also for the unusual and focused location. Spaces could be rebuilt or redesigned according to artistic need. This lack of constraint followed through into an absence of themes, sponsors or state directives. The whole was dependent on Toyama prefecture and Toga village funding, but the festival followed Suzuki's personal preferences.

Sceptics of the festival (as well as an initially circumspect Suzuki) were surprised by the audience numbers, at capacity level from the beginning. Visitors came from across Japan and from around the world. This festival differed from larger or urban events because most people saw most productions and stayed in the locale. Once in Toga, they were captive, residing there and accepting what was offered rather than selecting from a wide-ranging programme. This limitation did not constrain them. The festival took on a holiday atmosphere with its own rhythm. So it was that the theatre spaces could become temporarily 'public' or 'open', in the broad sense that Suzuki has defined this, as outlined in Chapter Three.

The Japan Performing Arts Centre (JPAC) was founded in 1982 in part to organise this annual event. With Suzuki as chairman and Ikuko Saito as General Secretary, JPAC formalised the work that WLT was already doing, but it was more focused on aspects of producing and funding. It could also institute an ideological brief, based broadly on collaboration and the promotion of understanding. Officially, JPAC is a non-profit public organisation, whose founding intention was to organise the Toga Festival, produce performances, lead training sessions, hold conferences and set up a performing arts library. Although the last two of these multiple aims have scarcely been realised, the other aspects have all been achieved. Overall, production and organisational aspects of Suzuki's work appear (from the outside and judging as one who has attended Toga festivals as both spectator and performer) to be thriving and smooth-running.

In spite of past success, radical restructuring was announced at the 1999 festival, supposedly the last one. This was endorsed by the presentation of SCOT's performance of *Sayonara Toga* (*Farewell Toga*). Suzuki felt that the festival had lost sight of its original aims and fresh vision was needed for the future. Since the year 2000, Toyama prefecture and the village authorities have had more input into the management of the facilities. JPAC wants to hand over more responsibility for future artistic developments in Toga and needs partners to share the administrative load. Details were being thrashed out at the end of 1999. Suzuki was asserting the right to still have access to the spaces, maintaining a foothold (though a diminished one) in the village and in the buildings which he had conceived and created.

Suzuki has been involved in several similar festivals and such projects will not end with Toga's demise. In 1988 he was appointed artistic director of the biannual Mitsui Festival in Tokyo. More recently (in 1999), Suzuki brought the Second Theatre Olympics to Shizuoka under the title 'Crossing Millennia'. The Third Theatre Olympics took place in Moscow in 2001. This international collaborative venture was founded to promote contemporary versions of ancient Greek and classical drama, to thereby regenerate theatre. With Suzuki, it is co-led by Greek director Theodoros Terzopoulos, Yuri Lyubimov and Robert Wilson, among others.* After its inauguration in Delphi, Greece, in 1995, the festival moved to Shizuoka, where there could be a larger scale of activity and a greater potential visiting audience that did not require accommodation than in Toga. The Theatre Olympics instigated the ongoing presence of an annual event, the Spring Arts Festival Shizuoka. Such enterprises (there have been many more, including a 1993 Polish Festival in Mito)

---

* Other members are Nuria Espert (Spain), Antunes Filho (Brazil), Jürgen Flimm (Germany), Tony Harrison (England), Georges Lavaudant (France), Wole Soyinka (Nigeria) and the deceased Honorable Founding Member Heiner Müller (Germany). The Theatre Olympics' main office is in Athens and the Asian office is in Shizuoka.

contributed to the death of the Toga Festival. Yet they all fed on the reputation and contacts that the founding festival made and have at times even shared performances and costs.

Such a range of projects necessitates extensive administrative support, which is now spread among SCOT, JPAC and SPAC. All have Suzuki in leading artistic positions. Inevitably he has expressed great interest in the operation and dynamics of companies, which he has addressed in his writings and performances. He has led (and in most cases founded) the Waseda Free Stage (WFS), the Free Stage, WLT, SCOT, JPAC, Acting Company Mito (ACM) and most recently SPAC, with whose resident theatre group he now mostly works. The large total membership of these companies operating simultaneously necessitates a strict regime. SCOT alone has consistently fluctuated at between thirty and forty members.

The training is one way of uniting these organisations, and company members participate in this from day one. Psychological research has shown that groups establish strong interpersonal ties through tackling difficult tasks like the training, which demands intense emotional input. The training proposes one model of interaction, with the leader separated from the otherwise equal trainees. Job definitions are more fluid than one might find in typical Western theatres, to help create this sense of equality, though there are still divisions between technical areas such as lighting, administration and acting. Broadly speaking, the actors must help with the whole public and administrative sequence of which their performance is just one small part. Correspondingly, the administrators and technicians must likewise understand the artistic mission and creative processes of the actors, the director and the company. The training supports this. Work is shared, roles are conflated and all members assist with office work and technical support. No actor can rise above the menial task of cleaning the living or rehearsal spaces. In the 1980s there was a two-year probationary period for newer members, who might only progress to acting after successfully fulfilling this. This not only gave them time to become familiar with the training, but also inducted newcomers into company conduct and laws, both explicit and implicit. Probation has since become less formalised, with new members taking on minor stage roles as and when necessary. Today a distinction is made whereby 'leading or senior members' (those who have been with the company longest) take over responsibility in Suzuki's absence.

The training upholds Suzuki as the tough taskmaster or *sensei*. A *sensei* is a spiritual and therefore individual guide as much as a technical one. The performer's engagement with the process of instruction has to be total, with nothing beyond the director's grasp. Rather than being ends in themselves, commitment and discipline should lead to the performer's self-fulfilment and self-discovery, as is the Buddhist way. Undoubtedly, other dynamics and interrelationships complicate such ideals. Outside training and rehearsal, for example, Suzuki appears much more relaxed with his performers. Yet discipline, absolute authority from the top and humility seem to be guiding principles.

The fact that Suzuki has called Toga a 'home' implies that his company is a family, a common hierarchical model for Japanese social and artistic groups. Suzuki analyses the difficulties of collective organisation and the *iemoto* system in 'House and Family' in *The Way of Acting*. The *iemoto* is a 'family' system still found in *noh* and other traditional arts, based on 'houses' led by a master. Skills and authority are handed on to a son or equivalent figure (usually a 'lesser master' who has his own students), for they do not have to be tied by blood. This patrilineal model has existed in an approximate form since the eighth century, surviving partly thanks to the secrecy, rigidity and loyalty that it encourages. Suzuki's companies have not followed the *iemoto* system exactly, but have adopted some traits, including his role as a master figure and an emphasis on discipline and loyalty.

Suzuki's understanding of groups is based on extensive personal experience and the constant fluctuations in the various theatre companies he has led throughout his career, beginning in his student days as chairman of the WFS. He considers group organisation to be the core of his activity:

> If one is going to ask on what foundation theatre is based, it's not the dramatic text, and it's not the actor performing on stage, but rather the attempt of isolated individuals to create a fictional group, with temporarily structured rules [. . .] by passing through the rules of the group, a person becomes an individual.[17]

Suzuki's 'individual' is more an artistic than a social being. Residency in Toga for several months of the year and international touring compound the personal demands made on group members, who might be away from their private home for long stretches of time. This difficulty is common to many theatre organisations but was exacerbated by the relocation to Toga. One feature of Suzuki's companies (found in most other Japanese organisations) is that the group takes priority over the individual, who must substitute their own desires for those of the collective. Ironically, Suzuki argues, it is only through self-constraint and personal sublimation that one can fully realise one's own individuality. This is not a denial of individualism but an analysis that differs extensively from reasoning familiar to Westerners.

The complications of group living and creativity are something Suzuki's productions have addressed, as the following comments from the programme for *The Tale of Lear* show:

> all groups are based on the principle of exclusion and the dynamics of sadomasochism. In any group certain individuals claw their way to the top and others are humiliated and destroyed. We can't live without groups but life within groups is dangerous. Shakespeare's text explores this dialectic of the impossibility of living alone and the difficulty of living in groups.

Whether one endorses such a view (with its pessimism and troubling acceptance of violence) and whatever the reality within Suzuki's groups, he is not blind to such issues. He has clearly articulated them and is working through such conundrums in his art and writing, however this impacts on personal relations. I have little insight into group dynamics in SCOT or SPAC. His performers do not appear to be subjugated slaves and they readily acknowledge the difficulty of what they are all attempting. Several have given Suzuki decades of their life to achieve these shared ideals. Some senior members have even left and then returned, perhaps addicted to the intensity of such work. At least the performer is forewarned when considering employment with Suzuki.

The concept of artistic and social freedom within the parameters defined by Suzuki is particularly problematic for Western observers or associates, who might be used to more liberal or equal ways of working, or at least ones in which authority can be openly questioned. Observers have described Suzuki's harsh and even abusive treatment of the performers in training and rehearsal. Minoru Betsuyaku called Suzuki 'a director skilful in developing mutual animosity with actors . . . which served as a contact-detonating device for creativity'.[18] Tsuka Kohei noted how 'Suzuki censures actors by criticizing every fault they have. Sometimes the censure even includes the actor's personality, family and lifestyle.'[19] James Brandon described Suzuki's fanaticism and occasional instructional 'slaps on the head' in his 1978 article. Nearly a decade on, Marie Myerscough called him 'almost tyrannical', a very hedged statement. Interestingly, these critics and collaborators have not automatically condemned such behaviour. Perhaps they have noted that it was accepted with understanding or complicity by the performers, and have attempted to view these processes emically.

In interview, American actor Kameron Steele gave the following telling account of a rehearsal of *Dionysus* with Suzuki:

> The first time he ever really grilled me in front of everyone was my first summer in Toga. I was a wheelchair* guy and I messed up. It was terrifying. He was screaming at me. The whole outdoor theatre was black except for a shining pair of glasses floating around in the auditorium, and the lights were glaring in my face – really serious. This was the first time I really understood what blasphemy was [. . .] This experience made me realise that things meant that much and were that important.

Steele's colourful narrative suggests an innocent abroad having his expectations shattered. The performer stands isolated in the great outdoor amphitheatre, facing a moment when there are no options, surrounded by an impenetrable, literal and metaphorical darkness and foreignness. Perversely, the challenging experience was enlightening for Steele. His alienation had significant results, confirming the notion that such combative relationships and struggle can be instructional and yield rich rewards. It can be a justifiable means to an end, though such a process is not for everybody.

The desire for such interaction and the ability to cope with it inevitably depends on the individual, though this is influenced by cultural tendencies. Doubts about these group dynamics are not

---

* This refers to Suzuki's use of wheelchairs for the chorus in performances such as *Dionysus* and *Electra*. See Chapters Three and especially Five for more on this.

exclusive to Westerners alone, though. Young Japanese performers today might question Suzuki's harsh treatment, yet the history of their culture also means that they might be more willing to accept it. There is no union membership in SCOT or SPAC and notions such as strong leadership, mentoring, humility, subservience and discipline are still deeply embedded in Japanese society. It is the very conflict between these and more open and individualistic Western approaches which have created the tensions that result in family breakdown and youth suicide. Work and educational pressures have steadily increased in Japan, as the ubiquitous example of the hardworking *salaryman* drinking late with his boss attests. Extreme company loyalty, jobs for life and work taking precedence over personal commitments have been central tenets in Japan, seen most explicitly in the larger corporations. Yet such ideals have been challenged by recession, corruption scandals, unemployment and Japan's economic downturn in the 1990s, alongside ongoing openness to outside influences and systems. Work and family roles are in flux. Although it is unquantifiable, the broad devaluation of these principles has surely affected Suzuki's *modus operandi*, or has at the very least altered the attitudes of his company members and the context in which the group operates.

Close kinship combined with authoritarian leadership can help create a strong and united vision while also enabling individual triumphs such as Shiraishi's. Whatever the observer or participant's background, and however much they might doubt the need for such autocracy, the admirable control and precision this can produce in performance is undeniable. Whether it is the *only* way to achieve such results is more debatable. A path that negotiates discipline and pleasure is fraught. Suzuki would probably argue that strict but familial relations are especially necessary to help build companies in a context where artists gain state or public support with the greatest of difficulty. The financial security and comfort which he has achieved for his company members and the lengths to which he has gone to create their home are two objective yardsticks by which to measure Suzuki's success. Yet the constant fluctuation in membership and the departure in the 1990s of several long-term members of SCOT indicates that these are not the only criteria that should be applied.

Another possible gauge of how Suzuki functions is the fact that he has collaborated with several outstanding artists and administrators for substantial periods of time. He has also put immense energy into promoting other Japanese and overseas artists at festivals in Japan. Equally affirmatively, the next chapter contains several Western performers' positive responses to Suzuki's approach and method. Only detailed, almost anthropological study could cast objective and unemotional light on such complex and personal relations. With a background in Polish theatre, I have often encountered reservations and concerns about unequal gender relations and autocratic directors, issues exacerbated when those practices interface with Western perspectives. Such experience confirmed that this is a fraught and delicate area, which general or swift judgements can only further confound.

This chapter's brief positioning of Suzuki within an artistic and social context and within his own groups has been a partial and suggestive view. However, an overarching pattern does emerge of Suzuki's increasing internationalisation, a journey that emulates Japan's own difficult path at the end of the twentieth century. This route has been complicated by dualities that combine to make Suzuki's background and context hard to categorise and summarise, but also rich and satisfyingly complex. It is probable that increasing globalisation will only entangle such interrelationships further.

The next chapter will determine Suzuki's present standing by considering some of the influences he has had on contemporary thinking about performance and on current practices. It will also risk making predictions about the future impact of his work. The book then moves from analysis of his performance spaces and his theorisation of these to an assessment of the non-material aspects of his theatre practice, focusing on training and then performance. Some matters are touched on only sketchily: there is no room to outline a history of Greek or Japanese classical theatre before describing how Suzuki adapts these, for example. The reader must accept this shorthand and my assumptions. This caveat grows from the desire to focus on Suzuki's processes and some productions in detail, rather than the sources from which they have derived.

Mine is also an ideological position. I want to continue to shift the balance in performance studies away from the literary towards experiential, phenomenological perspectives. Performance analysis should recount clearly what happened, with all the problems of subjectivity that this entails, before obfuscating the event itself in theoretical acrobatics. This is nowhere more necessary than in intercultural analyses, where attempts to decipher multicultural referencing can obscure understanding of the performance itself.

Literary-minded readers might want to know more about adaptation in Suzuki's work. Chapter Five focuses on dramatic performance rather than the literary text, which is partly a response to the nature of Suzuki's work. As a director, his selection processes seem personal and arbitrary rather than methodical, making it hard to pick out recognisable strategies. The few textual documents of performances that do exist give scant insight into how they are performed, heightening the limitations of close textual analysis. What is offered is a clear understanding of performance and its complex processes and an intimate knowledge of actor training and its consequences.

There are several difficulties to be resolved in writing about Suzuki's productions, not least the very specific referencing to Japanese circumstances and culture, as well as the obstacle of language for a non-speaker like me. His work is personal and hard to unpick even for cultural 'insiders'. Of course, there is no fixity in such positions. What makes performance so exciting is the fluidity between boundaries, such as inside and outside, that it encourages. Yet performance analysis that is dependent on semiotic or literary frames of reference is inappropriate in such a context. Besides, many others have enquired into interpretation and adaptation in Suzuki's work and have made comparisons with source texts (see especially Carruthers, McDonald and Mulryne in the bibliography). What Suzuki does with texts – his abridging, cross-referencing, quotation, parody and adaptation – is complex and original, and needs to be explained further, but it is not the main focus of my analysis.

I intend to concentrate more on the act of performance and choices in staging rather than the literary contortions and cultural referencing of Suzuki's *œuvre*. I hope to override some of the limitations of my position as an 'outsider' and move towards an emic approach. This is informed by the fact that I have for several years attempted to practise and embody the principles and form of the

Suzuki method as part of my research. My way in to the challenging experiences of his performances and his questionable ideal of universality is through the training. This emic perspective, decoding his performances from the inside as it were, seems indispensable because of the nature of Suzuki's practice. His productions are so physical, rhythmical, spatial and energetic that one can usefully analyse them as a linguistic and cultural outsider. Suzuki has written that 'Theatre, like life, is understood through experience, not explanations'.[20] Although of course I often have to explain, I hope my analysis contributes to clarifying how this distinction translates into a discourse about performance.

I will no doubt frustrate Asian cultural experts. Japanese history, culture and arts are not the focus of this book and are only mentioned in passing. There are clearly links between Japanese theatre and Buddhism, Shinto and Taoism, yet these connections have not been overtly made by Suzuki (at least not in works in English) and so are incidental to this study. They provide a context for his work (influencing his relationship to the natural environment, for example) but this is only in the tangential way that Ibsen's plays are rooted in Christian ethics but are not religious plays. Suzuki's existential views can be related to Buddhism but they are just as likely to have arisen from his contact with French philosophy in the 1960s.

Japanese performing arts have attracted many specialist commentators, whose work I hope I have correctly and respectfully acknowledged, either within the body of the text or in the bibliography. They must forgive my lack of reference to very specific influences on Suzuki, such as notions like *honkadori, sekai* or *joruri* which are derived in part from traditional theatre. These would probably mean little to those being introduced to Japanese theatre through Suzuki.[21] It is not the task of this book to catalogue all these sources, but to mark out patterns, trace influences and reveal possibilities, and to open these to readers who might not be closely conversant with Japan and its arts. While I will travel nowhere near the interior of Japanese culture, I will hopefully reposition one small aspect of Japanese performance within a Western context, without falling into the most worrying etic and superior or patronising perspectives of interculturalism. Suzuki's work is Western while it is also Japanese, as I wish to demonstrate. It is vital that more studies like mine continue to narrow this gap and attempt to deorientalise Asian theatre without reducing it.

To help build an emic position and steer the reader away from elementary prejudices, I want to make two brief observations on Japanese ways of seeing. Suzuki's performances are surprisingly self-referential and often recycle previous materials, characters and even stage objects. Waste-paper bins covered with the Marlboro logo reappear in productions as far apart chronologically as *Night and the Feast II* (1977) and *Electra* (1995). The notion of originality in Japan does not hold the same prestige as it does in the West. This stems from a heightened appreciation of traditions, but also a Japanese perception of creativity, which Thomas Havens has elucidated:

> Creativity has been a cardinal esthetic value in Japan only in this century, mostly because of stimulus from Europe. The traditional Japanese arts rarely prized innovation for its own sake, and even today they carefully regulate who may alter a time-honored script, technique, or piece of choreography [. . .] Creativity as an absolute is a foreign idea.[22]

This pertains mostly to traditional practices, though some insiders, like the *noh* performer brothers Hideo and Hisao Kanze, have challenged the conservatism even of these forms. But such a perspective does filter into unashamedly avant-garde experiments like those of Suzuki. Although it is imprudent to overemphasise an opposition between Eastern and Western ways of seeing with these worlds now so interwoven, we should recognise some nuances of difference. It is vital not to measure Suzuki's output purely by Western standards that prioritise originality. This is not to justify the stagnation that Takeshi Kawamura has observed, mentioned in the next chapter (see page 55), but merely to put it into context. The mission of defining *Nihonjinron* has not been without its consequences.

The other aspect I wish to highlight is fragmentation in Japanese culture. What might appear to be consciously postmodern structuring and quotation in Suzuki's work has deeper, older precedents in Japanese society. In his definitive book on *kabuki* written in the 1950s (updated a little in 1973), Earle Ernst notes that:

Existence is manifested in disparate, discrete moments in which
neither the artist not the object he observes has durability. He
cannot 'order' such an existence; he can only seize upon actuality in
the moment, since the moment is the only actuality [. . .] the
discontinuous glimpse of actuality, the brief juxtaposition of
incidents, are the materials with which the Japanese artist works.[23]

The effects of this Buddhist world view might explain Suzuki's
disposition towards 'wretchedness', mentioned earlier. As much as
you might find solace, you might equally feel despair at such a vision
of impermanence as Ernst outlines. This sensibility perhaps explains
the desire for order and discipline often observed in Japan. It also
might elucidate why the Western observer views some of the
illogical jumps and connections, the dislocations and collage of
Suzuki's productions, with complete bafflement. Ernst is identifying
an important mode of perception that underlies all Suzuki's
practices. It requires a mental and cultural leap for the Western
observer and reader to span such differences. I want this book to act
as a sturdy and trustworthy bridge.

In many ways I am writing a theatre history, and nowhere more
so than in my description of Suzuki's productions and the evolution
of his spaces in Toga. But I also mean to tunnel deep inside some
central issues for contemporary performance, in a way that unearths
fresh material, particularly regarding training and performing. I want
also to show how the underground might keep its feet on the
ground. Understanding and defining the physical principles and
techniques which lie at the heart of Suzuki's craft and vision is
fundamental to my analysis. In the process of documenting and
articulating these, I hope I accurately and faithfully recount the
practice and give some insight into some of the central theories of a
major twentieth-century theatre director.

T W O

·

SUZUKI NOW

Richard Schechner's editorial foreword to the *Drama Review*, Spring 2000, greeted the new century. Alongside Robert Wilson, Robert Lepage, Laurie Anderson, Eugenio Barba and others, he lists Tadashi Suzuki as one of those experimentalists who have ensured that 'many of the battles over the "future of theatre"' have been won – for the moment, at least. In the same issue there is an interview between Suzuki and the *butoh* pioneer Tatsumi Hijikata, originally recorded in April 1977. Suzuki also crops up in other articles that reassess Japanese theatre at the end of the twentieth century. He is not going to go away, as such acclaim and reevaluation attest. Instead, his practice is now instanced in a broader context than training or interculturalism. David Wiles mentions Suzuki's Greek productions in his *Greek Theatre Performance: An Introduction*, also published in 2000. With almost forty years of activity in the professional theatre, an overview of Suzuki's achievements and contribution to twentieth-century performance is long overdue.

This chapter will assess the present standing of the director. It will also look forward. What is the future of Suzuki's practice? How will the work of SCOT, SPAC and Suzuki himself progress? Will he continue to expand his empire and will his training endure? What more can we expect from his colleagues and collaborators, past and present?

One danger with controlling processes as closely as Suzuki does is that the practice dies with its instigator. This is unlikely to happen wholesale with Suzuki for his training method can continue independent of him, but it is doubtful that a disciple-director will emerge, as has happened with Jerzy Grotowski. Following the Asian master–pupil tradition, Grotowski formally handed his work on to performer and collaborator Thomas Richards before he died in 1999. Grotowski was profoundly influenced by such non-Western aspects of theatre-making. But, so far, Suzuki has not consciously ensured the perpetuity of his lineage, as might be expected of an Asian artist. This is not to deny Suzuki's impact on directors like Jacqui Carroll of the Australian company Frank or the American Anne Bogart, but there is no established 'family' who will guarantee the continuity of his theatre style and aesthetic, as one might find within *noh* or as with Grotowski. Perhaps it is too early for him to do this. But I also forecast discontinuity because of the singular historical circumstances which conditioned Suzuki's artistic consciousness and on which he persistently draws.

No doubt Suzuki's practice will keep evolving but I believe his major achievements are behind him: his collaboration with writer Minoru Betsuyaku in the 1960s; his 'Japanese' and intercultural performances, the rise of actress Kayoko Shiraishi, as well as the founding of his training method in the 1970s; his international festival and workshop programme in the 1980s; and consolidation and material projects such as the planning and building of the major arts complex in Shizuoka in the 1990s. This is not to signal the end of Suzuki's activities but merely to use this juncture between centuries as a yardstick. By examining potential legacies, it will be possible to establish how much Suzuki meets the challenges of the present. With so much already achieved, it is hard to predict where he can go next.

The analysis of Suzuki's productions in Chapter Five focuses mostly on pieces created before or at the beginning of the 1990s. Shiraishi left SCOT in 1990 and an actor of equal stature has not yet emerged to replace her. Even in the early 1970s, critics eagerly anticipated a performance to match the success of *On the Dramatic Passions II* (1970). They were disappointed initially by Suzuki's repetition of ideas and approaches, but he soon proved them wrong with *The Trojan Women* (1974). Yet judging by critical reception, no piece has since surpassed this. Suzuki's influence will continue to extend not so much through his own theatre direction but more through a ripple effect, as ideas spread out from his catalysing input. Later in this chapter (as one way of assessing Suzuki's current importance), there is an examination of how his method and practical philosophies have inspired several American performers from SITI (the Saratoga International Theatre Institute), which was co-founded by Suzuki and Anne Bogart in 1992.

As well as the ongoing work of collaborators past and present, inspiration will keep flowing from Suzuki's writings which will inevitably survive him. These remain absorbing because of the personal history and endeavours they demonstrate. Readers today will recognise the financial difficulty of setting up a rural retreat as he did in Toga, but might still harbour the desire to do so and appreciate the artistic value in such a move. The formation of ensemble-based companies is currently a fashionable ideal, however much this has been challenged socially by the prioritising of individual needs over and above communal ones. As performers transfer between directors every three months or so, the sharing of a vocabulary and a practice and a sense of continuity in their personal development becomes paramount. Suzuki training can provide this, as my interviews corroborate. Theatre artists are also still investigating the role of traditions within contemporary performance practice, whether their own or others'. With the rich insight gained from decades of hands-on experience, Suzuki's writing has addressed all these issues in depth.

Aspects of Suzuki's practice, such as the training, might possess a timeless appeal, but some values have become time-worn. The traffic of his own ideas has in part revealed this, though he has not always explicitly acknowledged it. The Toga International Festival served a vital social and artistic purpose at a critical time of Japan's opening up, but this need has now been answered in numerous ways. The festival has been emasculated by Japan's ongoing love affair with Western culture and increased internationalisation in the wake of global economic dominance in the 1970s and 1980s. The launch of the Tokyo International Festival in 1988 and overseas programmes like Britain's Japan Festivals in 1991 and 2001 have overshadowed Toga's role as a melting pot for cross-cultural meetings.

The Theatre Olympics and an annual festival at SPAC have recently absorbed much of Suzuki's organisational energy. Shizuoka can host an international assembly of Western and Asian experimental and classical productions far beyond Toga's intimate capability. Suzuki suggested in his book *The Way of Acting* that 'If such a festival [like Toga's] had been staged in a resort area such as Karuizawa, Nagano or Shizuoka, it would have become merely a kind of mini-Tokyo attraction.'[1] He has evidently shifted a long way in twenty years. Fear of absorption into the metropolis has ultimately not deterred him. No doubt the economic support and practical viability of Shizuoka was a significant motivating factor in its construction, but it nevertheless leaves Toga stranded. The Theatre Olympics and SPAC Festival have usurped Toga.

Progression and reformulation are evident in Suzuki's theorising. In the issue of the *Drama Review* previously cited, Carol Martin maps a brief personal view of post-World War Two contemporary experimental Japanese theatre. She notes how

> some theatre artists have rejected the essentialism of *angura* and its formulation of a 'Japanese body' in favor of an eclecticism that does not demand a unified Japanese consciousness but recognizes the complexities and heterogeneity present even in a society as homogeneous as Japan appears to be.[2]

This opening-up and shift towards internationalisation describes Suzuki exactly, revealing his ability to reinvent himself. The world has moved quickly on and Suzuki has scrambled to keep up. Theatre artists can become so absorbed in their practice that they lose sight of the bigger picture, but generally Suzuki has been insightful and ahead of the game, mapping rather than being mapped. However, the republication in several books of his article 'Culture is the Body' signals consolidation of old ideas rather than new inspiration, as the recent reprint of the Hijikata/Suzuki interview from 1977 also reinforces.

Suzuki initially emphasised the Japanese anthropological and historical sources of his training, typified in the stamp and the squat. These derived specifically from premodern performance and social practices, including ways of sitting or walking. In James Brandon's 1978 article, Suzuki declared that 'Through the disciplines I want to arouse the unconscious "Japaneseness" of their acting.'[3] In the early 1980s, Suzuki began to obscure this cultural specificity and move away from this affinity with *Nihonjinron*. In *The Way of Acting* (1984 in its Japanese imprint), he refuted claims that his training was easier for Japanese than Americans because their legs are shorter! He moved towards a universal position as he opened his workshops up to Western participants. William Beeman's article 'Tadashi Suzuki's Universal Vision' (1982) reinforced this shift. Suzuki's position was perhaps affected by time spent teaching in American institutions, some of which were then engaged in formulating intercultural theories. Yet it clearly shows his canny flexibility and pragmatism as he realised the wider application of his approach to acting outside the context of his own company and country.

The universality that Suzuki then proclaimed, and the interculturalism that followed his intraculturalism, has in turn been interrogated by postmodern thinking. Suzuki exemplifies an eclectic mixture of postmodern practice – with quotation, parody and juxtaposition – and underlying modernist inspiration from existentialism and surrealism. His work cannot be neatly pigeonholed. In a country that has lived through historically defined eras linked to its emperors, which has veered between isolation for two and a half centuries and post-Second World War American occupation and Westernisation, and where the past has been erased continually to make way for the new, etic or externally imposed categories are also inappropriate. Suzuki's framing devices and metaphors attempt to create unity out of his textual fragmentation and eclectic sourcing. Yet it is the very modern concept of the martially trained and controlled body that orders, energises and concentrates Suzuki's deep underlying cynicism, irony and playfulness.

Suzuki's desire to create universal theatre is not wholly assisted by his sourcing in Japanese culture. He attempts to engage with a wider audience through localised referencing, but this is frequently exclusive to Japanese spectators and those of his generation. Once taboo military songs or 1960s Japanese pop music, for example, signify little to Westerners or Japanese youth today, though they might sense the militarism or the kitschness in these. What does Shiraishi's recorded recitation of Lady Macbeth's lines in the festival extravaganza *Greetings from the Edges of the Earth* convey to a newcomer to Suzuki's work? Though universal is not simply a synonym for accessible, and universality is more an ideal than a simply achievable practice (as Peter Brook's naïve journey through sub-Saharan Africa revealed as early as 1972), Suzuki's introspection and self-referentiality often preclude breadth of reception. His conceptual layering mystifies audiences as they are simultaneously struck by the performers' energetic clarity.

The development of a training method helped Suzuki focus on and understand the nature of performing more than it illuminated issues of *mise-en-scène* or dramaturgy. It benefited the physical aspects of his performances, such as staging, which has received particular acclaim. Whereas his training is rigidly precise, his dramatic composition is erratic, even though he repeatedly reuses certain devices. His interpretations of classical texts have created resonances worldwide (thanks in part to the techniques of Shiraishi and other actors), yet they have simultaneously often appeared bafflingly cryptic. His directing would benefit from similar enabling formulae such as his performers found in the training.

Suzuki believes performance should communicate primarily on a physiological, rhythmical and energetic basis that can be universal. The influence of phenomenology shifted him away from Betsuyaku's playtexts towards an assessment of theatre as something that does not centre on written language but on that which is spoken or uttered, the embodied text. In his productions, the foregrounding of the actors' abilities that arose in his collages then gave way to the director's idiosyncratic adaptation of playtexts. In training, his emphasis on body movement shifted on to the 'movement' of the text, with the voice and breath dynamising the space and shaping the audience's response. Suzuki's idea that the voice is also a form of gesture shares more with modernist practices such as Jerzy Grotowski's and Eugenio Barba's than with dislocating post-modernism.

Total integration of the utterance of words with the body and action is an ideal. Chapter Four shows how differences in languages mean that vocal techniques do not transfer easily across cultures, as Suzuki himself has identified with *shingeki* productions. But even within cultures, as much as they are biologically integrated, the voice and body also operate independently as vehicles for conveying content, with the former linked to cognitive and not just somatic processes. Even if the text is unified with the body to become a physical gesture, it does not make that gesture universally readable. Further exploration of this relation between the voice and body, between text and action, is vital to the advance of theatre as a live medium rather than as literary text.

Today, the Suzuki method is situated beyond the limitations of localised specifics, such as leg-length, even if such formulations were unfounded. It approaches a universality that his productions cannot achieve. Audiences and scholars now possess more sophistication in reading performance on a biological and visceral level, as Suzuki proposes, rather than simply as 'text' laden with cultural codes and significance. The ascendance of dance and physical theatre and an increasing interchange with Asia and Africa have led to greater appreciation of the rhythmic, kinesthetic, energetic and musical dimensions of performance. The lessons of Theatre Anthropology with their emphasis on pre-expressivity and interrelated insights from interculturalism have helped progress this awareness, as has the academic shift from Theatre to Performance Studies. Semiotics alone is inadequate to translate or interpret the experience of performance. Equally though, physiological, kinesthetic and sensory aspects cannot be focused on to the exclusion of meaning, particularly when classical textual material is being adapted. Whatever the analytical methodology, the simple idealism of a universal theatre has been dismissed as unfeasible. It is not surprising that, in Eelke Lampe's 1993 article, Suzuki said: 'There is probably no such thing as a universal theatre but there is a possibility for theatre artists to address universal problems.'[4] This adjustment away from experience on to subject matter and the honesty of this admission show a revealing progression in Suzuki's practice and theory.

The political limitations of universality in Suzuki's and others' œuvres have been noted by Tadashi Uchino.[5] With the benefit of hindsight, he regrets that the Toga Festival (however significant its original mission) enabled Japan to adopt Western experimental theatre and turn it into another commodity. He highlights the naïve 'cultural relativism' that flourished under the idealistic umbrella of universalism advocated by several Japanese theatre artists in the 1980s. This only entrenched Japanese xenophobia in syncretism rather than encouraging investigation of what the other is. For Uchino, this reverse 'Orientalism' (the distorted depiction of other cultures outlined by Edward Said that has been generated predominantly – though not exclusively – by the West about the East) fatally depoliticised Japanese theatre.

This charge at Suzuki cannot be levelled without qualification, since he attempted intelligently to integrate Western texts, concepts and performers into his theatre. He amplified differences as much as he preached synthesis, avoiding bland homogeneity. What Uchino confirms, though, is the progression of artists like Suzuki from the radical fringes of Japanese theatre into the mainstream. Suzuki has been consistently 'apolitical' if not socially engaged, but his playing with form was initially radical and challenging. Since the 1980s his performance work has moved literally and metaphorically from the fringe to the centre, as the examples of the commercial production of *Sweeney Todd* (1981) and the development in Shizuoka illustrate. Peter Eckersall contextualises this progression: 'The vastly different context for 1990s theatre has undermined *angura* as a site of radical culture. As long-time observer of new Japanese theatre Akihiko Senda argues, "the relentless logic of capitalism has unified us all".'[6] Such a statement reflects badly on the edifices of SPAC, described in Chapter Three, with its leisure-oriented aspirations. If Suzuki was still considered avant-garde at the end of the last century, that description cannot be applied in this one. Suzuki's recurring metaphor in performance of man's sickness and his unwillingness to propose alternatives and only ask questions, becomes untenable as society grows increasingly dystopian. The illness remains undiagnosed and his theatre teeters precariously on its feet.

Universality is also tested in collaboration, where cultural differences challenge such idealism. How can universal aspirations be applied in a process, as people work together across cultures? Sexual politics is one fraught area. The training has been described negatively as aggressive and a primarily male domain.[7] It might encourage aggression but this is not necessarily bad, or exclusively male. Counter-arguments run that women are 'empowered' by the training, a phenomenon I have observed. The method's principal teacher or master (this does show some of the distance still to be travelled in discourse) is also a woman, Ellen Lauren, as was Suzuki's lead actor for twenty-four years, Shiraishi. Although they are subservient to the artistic director (as in the majority of theatres), they are also given extensive autonomy. Gender also became an emotive issue in Australia during the co-production of *The Chronicle of Macbeth* (1992). Several performers struggled to accept what they considered Suzuki's masculine authoritarianism as company director and artist. This was exacerbated by racial issues, with the inclusion of the American Ellen Lauren as Lady Macbeth in an otherwise Australian and male company.

Concerns about gender relate also to the content of performances. Carol Fisher Sorgenfrei has written that

> several of the most influential male theatre artists in contemporary Japan exhibit strongly gynophobic tendencies. Shuji Terayama, Tadashi Suzuki, Juro Kara, and Shogo Ohta demonstrate the conflicted male attitude toward mothers, female lovers, and wives. Each depicts women not so much as individuals but as beings defined by sexuality and power designed to fulfill male psycho-sexual fantasies based on fear. The resulting images can be disturbingly sado-masochistic, with the females represented as castrators, dominatrices, or slaves.[8]

Sorgenfrei surely has a point. Suzuki's *Clytemnestra* did depict such a negative, subordinate picture. However, he tries to present the plight of Japanese women critically. Part of the impact of *On the Dramatic Passions II* was its eye-opening and provocative portrayal of a typical Japanese woman, who is chained and fantasises about love and release. Shiraishi's madness and scatological actions undermined any sexual appeal in her entrapment. *The Trojan Women* also inevitably portrayed women as slaves, but Suzuki presented shocking scenes of violent rape sensitively and without voyeurism. It was also explicit that these women had become slaves as the result of men's violent squabbling. However negative such representations, to no extent were they presented for male delectation as critical responses attested.

Suzuki's productions broadly scrutinise human relations without offering solutions. He depicts men as cynically as he depicts women, showing despots, senility, passive cultists or irradiated victims of Hiroshima. Authoritarian control and sexism might be endemic in Japan, but Suzuki is highlighting the mechanisms of power as they appear in all cultures and across genders, critiquing group structures and allegiances, as in *The Bacchae* (1978). He never provides answers to social problems but aims to enlighten through provocation rather than by proposing alternatives, as Bertolt Brecht did. Necessarily, therefore, he does not eschew negative reception, especially in countries where there might be much more constructive gender relations than in Japan and more positive role models. Sorgenfrei's observation helpfully depicts a tendency but misses the mark with much of Suzuki's vast *œuvre*. But as Japanese society becomes more dystopian and gender relations break down further, to criticise without suggesting remedial action seems increasingly irresponsible.

Nowhere are the difficulties that arise in cross-cultural contact more evident than in Suzuki's enterprise with Anne Bogart. The inertia of this project raises doubts about the feasibility of international collaboration. Is such cooperation possible, especially with a director like Suzuki who has a long track record and a very singular vision? He has extensive experience of partnerships, though not with other directors, where the attribution of responsibility is complicated. He has been artistic director of mixed-race productions, such as *The Chronicle of Macbeth*, but these cannot be considered collaborative *per se*. What went wrong with the Saratoga International Theatre Institute, a widely anthemed joint venture?

Anne Bogart co-founded SITI with Suzuki in autumn 1992 in order to create a new international theatre centre. SITI's maiden statement was general enough to commit both parties to little beyond two co-productions a year and practical cooperation. One intended core activity was integrated workshops in Suzuki training and Viewpoints (Bogart's improvisational dance-based compositional technique). Initially, this was for an annual summer residential course at the independent liberal arts institute Skidmore College, Saratoga. Workshops in both techniques have since spread to New York and other American cities, and are the most successful aspect of the collaboration. Suzuki and Bogart carried on autonomously making their own performances, sharing some performers and hosting each other's works. But co-productions did not happen and by 1997 the international dimension to 'transcend cultural barriers' had narrowed into a predominantly national brief that would 'redefine and revitalize contemporary theater in the United States through an emphasis on international cultural exchange and collaboration'.

It is hard to see what would sustain Suzuki's active interest in such a project. He had already been involved in this to a small extent for more than ten years through his participation in training programmes at American universities and colleges. Perhaps the birth of SITI was motivated primarily by the survival of both founding companies in systems with extremely limited state subsidies, seeking strength in numbers and to attract money that can accrue from international exchange and liaison. This is, of course, a sensible and pragmatic way forward but does not predicate artistic cohesion.

The workshop course in Saratoga was scheduled close to the summer Toga Festival. This timing was constructive, allowing Bogart's pieces, *The Medium*, *Small Lives/Big Dreams* and *Orestes*, to play in both places, and Ellen Lauren to also perform in Suzuki's productions of *Waiting for Romeo* and *The Bacchae*. In spite of such mutual potential, tensions arose. Eelke Lampe struggles to be positive, but even in her inaugural article signs of strain and irreconcilable differences emerge, the 'Collaboration' of her title yielding to 'Cultural Clashing'. Interculturalism encourages artistic negotiation of such disparities but differences can easily become insurmountable on the ground. Suzuki considers 'struggle' and 'battle' fundamental to performing but not necessarily to administrative cooperation.

Lampe's critique in her September 1994 piece in *Anne Bogart Viewpoints* goes further, pointing out that Bogart was working mostly with American actors and that SITI was operating bi-culturally between Japan and America rather than multiculturally. Suzuki was still employing cross-cultural casting, though this again was bi- rather than multicultural. The main drive of the project was in fact international rather than multicultural as Lampe implies, but this distinction aside, cracks in the structure became irreparable. Embarrassingly, Suzuki was the only non-American at one symposium in the United States. The year 1996 was the last time Bogart took work to Toga.

To my knowledge, nothing has been written or stated publicly about the shift in ownership, but in 1994 Suzuki handed over responsibility for the Skidmore training programme to SITI performers and Lauren, putting his energy instead into the Shizuoka arts centre. He has continued to collaborate with individual artists such as Lauren, and on paper is still designated a co-founder, but SITI is now Bogart's project and is the name of her group (known also as the SITI Company). Reviews of their productions, *Cabin Pressure* and *War of the Worlds*, at the Edinburgh International Festival in August 2000 made no mention of Suzuki, and the programme names him only in passing.

The poor reception of SITI's work in Scotland was consistent with the panning that critics gave the whole official theatre festival programme. Most reviewers found the metatheatrical playing of *Cabin Pressure* (which was about actor and audience interaction) embarrassingly naïve and conceptually sloppy. Many also found the level of acting extremely poor, if nevertheless 'stylish', a word that appeared in several reviews. This certainly belies the great success SITI have achieved in America and elsewhere and might reflect a lack of appetite in Britain for postmodern practice such as Bogart's. But it also shows the validity of Suzuki's sentiment that training is only a 'grammar'. However good the training and receptive the performer, commendable performances do not automatically ensue. If Suzuki's vision is to be carried forward through his training and through collaborators like SITI members, it may not always be evident. More pertinently, it may not always do him good. However stylish, possessing technique is only part of the job.

There is little doubt, though, about the positive effects training and rehearsing with Suzuki have had on many Western performers. Recurring preoccupations (shaped by Suzuki's world view) arose in interviews I conducted, which can be summarised as follows: the need to counter individualism by creating theatre groups or communities; the restrictions of taboos within performance practice and the value in altering accepted norms; and the necessity of breaking away from realism. Even the fact that such issues are part of these performers' discourse validates the contribution Suzuki has made.

The most important of these matters for me (which I will deal with first) is the challenge to realism in Suzuki's practice. This arose originally from his frustrations with *shingeki*, outlined in the previous chapter. This oppositional aspect explains the affinity between Suzuki and Bogart, for he believes she is taking on the backbone of American theatre: realism, and the Stanislavski derived system of acting which supports it. By refusing to breathe the theatrical air that is so all-pervasive around her, she has created a vacuum that demands to be filled by something new.[9]

This vacuum has partly been filled by Suzuki's own method. Yet can Suzuki's training fulfil such high expectations and help forge an alternative tradition to realism? This conjecture is hyperbolic. However, his approach certainly provides fresh perceptions and structures with which to tackle a range of texts, naturalistic or otherwise.

Ellen Lauren also diagnoses the current failing with much contemporary theatre as resulting from realism's limitations. In interview she stressed that we are continually confronted by televised and mediated images, including

> acts of violence, an extreme use of human energy that we often don't know lives inside us all. Some recent plays don't necessarily break open in a creative, expressive way the potential that plays once had to express the human spirit and the quality of energy of which the human being is capable. Such animal energy, as Suzuki calls it, is found in the hearts and minds of characters from Euripides, Shakespeare and even Chekhov. It is through exploring the physical condition of these characters, the 'state of energy' they are in, that we discover what it means to be human in its fullest capacity.

Lauren is right to suggest that theatre can scarcely keep up with the hyperrealism of film and television or even of life itself as the media presents it. The plays of Mark Ravenhill and Sarah Kane con-textualise her comment, representing what has been dubbed a 'new wave'[10] of writing that uncompromisingly exposes the violence in real life. Detractors have considered these naïvely attention-seeking with their shock tactics, but they do evidence the contemporary theatre's struggle to compete with television drama and with mediated reality, even if it is too early to define this as a new wave. Lauren wishes to counter this problem, which for her depends as much on the nature of performing as upon textual material. Suzuki does not proffer new models of writing as such, but suggests reinvigorated modes of performing to help depict the extremes of expression found in much classical drama.

Individualism and isolation among Western performers, promoted by funding structures, concepts like 'finding your character' and the fetishised introversion of Lee Strasberg's Method, have all generated a desire for greater complicity among fellow artists.* Those I interviewed professed a similar aspiration to establish a home as Suzuki did with SCOT. Inspired by the singular purpose of the theatre buildings in Toga and the concentration possible in the village, they are not, however, considering such a permanent rural retreat. Their answer is not yet a geographical relocation (the Saratoga workshop course is only three weeks long) but an introspective search, finding within a consistently trained body a sustainable and less fluctuating relationship with the theatre.

Home can be discovered through a familiar use of the body, in the way that a *noh* performer can embody a space, as suggested in the next chapter. The SITI performers have found unity through a common training programme. A family grows from this familiarity, as kinship and community are established by shared experience, systems, principles and vocabulary. This family can then 'breed' its own 'children', as Lauren indicated in interview:

> In teaching as many students as we [SITI] have in New York, there has now become quite a community who've had some exposure to this training [. . .] This training can provide a very real vocabulary that actors can speak together; you can immediately become an ensemble, working in the same world with a similar sensibility.

The notion of actors sharing 'sensibilities' and one 'world' may seem limiting or homogenising. For Lauren, though, the application of Suzuki training does not demand uniformity in creative terms and is focused mostly on enhancing technical understanding. Besides, SITI's utilisation of this Japanese approach is intended to counter the rampant individualisation which is endemic in the American star system and which pervades the world of theatre as it does film – a

---

* The choice of alternatives is not quite as clear-cut as I may appear to be suggesting. Criticisms and counter-arguments have been fully argued in a sparky debate between Anne Bogart and voice teacher Kristin Linklater moderated by David Diamond, titled 'Balancing Acts', published in *American Theatre*, January 2001. The desire to find alternatives to Strasberg's method and for such issues to be aired was proved by the passionate letters in response to the article.

tendency that is increasingly infecting British theatre as more and more celebrities like Nicole Kidman and Jerry Hall take off their clothes in London's West End.

Suzuki training provides an opportunity to extend the performer's 'comfort zone' of another kind. For Suzuki, home also implies the formation of standards by which to judge your work. Tom Nelis refers here to rehearsals with Suzuki, but the method attempts to formulate equivalent demands in training:

> What Suzuki is interested in is taboo in the United States. The only experience equivalent to working with him is being held up at gunpoint. When you think your life is on the line your survival mechanism kicks in. Professional artists are not allowed to do that and undergraduates do not expect to be treated that way. It's called 'maltreatment'. The fact that *that's* where you have to go is totally unexpected. It's not part of our culture.

Nelis believes that political correctness in America bleeds into the theatre and limits directors and teachers. His subtext is that self-censorship circumscribes the energetic and emotional field in which the performer operates. This restraint is also culturally and socially determined. To articulate this, Nelis employs emotive and sensationalist language that draws from daily life, further entrenching the dominance of social frames within performance. Nelis is seeking appropriate metaphors to define the otherness of working with Suzuki, but he ironically sites his discussion within social parameters.

As well as enabling the shift out of the daily and the social, Suzuki's and other Asian approaches cultivate appreciation of repetition. Earle Ernst has recognised 'the Japanese concern for continuity of a family and [. . .] the propensity to respect precedent rather than investigation'.[11] In the West it is often mistakenly believed that innovation arises from the new rather than the familiar. Funding structures reflect this demand for originality. But constancy of practice is surely central to most creative approaches, with few exceptions, as Lauren stresses:

> This idea that the training is mind-numbing, or that the repetition of it is militaristic or limiting to the imagination, is, frankly, narrow-minded and a complete misunderstanding of the scope of

this work. It is hard to keep your imagination and your inner world going while you're doing something over and over again, but that's the very foundation upon which rehearsal and the creative process is built. Virtuosity is accomplished by a series of logical steps that build a runway from which to get airborne. The purpose of the training is flight. But at least 80% of the time the runway is built from repetition and will, from sheer perseverance.

Suzuki training's creative elements (and the gratification arising from these) are peripheral, so that its enactment demands a personal and committed response, generated by the performer's own application and diligence. You battle with your own boredom threshold and the requirement to imaginatively keep the exercises alive. This provides a fertile foundation for innovation.

The idea of following a 'way' and the importance of perseverance have become etic clichés within Western perspectives on Japanese culture. The title *The Way of Acting* endorses this (though it stems from J. Thomas Rimer's reinvention of the Japanese original, which is 'The Power of Transgression'). The notorious Japanese television competition *Endurance,* in which individuals struggle with ridiculous, distasteful and often dangerous tasks, such as eating worms for the viewers' amusement, symbolises this trait. It also demonstrates the sophistication of the Japanese in their rationalisation and exploitation of such perceptions. Suzuki training cuts through truisms and self-parodies. It provides an accessible and immediate process which embodies such principles without romantically elevating them. Practice cannot help but teach truths and force self-confrontation, as any dedicated martial artist would testify. There is no room for the pleasure or relaxation of parody in Suzuki training, especially when the pain and effort kick in.

Without wishing to reinforce stereotypical views about the training as military drill, the personal pleasure and satisfaction that engaging in such communal action can invoke should be emphasised. Janet Goodridge has noted that

> During preparations for a revival of Arnold Wesker's army-based
> *Chips with Everything* (Royal National Theatre, 1997) actors who had
> experienced military training, and some of the others who had
> been rehearsing, remarked to interviewing journalists on the

satisfaction they felt in the correct performance of synchronised, precisely timed drill. McNeil describes his experience [. . .] 'a strange sense of personal enlargement . . . becoming bigger than life, thanks to participation in collective ritual'.[12]

We need to move beyond paranoia about the dangers of Fascism (Goodridge inevitably then makes a link to Nazism) and consider the biological rather than social impact of choral movement in training. The desire for rhythmical cohesion and synchronicity is not specifically Japanese or the domain only of right-wing artists such as Yukio Mishima. Audiences enjoy and critics respond warmly to such timing and mutuality, as the success of Theatre de Complicite's technique evidences. Lessons of the past are contained in many Asian and traditional Japanese performing arts like *noh*, where they have been handed down by *noh*'s fourteenth-century pioneers Zeami and his father Kanami for Suzuki's artful extraction. The problem Westerners might have with some of these notions and practices reflects more on them than on Suzuki, showing the limitations of a dominantly etic perspective. Few actors would deny the need for such rigour and precision and would realise that such a 'way' is not the only 'way'. It is also a means to an end.

The training fulfils several vital roles for performers like those in SITI and Frank in Australia. It encourages bonding, enables exploration of acting outside naturalistic conventions and offers a rigorous daily practice and principles. With these the performer can move away from working on character and text to working on themselves and their relationship to the audience. For Suzuki, 'Culture is the body' rather than the text or other fictions. He recognises that we are only ever ourselves, whatever else we hope to or intend to represent. Suzuki's culture might not correspond with everyone else's but we should at least recognise the contribution it has made and can make. We might not want to practise Suzuki training, live and work in a remote village, or be held under the authoritarian sway of a single director, but we may well look back on this example with affectionate nostalgia and longing – for its discipline, commitment, standards and the vision it embodies. I certainly admire all these, though not without reservations.

With such an autocratic director and rigid training method, it is vital to ask if there is life for performers after working with Suzuki. The problem is not that they have been trained in a specific body use, for the principles espoused in the training can be widely applicable. Rather it is the close-knit company life and the humble relationship to the director from which it is hard to disengage. Several performers have described how difficult it was to leave SCOT and some did so unannounced or overnight in order to avoid confrontation with Suzuki. Japanese group models like SCOT (with a collective operating under the dominant artist figure) have been challenged by both internationalisation and ensuing oversensitivity about group structures and autocratic leaders, as suggested in the previous chapter. The murderous Sarin gas release by the Aum Shinrikyo cult on a Tokyo subway in 1995 also discredited such communities. Suzuki has always firmly denied that his group is a cult of any kind (however different it might appear from the outside), but these events inevitably stimulated public and personal questioning of organisations such as this.

This seems an appropriate moment to briefly assess Kayoko Shiraishi's career post-1990, for it is she who most epitomises the practice and who therefore might have been most trapped by it. In fact she has continued to work successfully as an actress in Japan. In 1992, she performed in the American director Julie Taymor's *butoh*-inspired version of Igor Stravinsky's *Oedipus Rex* at the Saito Kinen Festival in Tokyo, which included Taymor's hallmark giant puppets. In 2000, she presented a solo presentation of ghost stories, *One Hundred Stories,* at arts centres throughout the United States. Most notably for British audiences, she appeared as Titania/Hippolyta in Yukio Ninagawa's production of *A Midsummer Night's Dream* (at the Mermaid Theatre, London, in 1996) and as the mother figure Nadeshiko in Shuji Terayama's *Shintoku-Maru,* also directed by Ninagawa and brought to the Barbican a year later.

This casting and the international status of the directors Shiraishi has worked with show the respect she commands. Ninagawa is Suzuki's main directorial rival, of the same generation and with a similar background. He has achieved much more success in Britain than Suzuki, who was sunk by his 1994 Barbican production of *The Tale of Lear,* discussed in Chapter Five. Ninagawa has earned this position with safer and less deconstructed interpretations of classic plays than Suzuki does, and in a more popular style. These have also had a mixed reception, but Ninagawa has consistently been invited back to do more, thanks in part to the energies of producer Thelma Holt.

If we take these productions as representative, Shiraishi has sustained her success and adapted to other directors with impressive flexibility. The imprint of the training and her twenty-four-year experience with Suzuki may be indelible, but this did not prevent some very favourable reviews in both productions. Some were also naïve. One reviewer called her a 'kabuki actress'. Most critics commented on the surprising timbre of her voice and the almost animal sounds she emitted in the Bottom/Titania love scenes. In The Guardian, Brian Logan described how

> Titania soon dispels such tenderness – she's got a voice like a scratched blackboard and a chalky-white face with such a capacity for grotesque and fantastical expression, it's refreshingly clear that she hails from an acting tradition light-years from our own.[13]

Alastair Macaulay in the Financial Times was less positive:

> To these oriental ears, most of the actors speak Japanese as if it were a form of barking. When Titania is telling Bottom 'I pray thee, gentle mortal, sing again/Mine ear is much enamoured of thy note', she sounds like a Pomeranian who has been stung by a wasp.[14]

Macaulay confirms reservations raised about Suzuki's actors' text recitation in Chapter Four. Whether Suzuki is merely extending a typical Japanese mode of vocal delivery or has influenced Ninagawa through Shiraishi, I am uncertain. Yet the example of Shiraishi proves that there is life after SCOT and it is possible to traverse 'light-years' and work elsewhere with the principles and even the voice that Suzuki has cultivated.

The interaction that has grown out of Suzuki's work in Australia reveals potential hazards with collaboration. The 'Austral Asian Performance company' Frank are connected to Suzuki primarily through John Nobbs. After his appearance as Banquo in The Chronicle of Macbeth, he was invited to take other leading roles in Suzuki's productions, including the Reverend Father in Dionysus (1990). This link was deepened when Frank's co-artistic director Jacqui Carroll was awarded an Australian Creative Fellowship to study Suzuki's directing and training. The company has now taken performances to the Toga and Shizuoka festivals and taught workshops internationally that have been mandated by Suzuki.

Founded in 1993, Frank is building on positive critical responses in Australia. Their publicity reveals an intimate connection to Suzuki. Yet it is one thing to respect their mentor and occasional collaborator, quite another to be so entwined that they are identified mostly through his practice. On paper their repertoire and the mode of adaptation suggested seem derivative, with productions of *The Tale of Macbeth*, *Romeo and Juliet* and *Oedipus Rex*. Even newspaper reviews acknowledge Frank's indebtedness to Suzuki. SITI have progressed further from Suzuki to become fully independent. Frank's connection to Suzuki is no doubt sustaining and life-giving, but their twice-weekly training in the Suzuki method need not circumscribe their performance repertoire. The company can break free from what is simultaneously stimulus, lifeblood and stranglehold.

The training is the dominant means by which Suzuki's total practice has become known. The growth of interest in approaches to acting, such as Michael Chekhov's, that offer alternatives to Stanislavski has meant that Suzuki's method no longer stands as isolated as it did when Brandon encountered it in 1976. Suzuki's 'way' may offer little to artists other than the performer, and Suzuki is rightly dubious about prescribing models for directing. However, it is the performer who will remain at the centre of the performance process. The development of multimedia and digital technologies is a vivid challenge to notions of Suzuki's such as animal energy. Yet our most complex technology is still the human body and in particular the brain, whose parameters are still largely unmapped. Suzuki has demonstrated that it is possible not to drown the performer in non-animal technologies, while making powerful performances in large spaces. Through the body he presents alternatives to intensifying mechanisation.

If we wish to keep the theatre alive in this century we should hold on to this capability. Australian performance artist Stelarc offers one integrated way forward, combining his body's muscular dance with advanced robotics and performance dissemination over the

Internet. Japanese scientists are the world's greatest innovators, potentially enabling multiple Stelarcs. Ironically, Japan has also given birth to some of the most technically complex and enduring performer techniques. Suzuki has stated that 'One reason the modern theatre is so tedious to watch, it seems to me, is because it has no feet'.[15] However hyperreal, virtual or up in the air circus- or computer-inspired performances might become, we need performers who can keep contact with the ground.

Rumours persist that Suzuki is more interested in business and buildings than art. The energy put into starting up the new complex at Shizuoka has inevitably deflected his focus away from performance work. The question mark raised earlier – how to surpass *On the Dramatic Passions II*? – is even more pertinent now. What can Suzuki do next? Although we should treat the criticisms of rival director Takeshi Kawamura of the experimental company Daisan Erotica with caution, they do reinforce a sense of creative inertia. Kawamura lumps Suzuki in with *butoh* and with Juro Kara: 'At the beginning of the 1980s their aesthetics became static. They were not exploring any further. They had established their aesthetics and they were enclosing them within what they had established'.[16] I would not totally endorse Kawamura's view that Suzuki's aesthetic has been completely static during these twenty years. The diversity of his responses to a range of source materials, for example, has helped to alleviate the repetition of his framing and style. Yet the 1999 performance of *Sayonara Toga* was a collage of old bits stuck together with scarcely an attempt at integration or elision, and showing scant vision.

THREE

•

SUZUKI'S SPACES

Tadashi Suzuki first visited the small mountain village of Toga in 1976.

> I remember the day very well. It was February 12, 1976. The place was buried deep in heavy snow and the drifts were blowing badly. There were five old farmhouses there which had been moved and were no longer in use. I made arrangements on the spot to borrow one of them.[1]

This is how he describes his initial impression of the place that was to become his family and company home, an arts complex of four theatres and site of a seventeen-year festival of international significance. The image of snow blanketing everything and the bleak emptiness presented a blank sheet on to which Suzuki could stamp his own practice.

The trip to Toga followed a nationwide search for an appropriate venue in which to re-establish the Waseda Little Theatre outside Tokyo.

> It seemed to me that in terms of traditional Japanese styles of architecture, there were only three possibilities that could provide the proper conditions: a castle, a Buddhist temple, or a mountain farmhouse, particularly the kind with a steeply pitched roof.[2]

The authorities would be unlikely to let him change a temple, and castles were few and far between. Suzuki was also not sure that he would even be allowed near the latter. He therefore chose to look for a farmhouse and someone recommended he visit Toga. Once there, he knew that the local domestic architecture had the right potential because its internal structure allowed enough space and height for a

57

small stage, auditorium and lighting. So began one of the most significant developments of a theatre community and its base in Japan, if not the world.

This chapter will describe and assess in pragmatic terms Suzuki's concrete achievements with theatre architecture, such as the conversion of the farmhouse in Toga, as well as the environments the buildings occupy. It will then relate these to his theories about performance space and demonstrate how practice and theory intertwine and how his use of space connects with other elements of the production process, be it scenography, training or interaction with an audience. Suzuki's first fifteen years of exploration should also not be forgotten. This was in a more orthodox urban environment, before he realised his aspiration to create a centre for his company away from the distractions and assumptions of Tokyo's cultural scene.

The shift of experimental theatre artists in Japan towards outdoor and unorthodox spaces (several of them operating with portable tents) has been touched upon in Chapter One. Suzuki was also not alone in investigating *noh* theatres as a site or model for contemporary performance. This was taken up by Shogo Ota, a peer of Suzuki's, most notably in his 1977 production of *The Legend of Komachi* with the Transformation Theatre.[3] The piece's critique of contemporary life was framed by a silent old woman cooking and then eating noodles. It was presented on an actual *noh* stage, rented for the purpose, breaking the centuries-old norm that these be restricted to *noh* actors. Like Robert Wilson and Suzuki, Ota drew various acting principles from traditional theatre, in particular slow movement. Such investigations were not only a reflection of individual taste, but part of a wider trend. What stands out about Suzuki's enterprise and his reformulation of a *noh* theatre in the farmhouse in Toga is the remote location for this and the scale with which he challenged and reinterpreted traditional sources.

Space as Suzuki understands it is not just the stage on which the performer walks, nor the intangible entity which they attempt to control, and which their body occupies. Theatrical space refers as much to the total environment and context within which the event happens as it does to the actor–audience arrangement or the body alignment that the training enables so precisely. As such, theatre needs to extend outwards and be coordinated with the natural or local habitat. To attain this, Suzuki has collaborated with one of the world's leading architects, Arata Isozaki.

Born in 1931, Isozaki founded his architectural group Arata Isozaki and Associates in 1963, with whom he has designed significant buildings around the world. He has been active in curating exhibitions of architecture, art and culture, and has received many awards, including the Japanese Culture and Design Award (1993). Among his major works are: an exhibit based on a *noh* stage as part of '*Ma*: Japanese Time-Space' for the Autumn Arts Festival at the Musée des Arts Décoratifs in Paris (1978), which subsequently toured internationally; the Museum of Contemporary Art, Los Angeles (1986); Tokyo's Globe Theatre (1988); and the Team Disney Building, Florida (1990). As well as the Toga complex, he has also collaborated on two other projects with Suzuki: the Art Tower Mito, Japan (1990); and the Shizuoka Performing Arts Park (1997). Isozaki appropriates ideas from such diverse sources as the Vienna Secession and Marcel Duchamp. He believes in the validity of quotation and the reuse of successful design elements and themes from different periods and styles, a recycling which he calls 'maniera'. Chosen elements are blended to make a coherent, autonomous whole in works that must always be responsive and adapted to their cultural context. Such theories and practices (which he articulates in writing as well as in building) have made him the leading creative figure in Japanese architecture and an influential architect world-wide. Together, he and Suzuki have designed and built theatres, rehearsal rooms and arts complexes. Suzuki may be recognised predominantly for his training, but these material attainments need to be proclaimed for their breadth, imagination and pragmatic surmounting of obstacles.

The desire to locate theatre practice within a natural environment has had many antecedents. French director Jacques Copeau was the father of this notion of a return to nature, working with his company Les Copiaus in his Burgundy retreat in the early part of the twentieth century. For him, the rural context and its absence of conventions exposed the actors' habits and assumptions. He wanted to remove his company from the influence of the Parisian theatre's artifice. With Susan Bing, Copeau set up a school in order to coach and sensitise his actors to their renewed sensibilities. He also toured in local areas, shaping his productions with material relevant to these fresh audiences.

A strategy to decentralise theatre away from urban centres can also be seen among Suzuki's contemporaries – Jerzy Grotowski, Wlodzimierz Staniewski and Eugenio Barba. Grotowski conducted most of his programme of paratheatrical activities with the Laboratory Theatre in the forests of Poland between 1970 and 1981. This included workshops of varying lengths, many of which were outdoors. In 1976, after six years of collaboration with Grotowski during this paratheatre period, Staniewski took a group of actors and settled in the small village of Gardzienice (from which they took the company's name – the Gardzienice Theatre Association) in south-east Poland. They were searching for what Staniewski described as 'A New Natural Environment for the Theatre'. Barba founded Odin Teatret in the small Danish town of Holstebro in 1964, a project that was consciously provincial rather than rural. His relocation from Norway to Denmark was pragmatic, following an invitation by the town council to be their resident company after a nurse from the small town saw one of their performances on tour. Suzuki would probably have been aware of these practices and possibly those of his European antecedents, but he has not referred to them as a source of inspiration nor for confirmation of his own concerns.

These directors are all linked by their attempt to remove obstacles inculcated in established spaces, fixed conventions and prescribed economic and social structures, but the distinctiveness of their projects should be remembered. Fundamental differences in the intentions and actions of all those cited are evident beyond their shared rejection of given values and preconceptions and their search for the new. Copeau, like Suzuki, set up a rural training programme for his actors, though Suzuki more clearly sought a continuation of ongoing practices rather than an opportunity for radical reformulation. Suzuki's quest was primarily linked to the aesthetics of theatre space and the need to establish a viable company base where ground rules could be reinvented, rather than the search for creative sources to revivify theatre as with Staniewski. Nor did

Suzuki want to reinvent the performer as a 'man of action' by defamiliarising the artistic context, as Grotowski attempted. Barba more consciously defined himself as operating on the political and artistic margins than Suzuki, working in what he has named 'Third Theatre' and on the fringes of societies, which even stretched to embrace the Yanomami Indians of the Venezuelan Amazon (1976). This stemmed from Barba's own personal situation and history as an *'emigré'*, about which he has frequently written and as the titles of his books *The Floating Islands* and *Beyond the Floating Islands* suggest. Holstebro offered Odin Teatret a small annual grant and space in an old farm, so this rural residency depended primarily on economic rather than artistic criteria. Financial factors did play a major part in Suzuki's decision, but his move was motivated as much by a hunger for his own working space shaped by him, which coincidentally also turned out to be an old farm. Rather than emphasising marginality as Barba did, Suzuki wanted to make Toga *the* centre, and as such played an influential role in the global shift away from the urban context of theatre-making in the 1970s.

Of those cited, Suzuki is the director who has pursued this mission with the greatest material consequences, as this chapter will show. He has made considerable inroads into one of the major problems facing theatre artists today – how to sustain professional activity and find an appropriate environment in which to do so. 'Any actor who makes light of the fundamental physical relationships within the theatre space will discover that the matter of acting space becomes his most fundamental problem. The modern theatre has yet to work out a successful plan to deal with this problem.'[4] The director's primary task is to help the performer overcome this obstacle. Suzuki has done more to address this dilemma than even he might have anticipated at the time of his writing (originally 1984). The impact of his achievements on others may be limited by differences in the economic, cultural and geographical contexts, but he does offer transferable models for other artists and theatre cultures, suggesting concrete alternatives to received notions about the performance space. Moreover, he has found a way to sustain and nourish his own and his group's activity. In light of the fragmented nature of the performer's craft today, as they move between film and live event, ancient Greek and contemporary text, stylisation and naturalism, Suzuki's clearly defined spatial and architectural practice and the guidance it offers is as much as can be hoped for from any theatre director.

Toga Village

Suzuki's investigations into the possibilities of theatre space began most earnestly in the village of Toga, roughly four hundred miles north-west of Tokyo. The main residential part of Toga is in two halves, separated by a mountain ridge. An almost kilometre-long road tunnel, which was rebuilt and widened in summer 1988, bores through this. It was previously a rough-hewn narrow construction. The village's administrative heart lies on the western side of the ridge and contains the mayor's office, municipal buildings, houses, a temple, and a small hotel and shops, all clinging to the steep hillside. The eastern side is where Suzuki has built his base. It is hard to imagine how the two sides of the one village coexisted before the tunnel was built. It is an indication of the isolation and hardship of rural life earlier in the twentieth century. With images of Tokyo shaped by technological innovations dominant in Western minds and imaginations, it is easy to forget that Japan was primarily an agricultural country until rapid post-Second World War modernisation and industrialisation.

The eastern side of Toga, where Suzuki's theatres are located, is flatter and more open than the west. It stretches approximately five kilometres up the mountain valley alongside the River Momosa. The main road runs parallel to the river and has minor offshoots to ski centres, private houses and the Toga Performing Arts Park. Most of the river is controlled by concrete banks restraining the fast, cold mountain water that is a torrent even at the height of summer. The river is continually channelled off to the sides to create small feeder streams that can pour through controlled sluice gates on to the flat paddy fields that climb up the valley in steps. These are also blocked to trap and house fish in concrete ponds for the breakfast table or to water the neat gardens that are beside the houses. Water rushes down concrete gulleys beside the main road, as fast as the new cars that cruise up and down. Higher up the valley, towards the river's source, man's influence disappears as the road turns into a gravel track with no houses, where the river eventually runs its own course.

The village is an incongruous mixture of scales and functions, including the domestic and the grand, the personal and the communal. Houses are interspersed with a baseball pitch with floodlights, a huge gymnasium (this was used as a performance venue for Gardzienice Theatre Association at the 1993 Toga Festival), an international campsite and two ski centres. Some of the larger sloping-roof houses also provide tourist accommodation. There is a restaurant and a small shop next to the gym that sells postcards of the Toga Festival and tourist knick-knacks.

Toga also demonstrates a mixture of modern and ancient methods of work. Tourism rubs alongside farming and the two seem to coexist harmoniously, the former enabling the economic survival of Toga. Twice a day, the small Toga bus that can manage the steep hairpin bends speeds up and down the valley, which is overgrown with forests that start where the rice paddies finish. It brings newcomers as well as locals returning with provisions from Yatsuo town, twenty-five kilometres from Toga at the bottom of the valley, an hour on the bus.

A sense of order, peace and harmony pervades Toga. Shrines are dotted here and there on the road and mountainside. There are bright butterflies and birds, whose complex song rises above the constant hiss of cicadas. The paddies are all rectangular and rice is planted in neat rows. Marigolds line the side of the central road. House doors are frequently left open. At twelve noon taped music rings out from loudspeakers throughout the village to inform villagers at home or in the fields of the time. This is one of the few intrusions to interrupt the background noise of nature. This sense of tranquillity comes partly from the isolation. Yatsuo is fifteen kilometres from Toyama city airport, just outside Toyama, from where it is an hour to Tokyo by plane or four hours by bullet train, the *shinkansen*. The Toga road winds so steeply and with such precarious bends that it increases the sense of seclusion: few would want to drive to Toga for the sake of it. Beyond a love of nature, what would drag you here, where the road comes to a dead end? The difficult terrain makes Suzuki's achievement all the more admirable. It also makes his reasons for establishing a base here seem, on the surface, all the more perverse.

In such an intimate village setting, Suzuki could not avoid the many and various local challenges. Indeed, he refers frequently to struggle and battle as essential conditions of life. One national and also global issue which Suzuki has continually addressed is how to maintain rural populations by keeping young people in such areas. At the end of the Second World War, the total headcount of Toga stood at 4,800. It was 1,480 when Suzuki first arrived in the mid-1970s. At that time, the population was still declining rapidly. As agricultural labour became untenable, people moved into cities and larger towns looking for work. In *The Way of Acting*, Suzuki put Toga's population at approximately 1,200. The village now comprises about 1,000 people. At least this problem has stabilised for the moment, though it continues to be precarious and no one can be complacent.

Barbara Thornbury described the effects of depopulation in Japan in 1993: 'the continuing movement of young people from rural areas to major urban centres has hollowed out a number of communities.'[5] In her article she referred to a lead editorial in the *Japan Times* titled 'The Threat of Regional Depopulation' which explained that the population shift was ongoing and of national importance. In spite of this local 'hollowing', Toga manages to remain full of life and activities, mostly thanks to tourism. It is a busy holiday venue and the number of residents changes radically as rooms and the campsite book up in the summer and then in the winter for skiing. Toga is dubbed 'Snow Valley' and the authorities market the village vigorously, declaring its virtues to temporary visitors on numerous signs dotted along the roadside. The local authorities demonstrate equal enthusiasm for engineering and building projects, as evidenced by the taming of the river, the tunnel, the mountain road and a new school built in the late 1990s. What Toga has become bears scant relation to the size of its population and more to the aspirations of its residents and administrators. It has even twinned itself with the Nepalese mountain village Tukache 5,000 kilometres away, through a connection based on *soba*, or buckwheat, which is grown in both communities. Toga seems to act as a model village, demonstrating what is possible given energy, will and a lot of investment.

Suzuki's own plans have fundamentally contributed to this progression and his accomplishments are integral to the village as it exists and presents itself today. The Toga Performing Arts Park at the heart of the east side of the village is a clear indication of what conviction and vision can achieve. It includes several buildings which hosted the annual Toga International Festival. Toga's buildings have periodically cropped up since WLT's first performance in the old farmhouse theatre in 1976, resulting in a large complex that now includes theatres, a small office space and several accommodation blocks and houses that served the festival until its demise in 1999. There is even the Volcano Pasta House, established in 1992, providing sustenance for those attending the festival at its riverside location and hosting post-performance parties.

The Greek-style amphitheatre is the main focus of the park. Opened in 1982, it lies on the east side of the main road, overlooking a lake. In the middle of the water that teems with giant carp are two piles of stones. These miniature 'islands' represent a crane and a tortoise – the one rising tall and upright and the other sloping low in the water – and were constructed by Hiroshi Teshigahara, known as a master of *ikebana* (flower arranging). These are both symbols of longevity, for it is believed they live for 1,000 and 10,000 years respectively, and they appear frequently in Japanese gardens and lakes. The crane also acts as a fountain, its dark stones glistening in the falling water. On stage are two pillars, holding up nothing except the heavens and serving no direct function, but operating as a visual reminder of a *noh* theatre's four pillars that support the stage roof. The theatre has a steeply raked auditorium to keep the audience close to the action, with dressing rooms and storage space located underneath. Two *hanamichis* (or runways) stretch from both sides of the front edge of the stage to the lake's banks.

A *hanamichi* is an essential element of the *kabuki* stage, similar to a footbridge and constructed with planks. Etymologically, it means 'flower path', its name possibly derived from the fact that admirers used to lay flowers on it at the performers' feet as a sign of respect. Traditionally, it extends through the spectators and is usually located stage right, leading to the back of the stalls. Occasionally it is mirrored by another, stage left. An actor might hold a *mie* (or frozen pose) before exiting quickly down the *hanamichi* in thrilling proximity to the audience. The *hanamichi* accentuates entrances and exits, parades or high points of action.

On Suzuki's stage (or *orchestra* as it is called in the traditional Greek theatre) the two *hanamichis* allow long dramatic entrances and exits from either bank of the lake, and lead away from, rather than into, the audience. They thus have a similar energetic potential to *kabuki* theatre, amplified by their length. Runway is an appropriate term, as the SCOT actors speed along them in their wheelchairs (see Chapter Five), sometimes entering along one and exiting along the other, barely spending three seconds on the actual stage. The *hanamichis* allow both a distance and a speed that it is hard to create without constantly circling, as the actors do in Tadeusz Kantor's production of *Wielopole Wielopole,* or moving swiftly on and off from the wings. They are not, however, a part of the original design of the theatre, but were added after experimentation with a temporary runway. This mimics *kabuki* theatres where sometimes a second impromptu *hanamichi* is installed. Such addition is testament to the possibilities and flexibility that creating and managing your own space allows in a relatively uncontrolled administrative environment.

Nine rows of seats sweep in wide semicircles with a total seating capacity of around eight hundred. As members of this audience you enter the top of the auditorium by one of four points and look over the stage and lake towards the trees, which are reflected in the water. Beyond rises the wooded slope of the other valley side, providing a natural backdrop. During performances these trees are magically lit up with high-powered lights. The theatre itself nestles within trees and is approached by a gravel path, creating a further sense of isolation from civilisation. From your seat you see few signs of habitation, although at night you might occasionally notice car headlights on the main road. The whole is open to the elements and nature's sounds and smells.

Although the amphitheatre is made from concrete and the stage is black, it is not an incongruous sight within the mountain setting. In front of the seating and before the stage there is a small semicircle of gravel. This can become an overspill area for the audience, but it also creates a space made from natural materials at the centre of the construction. It gives a little distance between the stage and auditorium, in part enabling good visibility but also adding to the remoteness and other-worldliness of the 'beings' on stage. The architecture of the whole emulates Greek antecedents, but is modern and practical. Aesthetically, it recalls the principles of Japanese gardening, with the partial use of local materials such as the gravel and water, its integration into the pre-existing landscape, and its symbolic crane and tortoise islands. In exposing and lighting the mountainside, for example, the design draws out what already exists as much as it imposes its own imprint.

The space is open if you wish to see behind the scenes. Suzuki wants to reveal all aspects of the theatre process. You can even sit in the theatre auditorium by day to watch company rehearsals. In the daytime, on the track that runs behind the lake, you might observe technicians setting up fireworks for the spectacular production *Greetings from the Edges of the Earth*. When the company is striking what little set there is, you can spot SCOT members punting across the lake on a raft to undo the wires on which fireworks are strung. These create a line of light that showers down on to the water, the reflected image doubling the fireworks' radiance. More mundanely, you can see the plastic sheeting that leads from the dressing rooms through nettles and reeds to the lakeside entrances on to the *hanamichis* – a rough path for the wheelchair men. It is not that the wizardry of the design is revealed to show the 'magic of theatre' or other such clichés, but simply that little is conducted privately or consciously out of sight.

The scenography for performances outdoors and in the indoor spaces has a similar openness, though in a visual rather than public sense. Designs are usually basic and functional, with few fixed structures. This endorses an emphasis on the body in the space, which is defined, amplified or supported by simple movable props, such as wheelchairs, flags, umbrellas, laundry carts, dustbins or a table on wheels. In the farmhouse theatres, grilles or material are hung to create moods or cast shadows, enhanced by sweeping side lighting. There is little obscuring or transformative décor in Suzuki's productions, as reiterated in Chapter Five, but instead carefully selected symbolic objects and materials. The architecture and shaped natural environment become the main focus of the scenography.

Almost adjacent to the amphitheatre are two buildings which serve as the administration centre for the park and the festival. One houses the JPAC office, which for the duration of SCOT's summer residency in Toga keeps all the paperwork. This then has to be packed up and returned to the Tokyo office when they decamp. As the audience arrives in the early evening, this building is in a commotion, its sliding doors open for all to see the frenetic activity inside. Outside, tables with awnings to keep off the fierce heat are erected, where tickets, programmes and company literature such as the SCOT book are sold. The building opposite is for Toga village administration and houses a public telephone and rest room. The latter is adorned with photographs of productions from previous festivals and contains a video player to show some of these. Both buildings provide small rooms for meetings, administrative or artistic. The two worlds coincide, inseparable and mutually supportive.

The gravelled outside area between these small buildings becomes the 'foyer' as the audience congregates and darkness falls. You leave your car in a car park across the river from the theatre and are then guided by stewards to this collection point. You pass the local police (stationed to enjoy the event as much as patrol it) and walk across the Momosa on a bridge. The sculptures in the lake are lit and the amphitheatre glows with house lights, as does the entrance hall to the farmhouse theatre. All are reflected in the lake. Thatched roofs drip with water sprayed on to them to prevent danger from stray fireworks. Loudspeaker announcements shepherd you into lines according to ticket prices, so that seating can be coordinated. It is a big operation, deftly organised and stage-managed, encouraging compliance without coercion and a sense of anticipation and excitement.

David Tracey quotes Suzuki on this whole pre-performance process:

> One of the reasons I came to Toga was to explore how to create theatre in a space. The depths one must go to in thinking about this include what sort of road the audience came on, what experiences they had getting there, what they saw when they sat down, their surroundings. These are all factors for an artist. For me to have control over these things is vital to my form of stylisation.[6]

The journey and anticipatory wait almost become a rite of passage, preparing you for the theatre event. The scenography of the amphitheatre within the environment encourages you to look and observe, viewing the harmonious integration of man and nature. The organisational control the SCOT members exert over you is functional but helps create expectation and openness to what might come. This is enhanced by detachment from familiar routines and theatre conventions as you place yourself in others' hands. Your perception alters as you are welcomed into and participate in Suzuki's summer ritual, dominated by a celebratory festival atmosphere.

This transformative mood has been depicted in detail by Japanese critic Akihiko Senda in 'A First Trip to a Distant Village'.[7] This article was a review of A Night's Feast, but, more interestingly, it also charted the urban theatre critic's 'spiritual replenishment' in Toga. The events of A Night's Feast involved a lion dance by local artists, a section of the noh play Tsunemasa performed by the three Kanze brothers, and finally Suzuki's work. This was a short collage of previously performed sections of texts by Beckett, Chekhov, Oka Kiyoshi and Euripides, interspersed with loud music that included Carl Orff's Carmina Burana. Prior to the performances there were open rehearsals and training, revealing what Senda described as the group's 'quasi-religious discipline'. The performances were merely the culmination of these activities. On the afternoon of 28 August 1976, there was a free performance for four hundred or so villagers and in the evening some six hundred people packed into the farmhouse theatre for A Night's Feast.

Toga's isolation meant that Senda's trip took him away for 'virtually four days' for only one night of performances: 'The experience was a rare one, almost dream-like, one in which ordinary reality had somehow taken on an element of the fantastic [. . .] removed from our ordinary life and concerns, one is far more open to an unusual theatre experience.'[8] As a comparison, he recalled his visit to Epidaurus, outside Athens, where a Greek theatre also nestles into the hillside. This recollection came before the Toga amphitheatre was built six years later, but it is illuminating to see how this connection occurred to a visitor. The detachment from the daily that Senda described and the shift in perception this allowed both affirm Suzuki's intention to develop the site in the mountains as a way of encouraging fresh perspectives on the theatre event itself. The journey of the pilgrim directly accounts for the intensity of the act of worship at the place of pilgrimage itself; the two stages of the process are interdependent.

The evening in 1976 which Senda describes was a small beginning of high artistic risk. *A Night's Feast, Part 1* was the WLT's inaugural presentation in the village, but the huge turnout of both villagers and visitors was surprising and reassuring. It strengthened Suzuki's resolve to make theatre and make it there. The first generation of villagers who greeted the SCOT company were understandably puzzled and suspicious. Before their arrival in Toga, there would have been no more than two hundred visitors to the village at any one time. In one night, six hundred strangers appeared, a shock for residents. Trust was encouraged by making the free performance for the villagers an annual event. As the theatre company returned year after year, opening the work both to locals and a visiting audience, they were accepted with fewer reservations. Local people, trying desperately to keep their village alive, began to contemplate sharing this task with the 'outsiders' as one way to stem the area's economic decline.

The decision to settle in Toga was not predetermined from the beginning. Suzuki initially only planned to stay for five years. The company had continued to show their work (including a version of *Salome*) in rented spaces in Tokyo and elsewhere in Japan, without a permanent base. Pragmatically, their arrival in Toga arose from the fact that the company had lost its lease on their coffee-shop theatre space in 1976, which had subsequently been torn down. The cost of obtaining equivalent or better premises in Tokyo was prohibitive. In 1980, finances had improved enough to open a basement studio in Ikebukoro, Tokyo, for use during cold weather and to maintain a continuing presence in the capital. Suzuki made up his mind to leave Toga. On learning of the company's imminent departure, Toga's mayor begged Suzuki to carry on their activities in the mountain base. When Suzuki responded that the living conditions had to improve and that better theatre spaces were necessary, the village office decided to renovate the old farmhouse, offering 70 million yen towards the construction of a company home (roughly £400,000 according to the November 2000 exchange rate but 1980 prices). This was five per cent of Toga's annual budget and demonstrates an undeniable commitment. It also highlights the fragility of such a rural existence if the local government were prepared to commit such an amount to a risky project. With such backing and popular support, Suzuki accepted the mayor's request and planning began. The task of redesigning the old *sanbo* (as the farmhouse is known in Japanese) fell to Arata Isozaki. Like Suzuki, Isozaki is equally recognised as a writer and theorist who values the explanation of his work for cognoscenti and a broader public alike. The fact that both artists exploit and update traditional models, creating bold, challenging art with an explicit cultural and social purpose that can be defined loosely within a postmodern aesthetic, suited him for this reinvention. Their mutual love of artistic quotation and a complex understanding of space unified them and they have forged a long-lasting creative partnership and friendship. WLT had originally converted the traditional thatched *gassho-zukuri* house themselves (*gassho-zukuri* means 'constructed like praying hands', describing the steep pitch of the roofs which helps shrug off the deep winter snows), turning the large central kitchen into the stage area. This is where they had shown the several incarnations of *A Night's Feast*. The renovation of this space was Isozaki's first fully realised theatre project.

The desire to find a site that had not been initially designed as a theatre space began with Suzuki's attendance at Jean-Louis Barrault's Théâtre des Nations Festival held at his Théâtre Récamier in Paris in 1972. This theatre was 'extremely sober and simple [. . .] There was a special area made from several square rooms that must have once been used as living quarters [. . ,] it seemed more like a reused residence than a theatre.'[9] The theatre was in fact a converted house. Suzuki wanted to emulate this and recreate 'a space in which people had actually lived.'[10] Yet what Suzuki and Isozaki managed to forge was an even more difficult concept and a true hybrid – a theatre space that was both domestic and sacred,* where the daily and extra-daily could coexist.

In 1982, the farmhouse theatre was reopened, renovated by Isozaki to appear as it does today. To this building Isozaki added a

---

* Suzuki derives his understanding of this term from Romanian anthropologist Mircea Eliade, who differentiates between 'sacred' and 'profane' or 'worldly' time and thus space – see Eliade, *The Sacred and the Profane: The Nature of Religions*, Harcourt Brace Jovanovich, New York, 1959.

71

new entrance lobby, a 'space of light', where you take off and leave your shoes before passing through a small covered corridor into the dark interior of the *sanbo*. With many steps, the lobby leads you up the hill on which the *sanbo* perches. The concrete staircase also functions as seats on which to take off footwear or as an auditorium to view lectures or other small presentations on a central mini-stage. Although it is built lower down the hill from the *sanbo*, the hall reaches up to the same height as the *gassho* thatch, an echo. From a distance its slate grey-tiled roof looms up above the lake and amphitheatre auditorium. This is inspired by the *yagura* tower of early *kabuki* theatres, which originally housed a drum to announce the beginning and end of performances and which thus came to represent the spirit of the theatre.

Inside the *sanbo* you are struck first by the dominating black aluminium stage floor. This was borrowed from Isozaki's modified design of a *noh* theatre that was shown in France for his 1978 exhibition. It is central to the dark atmosphere that conjures the other-worldliness of *noh* performances, which Isozaki wanted to create in his original exhibit. Marianne McDonald has described the mood inside the farmhouse itself. This effect is particularly noticeable when you enter from the bright sunlight of a summer day.

All is painted black and the stage is lit by low-intensity lamps,
suggesting the original illuminations of Noh stages by candlelight
or lanterns. There is also a philosophical component to this low
lighting. Noh drama often showed the emergence of a divinity or
ghost from the darkness, as it were the primeval womb of the
world. This sense of oneness with the world was also the
experience of Greek drama for its original audience.[11]

Like Senda on his first voyage to Toga, the architecture inspired McDonald (a trained classicist) to link ancient Greek and *noh* theatres. These forms provide the inspirational axes around which Suzuki built his theatres in Toga as well as much of his performance work, as explained in Chapter Five.

Isozaki's designs made concrete Suzuki's belief in the need to rediscover the spiritual dimension of the theatre inherent in these two modes of performance. Suzuki reasons that obsession with naturalism and human psychology has ousted metaphysical qualities that he wants to reinstate. As well as the lighting and colour tones, the sense of a sacred space is encouraged by the intimacy of the whole design. Most of the audience of approximately 150 sit directly facing the twenty-foot-square stage on two rows of tatami (rice straw) mats, but the thrust means that a minority view the action side-on. Everyone huddles closely together on the mats, evoking the informal 'lived-in' atmosphere to which Suzuki aspired.

Much is constructed of blackened wood, with the notable exception of the stage floor. Beside the stage are two dressing rooms, one on either side. There is a control room by the main entrance with an adjacent office. The basic design of the stage area is almost identical to that of a *noh* stage, including the four central pillars (which were moved in Isozaki's design to create a larger stage) and the shiny floor, although in a *noh* space this would be uncoloured polished cypress wood rather than black aluminium. Isozaki also departed from the traditional décor, omitting the painted pine-tree backdrop (*matsubame*) for example, and placing large boulders under the stage rather than the clay pots which would traditionally be used to increase the resonance of the space. The construction borrows the essence and spatial dynamics of *noh* rather than the surface, allowing more adaptability than a direct imitation would allow. After all, *noh* theatres are made solely for *noh* performances. Isozaki's design also omitted *noh*'s long, angled entrance walkway (*hashigakari*) for which there is no room – a typical *noh* auditorium seats approximately four hundred people with a 320-square-foot stage and thus occupies a much larger total space. Instead, the *sanbo* has shorter entrances at either side of the upstage area. More entrances centre and upstage are enabled by revealing performers behind the sliding white paper and black lacquer screens, or *shoji*, which otherwise act as a backdrop. The whole building is circled outside by channels of running water.

Since Isozaki's second renovation of the farmhouse there has been frequent building in Toga, creating what is now known as the Art Park. Two years after the *sanbo* was finished in 1982, the amphitheatre was constructed, financed by the prefecture and the village on the understanding that it would also be used by them for other festivals and events. A thirty-room modern and rather utilitarian hostel was built at the same time. Other dormitories were added later in a more traditional local style. The humbler origins of the

73

company's presence in Toga should not be obscured in the light of what exists today.

The process was open to change, as recollection of the progression of events reinforces. From the perspective of 1986 and based on a news programme, Yukihiro Goto describes how

> In the near future the SCOT members will be settling down permanently in Toga village, establishing there a self-supporting theatre commune. He and his group will engage in farming as well as theatrical activities. Also the Toga theatre area is to be developed into a new mecca of international theatres – the 'New SCOT-Land'. As part of the project, in collaboration with the University of San Diego, Suzuki is currently building in the area a performing arts library and a new 500-seat theatre complex.[12]

The organic development of the Toga Park meant that plans inevitably altered. Isozaki's Studio/Library (reminiscent of a small modern church) was completed in 1987 and overlooks the river three hundred yards down from the *sanbo*. This studio has hosted many companies (including Anatoly Vassiliev's group from Moscow, which performed *Joseph and his Brothers* and *Fiorencia* at the 1993 festival, to name just one) but it has barely operated as a library, housing a few books in what might be called a reading room. The company did not begin farming as Goto suggested. Also contrary to Goto's expectations, Suzuki then began to develop more sites outside Toga (the Art Tower Mito opened in 1990) rather than consolidate a year-round presence in the village. The park did continue to expand and increase its potential to host international groups, with more spaces for accommodation and catering, but hindsight shows that the plans Goto outlined were subsequently reviewed and changed.

Toga has a tiny local population (and thus resident audience) as well as awkward access, that both mitigate against a permanent presence for a theatre group in the village. This is compounded by the inescapable factor of the local climate. As Suzuki recounted about his first visit, the village is snowbound in winter, with falls of at least three and sometimes six metres. The appealing blank sheet Suzuki enjoyed creates logistical complications. Snow usually falls at the end of November, but occasionally arrives as early as October. Access is therefore a fundamental obstacle, which explains why the company have normally balanced a long summer in Toga with a winter in Tokyo or another urban centre. Against such odds and a sign of their resilience, SCOT did organise two small winter festivals using the old *sanbo* in the 1980s. One year, there was heavy snow of about one metre every night and the actors had to dig their way out of their dormitories to reach the *sanbo*.

In part to counteract such climate constraints, in 1994 a new *sanbo* with a heating system (this was impossible to install in the old farmhouse) was built close to the administrative spaces, which can be used in colder weather. It can seat four hundred people but maintains the intimacy of the old *sanbo* by increasing both width and depth. With five rows of tatami mats, and beams and stage painted black, the new *sanbo* is a large-scale replica of Isozaki's original. Lights project up to illuminate the yellow straw thatch which is supported by three layers of cross-hatched timbers that get narrower the higher up they go. Black grilles placed in the ceiling throw striped shadows on to the stage and black cast-iron domestic wall lamps are used as house lights. There is an overwhelming smell of rushes, straw and wood. In the middle of this technologically sophisticated theatre space you do not lose a sense of the local nature. Whatever the limitations of such blunt duplication, this replica offers a practical solution to just one of the obstacles that mitigates so strongly against theatrical activity in this mountain village.

Suzuki's definition of 'local' refers as much to the indigenous people as it does to the environment. For him, artistic practice has to be integrated into its community, which was and still is almost impossible in a vast metropolis like Tokyo. This is partly pragmatic, to provide the infrastructure to support visiting audiences with accommodation, food and transport. But more vitally, it emphasises the social dimension of Suzuki's and SCOT's work: 'There should be a close relationship between the artists and their social environment, so they can affect it positively.'[13] Cooperation with an audience is fundamental to all theatre practice, particularly if the site is as isolated as Toga. Mutual enhancement is something Suzuki has written about at length in *The Way of Acting*. The advantage of such a project for Suzuki is primarily on a human rather than economic level, but financial reward can follow on from such interaction, for the village if not for Suzuki.

The struggle alongside the villagers fighting to save their dying community had, as Suzuki anticipated, a formative and cohesive effect on his artistic group and his own practice. 'In any terms you care to set down for commercial success in the theatre, our activities at Toga-mura fall into the red. We are held together by a kind of volunteer spiritual support that could only characterize a group with religious convictions.'[14] Through the necessity of collaboration with local people, a shared ambition arose to keep the village alive. Intention was supported by financial and practical aid, essential for building large structures like the amphitheatre. Suzuki has frequently expressed his empathy with Toga's mayor, whom he has invited on to the stage at various festivals to introduce himself and welcome the audience. This friendship and partnership has enabled the village to become a proactive entity defining and shaping culture, rather than a passive recreational site for city-dwellers.

As the notion of audience in Suzuki's theatre encompassed local villagers, so the whole village and its surroundings could become the company's theatre space. The performance of *Wasteland and the Wagtail* by British group Welfare State International at the first summer festival of 1982 took place on a mile-long ski slope above the village. It involved local people, employed in the winter to support skiing, and twenty Japanese theatre students for a preparation period of three weeks, ending with a barn dance after the performance for villagers and festival-goers. Such large-scale projects, extending the participatory community work that Welfare State International do in Britain, were enabled by the respect Toga villagers developed for WLT and then SCOT, that displaced their initial suspicions. There was mutual dependency and learning, with both groups fighting for what Suzuki sees in the long term as a near impossible cause – the survival of a tiny mountain village in an increasingly urbanised country. The change of title from the Waseda Little Theatre to the Suzuki Company of Toga, some eight years after the group's activities in the village began, epitomised and endorsed the symbiosis with which these two communities have interacted.

The construction of the park in Toga was an ongoing long-term and organic process spanning three decades. Buildings arose according to the influx of new funds and new demands, be they from SCOT, the villagers or an American university. Although each space serves its own specific function, they are all unified in their design by Isozaki and their location within the landscape. There was a steady increase in comfort and subsequently the length of time in which the company could operate in the village, without compromising initial principles, as the development of the *sanbos* demonstrates. As an audience member, you want to be comfortable and need to feel welcome, especially when you have spent so much time, money and effort to arrive there. A mood of harmony and pleasure was achieved spatially and architecturally, supported by the company's own welcoming attitude as they invited you into their home – a home that was invaded every summer by up to 10,000 visitors. After this hubbub of festival activity died away, the village returned to its quieter, more usual rhythms, sounds and isolation. Neither world seemed to irrevocably derange the other. It is this very life and commotion and this delicately balanced complementarity which ensured Toga's survival as a village and which sustained twenty-three years of activity as an international centre for the arts. It will be a quieter place without the festival.

Mito City

The development of an arts centre in this city would seem to be far removed from the principles that Suzuki enshrined in his buildings and their relationship to the environment in Toga. Mito lies an hour on the *shinkansen* north-east of Tokyo and has a population of approximately 100,000. The complex here is architecturally familiar to Western sensibilities, similar to modern arts centres throughout Britain, albeit with a more radical vision. Once Suzuki's company's home was firmly established in Toga, rather than reiterating the value of the rural environment for theatre-making, Suzuki followed through his aspiration to decentralise Japan's culture. As he has indicated, the choice of Toga was accidental rather than considered – 'any suitable place outside of the capital would have done as well as Toga'[15] – though the architecture did suit his purposes. We should not therefore be surprised that Suzuki also established a base in the quite dissimilar environment of Mito. After all, he freely admits he is 'naturally greedy'.

What Suzuki had learned about theatre spaces in themselves, as distinct from the total setting in which the buildings exist, could be put into practice and tested in Mito. In Toga, he had struggled to raise money and support along with the mayor and villagers, through the commitment of his group. With Mito, he did not have to fund the project, which must have felt a luxurious condition after more than a decade of his efforts in Toga. Such backing offered great opportunities. The city was making a large investment in the propagation of arts and culture, evidenced by the fact that approximately one per cent of its annual budget was given over for the new centre. Isozaki was invited to be the building's architect and he completed the complex in 1990. Suzuki was made artistic director of Acting Company Mito's (ACM) theatre in 1989, a position he held until he left in 1994. (There is only one of the original actors left in ACM at the time of writing, with most having departed to form SPAC theatre company.) *Dionysus* was premièred there in 1990, opening the theatre to Mito's public.

Art Tower Mito (ATM) is a modern complex which combines an entrance hall, concert hall, theatre (whose flexibility allows seating for between 472 and 636 people), gallery, conference hall, tower and plaza area. It is constructed from grey concrete with four above-ground floors and two below. A tower spirals upwards to a height of one hundred metres, a metal helix. The plaza leads people into the arts centre and provides squares of lawn as relief from the grey concrete and pillars of steel and the predominantly neutral colours. The focus of the plaza is drawn by a large grey rock suspended from steel cables, which is lit at night to reveal the spray from the fountain that engulfs it. Inside, all is made from stone of various colours, warm white plaster and revealed polished metal. The entrance hall contains a large organ and its pipes, recessed at one end. Even though the centre uses mostly natural materials like stone and marble, it bears no relation to Toga's *sanbos*. It is utterly urban and modern in its design. It is also an arts complex rather than purely a theatre, so has to be multifunctional and yet coherently planned:

> Art Tower Mito was conceived and designed with the aim of
> stimulating Mito's urban development, which had so far centred on
> the national highway [. . .] At Art Tower Mito, each facility, with its

respective focus on music, drama and art, has been made spatially independent, but, on the other hand, connected by common areas.[16]

The Toga and Mito complexes both attempt to present a unified aesthetic. Mito, however, is understandably more cohesive even though it is multi-purpose, for it was designed in advance as a single entity.

Differences between the two extend beyond constraints imposed by the urban and rural contexts. The evolution of ATM contrasts with the gradual development that took place in Toga. It also has quite another purpose. ATM houses two orchestras as well as ACM and coordinates events such as the 1993 'Polska' Polish Arts Festival which hosted the Gardzienice Theatre Association. This large ensemble played two performances, *Avvakum* in the entrance hall and *Carmina Burana* in the theatre, accompanied by contemporary Polish art exhibitions and seminars. The company performed in Mito after the festival in Toga, showing how Suzuki coordinated events hundreds of miles apart to help spread costs. Such a potential range of activities was anticipated at ATM whereas in Toga buildings sprouted or altered as the need arose and finances became available.

On the surface, the design of ATM bears few similarities to that Isozaki explored in Toga. The tower over the entrance hall in Toga recalls traditional theatre architecture. The one in Mito has a more local reference point, its roots in science rather than arts with its helix shape, and the hundred metres representing the 'hundred years of the city's modern form of government'. It thus operates more as an iconic advertisement for the building and the city as a whole. With such a dissimilar structure, purpose and context from the Toga complex, it is hard to see what principles Suzuki and Isozaki carried over from the established model into the new one at Mito, as they adapted to other demands.

A return to and updating of sources is a central concept that Toga and Mito share. Whereas Toga's amphitheatre and the *sanbos* resemble traditional Greek and *noh* stages, the ACM space is reminiscent of the Globe Theatre in its design. Isozaki was consultant for and principal designer of the Tokyo Globe, a reproduction of Shakespeare's original playhouse sponsored by National Panasonic that was completed in 1988, nearly ten years before London's own reconstruction opened. The theatre in Mito allowed Isozaki to improve on this design, erasing small errors that had become apparent in performance, such as the level stalls seats. In Mito, he raked these to create better sight lines. The ACM theatre is twelve-sided, its thrust stage ringed by three levels of curved, low balcony seats, with the stage at the centre of a circle. The dimensions of this area are made flexible through the use of trap doors. Black panels front the balconies, killing the light and partly obscuring the audience. The galleries are low to keep them close to the action. As in the Elizabethan model, a large capacity and intimacy coexist.

Even if the basic structure belongs to Shakespeare's day, the theatre represents the forward-looking spirit of the arts centre with hi-tech provision, though it has no large-scale stage devices such as revolves. What Isozaki carried through to Mito, that was begun in Toga, was a shifting of the process of theatre away from the viewing of pictures on a frame-like stage towards a more direct, interactive spatial experience. He has noted how 'revolutionary' Japanese theatre artists of the 1960s, like Suzuki, wanted

> to bring the audience and stage into extremely close contact with each other – allowing the audience almost to feel the actors' bodies, so to speak [. . .] an attempt to reestablish the relationship with the audience – in the form of dramatic space – that had existed in an era that produced both the Noh stage and the style of theater represented by Shakespeare's Globe Theatre.[17]

As Isozaki states, these two forms are linked temporally and by other commonalities such as their outdoor presentation. Both the return to traditional architectural sources and a subsequently dynamic and physical actor–audience relationship connect Mito's theatre with Toga's spaces.

In 'Theatres without Purpose', Suzuki has railed against the multifunctional nature of many municipal arts buildings. Although these are 'lavishly constructed', they tend to be 'only viable for making speeches with a microphone [. . .] A multi-purpose hall is really a hall with *no* purpose.'[18] Many spaces in Japan are also what Suzuki calls 'adopted', replicas of Western theatres built for *shingeki* performances. The ACM theatre is, of course, also based on a

Western model, but one that has more affinity with the long history of Japanese premodern theatre. It is not a simple replica but a more sophisticated fusion of the traditional and the contemporary. The Mito complex is an antidote to such imitative edifices which attempt to cater for all possibilities. It provides each autonomous activity with its own space, while aesthetically and structurally uniting them. Mito's theatre was designed to reflect the singular vision of one theatre artist, Tadashi Suzuki, rather than trying to provide for all tastes and styles or offer total flexibility. ATM was a reaction against bureaucrat-centred rather than artist-centred approaches to the arts that followed the economic expansion and resurgence of regional pride in 1970s Japan, which Thomas Havens has observed. This was the 'decade of public construction': 'The number of public art museums and performing-arts centers doubled during the seventies, partly inspired by aid from Tokyo but mostly by local pride.'[9] Rapid imitative developments are bound to lead to homogenisation and mistakes and the problematic tendency of designing artistic spaces for everybody and thus nobody.

The singularity of the ACM theatre has created an unfortunate predicament now that Suzuki has cut ties with the complex. A theatre that was designed for Suzuki's demands and which can therefore accommodate only minimal sets now suffers from the limitations imposed at the planning stage. There is little backstage area or wing space for storage, which restricts certain types of performances there, a difficulty that even arose with Gardzienice, whose sets were not extensive. The ATM theatre is perfect for Suzuki's minimal visual style, but this vision that he and Isozaki determinedly pursued now compromises other artists. Such fixed design concepts work only in the context of sustained long-term use. Otherwise you run the risk of creating white elephants or 'Theatres without Purpose'.

Shizuoka

The twenty-one-hectare Shizuoka Performing Arts Centre (SPAC) was founded in July 1995 by the prefectural government of Shizuoka as a cultural institute dedicated to the performing arts. It had a total budget of 1,272,500 million yen, equivalent to just over £8,000 million (according to November 2000 exchange rates). It is in many ways an amalgamation of the Toga and Mito complexes, borrowing the best elements from each. It takes its isolation from Toga and its location from Mito. The site is in the mountains just outside the large prefectural capital of Shizuoka, some 130 kilometres west and one hour by *shinkansen* from Tokyo. The complex is not far outside the city but feels remote. A bus from the city drops you in a car park, which stands on its own at the top of a hillside, incongruous and puzzling, an apparently purposeless enigma in the depths of the countryside. But on one side of the car park a map of the buildings hidden below indicates the extent of the project. Steps lead you down and into the park, which contains an indoor theatre, two rehearsal studios, dormitories, a canteen, a security and reception centre, an administrative hub and – the centrepiece – an outdoor amphitheatre. There are even two newly built spaces in the city itself which are run by SPAC – the Shizuoka Arts Theatre and Granship Medium Hall, which is part of a vast ship-shaped arts and convention venue. In the 2000 Shizuoka Spring Arts Festival, the Arts Theatre hosted Robert Wilson's monologue *Hamlet* as well as concerts, and the Granship presented African dance and the Odéon-Théâtre de l'Europe. These are large venues for international as well as local events, enabling major contributions to the prefecture's cultural life.

The park appears and functions differently from the Toga Art Park in several ways. The buildings were all built concurrently and are stylistically and spatially more integrated. Isozaki's functional and modern design lacks the history or traditional reference points seen in Toga, and relies instead on a pure and contemporary feel, as in Mito. The site is not linked to a particular community nearby nor to a specific regional architecture. The only signs of local life are the fields of tea bushes that are dotted around the park and which are farmed. The impression is given of spaces for a self-contained artistic community, nestled into and cut off in the hillside, a sense which the raised and out-of-sight car park reinforces.

Among the trees there is a compound of accommodation blocks that stand like small and narrow grey aircraft hangars. This is known as the Training Exchange Lodge and provides facilities for students, visiting artists, researchers and guests as well as meeting rooms.

Given the seclusion of the park, this allows people to stay and work in one place, supported by a canteen which can seat sixty-four people. The 1999 Theatre Olympics which launched the total complex (some buildings were only completed in March that year) needed to house many more than this. The park's facilities went part of the way to create the possibility of a self-sufficient on-site community. Yet the stripped-back functionality of the design suggests that this fraternity will only be passing through, the impermanence emphasised by the uniformity and utilitarianism of the buildings that resemble workplaces rather than homes.

The outdoor theatre, the Udo Open Air Theatre, occupies the centre of the park and is opposite the administrative hub across a large paved courtyard with benches and steps that create a potential stage area. The auditorium has fourteen rows of black-painted wooden bench-seats on white marble-effect stone, seating approximately 550 people. These are broken into three sections, the largest one in the middle. The auditorium is squarer and smaller than that of the Toga amphitheatre and stylistically it does not so much recall ancient Greek design. The building is predominantly concrete with battleship-grey walls and roof, black wooden pillars and grey slabs of 'Wakakusa' stone on stage, gathered in the nearby Izu peninsula, over which a wooden floor can be laid. Flooring, lights, lighting tower and other accessories are stored to the sides of the stage in open shelves, where lizards shelter from the summer heat. Lights hang above these at the end of first-floor galleries that run on either side of the auditorium, under which are the cloakrooms. As in Toga, nature provides an aural backdrop of cicadas and birds, and the unpredictable coexists with the rehearsed and meticulously planned. The 2000 festival programme stated that 'Performances held at the Udo Open Air Theatre in Shizuoka Performing Arts Park will take place even in the event of rain'. Like Toga, it combines sophisticated technology with natural simplicity. The stage gives way to what is called a 'Tea Walk' – four or five rows of bushes that are separated by two entrances or exits. Behind this, you see towering trees with thin and twisted trunks, which can be lit for performances. This backdrop and the design, with a narrower stage area and less depth of auditorium, make the space feel more enclosed and intimate than the Toga amphitheatre.

The central location and dominance of the administrative block (known as the Main Building) emphasises the functional and preplanned purpose-built nature of the whole complex:

> A vast green site large enough to accommodate Tokyo Dome four times over. The ideal venue for the creation, rehearsal, presentation and educational support for the performing arts. Built with this vision, ten facilities for the performing arts have been constructed in harmony with this lush natural environment. As a symbol of cultural exchange on a regional and international scale, the Shizuoka Performing Arts Park is a thriving center for the promotion of the Performing Arts in Japan and abroad.[20]

Suzuki was asked to be both artistic director of the whole complex and SPAC Theatre Company (from 1995), while Jean-Claude Gallotta is artistic director of SPAC Dance Company. Accounting and administration are organised by the prefecture, leaving Suzuki to spearhead the artistic work. The whole is run by a foundation which has an educational, creative, local and international brief. SPAC offers the four million people in the prefecture venues for the promotion of 'indigenous' performing arts, such as the choreography competition at the 2000 festival.

The combined presence of a dance and a theatre group explains the dual purpose of the Rehearsal Hall, which contains both a mirrored square dance studio and a hexagonal theatre space. The latter has a gallery built for observers to watch rehearsals. Both have lighting rigs and sound systems so they can double up as performance venues. The interior is all wood including the internal roof structure, which contrasts with the exterior's grey paint that unites it with the other buildings. Underneath the theatre studio is a dressing-room and washing area, and adjacent is a smaller section of the hangar-like Training Exchange Lodges.

The 120-seat elliptical Daendo Theatre is located on a hillside and is again grey on the outside and wooden inside. The whole building has a church-like shape, designed on the basic form of a cross, which deliberately gives it an 'almost religious flavour' reminiscent of Toga's studio. The theatre is appropriate for solo or intimate works (*King Lear* was SPAC's 1997 première performance here), and is also meant for symposia or talks. Its sacred aura is heightened by the play of light, designed as 'a symbiotic contrast between the bright, open upper level, and the lower level with its focus on the dynamic tension between seats and stage'.[21] The theatre perches on the edge of a hill, allowing a depth inside that is surprising and deceptive when one enters the foyer of an apparently shallow building. This play of levels and subsequently of contrasting shades is amplified by a ceiling that channels in natural light. Timbers circle and emphasise the 'hole' in the roof, which replicates a stubby church steeple. Two large doors behind the stage area can open to reveal the distant, unmistakable shape of Mount Fuji. The mountain is not only an internationally recognised symbol of Japan but also has great spiritual significance, its peak often tantalisingly shrouded in mist. The foyer which runs around the top of the theatre also has large windows on to this magical view. The building is integrated into the local and distant environment in a surprisingly dramatic way. The Daendo Theatre's drab low-key exterior that helps it merge with the habitat belies the life and spatial dynamics inside.

Toga was found almost by chance but was appropriate because of its domestic architecture; however, the location of Suzuki's work in Shizuoka stems from more subjective reasons. Suzuki was born here and as a child played in this area. He has therefore responded to the development of this site by the Shizuokan prefectural government on a personal note, as something of which he can be proud and of which he intimately knows the value. Shizuoka's official web site anthems him as a star attraction in pages titled 'Person of the Month'. Promotional publicity for the park is friendly and accessible, stating how it is to be a focus for the region's young people, stimulating potential artists while attracting and bringing together the whole family. It is minimally prescriptive about what will actually be presented but has a clear social ideology and an easygoing personable feel.

For Suzuki the directorship of this major art park corresponds with his aim to decentralise the arts, as both Toga and Mito do.

> Intelligent leisure activities and cultural events will permeate the
> areas surrounding Tokyo more and more, within 100 or 200 km
> (60 to 125 miles) of the city. People working there want to get out
> of their busy, crowded metropolis if it's for something fun. Those
> people will go to quiet areas like Shizuoka.[22]

Thousands trekked the long way to Toga almost as a pilgrimage. Shizuoka creates a similar atmosphere for quiet creativity and reflection but draws on a much larger potential local audience, be it the nearly four million people who live in this prefecture or the many millions more from Tokyo and its suburbs.

By way of comparison, few in Britain would think anything of travelling an hour into London to see a West End show. Yet how many would reverse this to go out of the metropolis? Stratford-upon-Avon is one of the few exceptions, though here the lure is Shakespeare's name and birthplace as much as the Royal Shakespeare Company's style and interpretations. Suzuki is attempting to change expectations about and patterns of our leisure time, by providing for the capital through the regions. By bringing an international festival, the Theatre Olympics, to a Shizuokan mountainside (which 76,000 spectators reportedly attended), he is taking Shizuoka to 'the forefront of the world'. As he suggests, it is an 'experiment', but one on a vast scale and of international significance. It shows not only the vision of this director, but also the support he can muster to fulfil it. A hundred pioneering ideas and imagination are worth nothing unless they can be backed up and made into actuality. This combination of business acumen, social concern and artistic sensibility is what makes Suzuki's material achievements so noteworthy and influential.

A   Sacred   and   Open   Home

The inspirational construction of so many performance spaces that are closely integrated into their local environments and communities raises specific questions about the audience–actor relationship in Suzuki's work. How does the fact that he has been able to construct his own theatres benefit this dynamic and what is gained from the considerable effort and expense which Suzuki has undertaken?

Artistic advantages in designing and building theatres according to personal priorities are immediately apparent. The entrance of the audience into and out of the total environment can be controlled, manipulating their experience beyond the time frame of the performance itself, as discussed regarding Toga. The spaces SCOT and SPAC occupy give them a range of venues to work within, expanding the performers' and technicians' capabilities as they shift from intimate indoor to epic outdoor scale. Performers must moderate and regulate themselves physically, vocally and energetically. The wood of the indoor theatres in Toga acts as both resonator and amplifier, whereas the amphitheatres demand greater levels of projection. Negotiating the difference is primarily a technical task for the performers but one that also leads into questions of style.

As well as shifts in scale, actors must cope with playing either end-on in the outdoor theatres and *sanbos* or in any other way that the flexibility of the studios permits. A high-energy presentational mode of acting complements the spectacle of performances such as *Greetings from the Edges of the Earth* with its fireworks and illuminated mountain. Conversely, the actors need to employ subtlety in the farmhouse theatres, where every detail of the face is evident, including the actors' sweat. The forward-facing presentation to the audience and the performer's sense of speaking through the gods must be adjusted in such intimacy. Suzuki's repertoire is eclectic and broad-ranging and his spaces demonstrate this. Such diversity and breadth does not, however, imply a subsequent lack of discipline or foundation, or generalisation. The sense of home enables the performers to feel secure within any space, which the training also encourages. Adaptability depends on confidence and stability.

Suzuki considers that being rooted is vital to the creation of a home for his company and he has frequently asserted its pivotal function in the nurturing of a creative group. This anchoring is not solely to realise a personal vision but also a social one: to create a sense of community primarily within the group which may then be extended to an audience. Unlike the urban complex at Mito, the Shizuoka and Toga parks are designed as composite integrated living and work spaces with dormitories and lodges. This is necessitated in part by the isolation of these sites but points more to the nature of theatre creativity as envisaged by Suzuki. It is an occupation that requires more than a nine-to-five existence and needs personal commitment and sustained engagement. It is not enough merely to turn up for rehearsals. Suzuki's private house is a five-minute walk from the theatre spaces in Toga. This proximity is both practical and symbolic of the responsibility all the company must take for the whole performance sequence, beyond the length of the performance itself. Suzuki suggests that theatre artists must have 'a place that we can always carry in our hearts even when we go elsewhere; we need a place that can serve as a source of inspiration and stimulation'.[23] This is not abstract or sentimental, but precisely indicates the rooted and spatial nature of the performer's practice. His railing against the multifunctional blandness of contemporary theatres pertains broadly to other aspects of our culture, wherever spaces have lost their specific and historically determined identity and turned into what anthropologist Marc Augé has called 'non-places'.[24] This usually arises through the demands of globalisation and consumerism which override and subsume differences. Augé has identified the homogeneity of locations such as shopping malls or airport lounges, in which we spend more and more of our time and which have become increasingly similar throughout the world. His theory could apply equally to theatre buildings, as the continuous criticisms about the characterless architecture and interior design of Britain's Royal National Theatre, for example, have highlighted.

For the theatre artist, *noh* offers an antidote to such uniformity:

> what is important is that because the bodies of the actors
> themselves can remember the indivisibility of the space in which
> they perform, they seem to have the ability to make a rent, an
> opening in the homogeneity. Because of their physical deviations
> from the movements of everyday life, the actors' bodies somehow
> seem equipped with some means to defy those amorphous and
> sterile perceptions of space that have evolved as modern culture has
> developed.[25]

'Home' for the contemporary actor can encompass a spatial template, which the performer embodies and which they can then impose on any space. In France, Suzuki observed how *noh* performer Hisao Kanze rebuilt for himself a fictive *noh* theatre's pillars and *hashigakari* on the unfamiliar Théâtre Récamier stage, rooting the body in the frames which his *noh* training had inculcated and internalised in him from childhood. Suzuki is not naïvely demanding that the performer must train from the age of seven, but is looking for more manageable strategies. The development of Toga as a home was intended to knit the company as a social and artistic unit, while circumventing Tokyo's bureaucracy and economic constraints. Artistically, it was to give a spatial foundation for the company's work in whatever context and wherever they might appear. The pillars on Toga's amphitheatre stage may only hold up the heavens but they recall the defined structure of *noh*, whose pillars help the *shite* (the principal actor) orient himself through the narrow eye slits in his mask. In *noh* theatre, these possess names such as 'the flute pillar' or 'the *shite*'s pillar', according to their proximity to the flautist or the actor.

With such physical intelligence, the performer can make the invisible apparent and conjure gods. In many *noh* dramas, the *shite* plays a supernatural being. The stage thus becomes a meeting ground between man and the gods or *kami* and the masked figure becomes an intermediary and go-between. Traditionally, performance spaces in Japan were often built on burial sites or at the border between two villages in liminal space, emphasising the link between the performers and the gods or spirits, reminding us of our mortality. *Noh* was originally performed in shrine or temple grounds, its foundations in religious and shamanistic practices. The *hashigakari* leads from the mirror room to the main stage, connecting the open performance space with the closed private place of transformation in which the performer dons the mask. On a small scale, this bridge depicts the first part of the journey of a rite of passage. The performer traverses the *hashigakari* with a long, slow walk after their meditation on the mask in the mirror room, this rhythm elongating the otherwise short distance into the shared public space. The notion of sacred space has deep roots in Japanese theatre.

In *The Way of Acting*, Suzuki notes how the *noh* performer's stamp is considered a means of waking up the spirits, who are thought to reside in the ground rather than in the air as in Western thought. The stamp can summon this dormant energy, as they are woken by the noise, amplified by the resonant pots under the wooden stage. In the *noh* space, the material and spiritual are united, as they are in Suzuki's theatres. Only with a fatalistic sense of our own mortality can we reach for the heavens. Suzuki's stages allow the performer to create a fictionalised or ritualised space, their personal actions becoming symbolic yet rooted to the ground by the body's precise gestures.

Acting for Suzuki is 'a transformation from the personal to the universal'[26] in a sacred space.

Through investment of time, energy and communal commitment, a space becomes cherished. When the public independently recognises the selfsame qualities, an open dialogue is established with understanding. For Suzuki, through rigorous daily practice and effort the space is transformed when 'The actor's body and the space reveal a mutual connection. I call a space which is thus connected to the actor's body a *sacred space.*'[27] The fact remains that much of SCOT's work is shown abroad in venues over which they can have little control. Suzuki is pragmatic and wants to make quality performances, rather than theatre that will work only in his spaces. Yet what he is arguing is that a sense of the sacred can be internalised and embodied. It is the performer that makes the space sacred rather than the space itself, although the design is obviously a contributory factor. (This is of course not foolproof, as the example of *The Tale of Lear* recounted in Chapter Five shows, but an ideal.) Such transformation is implicit in the nature of ritual, where the action lifts the performer and sometimes the spectator from the everyday on to a spiritual level. Intimacy within the act of theatre encourages the audience to feel involved in the event as a witness as they become emotionally aroused and physically confronted.

Being a theatre company, SCOT and to a lesser extent SPAC's homes are unavoidably also public domains. Privacy or secrecy are challenged by the fact that the spaces are opened up to an audience through the outdoor stages or in the observers' gallery in the Rehearsal Hall in Shizuoka. Like *noh* theatre's mirror room (a private chamber in the middle of the public temple grounds), some spaces and activities remain private. In Toga, the training is often conducted out of sight in one of the *sanbos*, with only the sound of the actors' stamping reverberating around the valley. But naming the Toga and Shizuoka complexes 'parks' puts an emphasis on access and leisure, as the publicity reinforces. The spaces are for the audience as much as the artist, with few areas hidden or restricted. Isolation in remote areas does not preclude the presence of visitors who can observe the creative process. They can stay after performances to meet actors, the crew, even Suzuki himself. Festival performances in the Toga amphitheatre were preceded by Suzuki and the mayor's welcome to guests. After *Greetings from the Edges of the Earth* a sake barrel was smashed open and the audience were invited on to the stage to drink. Suzuki has pushed this notion of 'open spaces' to the limit, re-emphasising the fundamental principle of theatre as a communal act – a collaboration between artists, artists and villagers, and ultimately between audience and performers.

This social dimension is what Suzuki so admired in ancient Greek theatre and what he believes has been forgotten in most contemporary performance. 'That sense of public space has been lost, rendering the art of watching a play quite close to the experience of watching a film or reading a novel. I strongly believe that we must return to open spaces.'[28] Open does not simply mean outdoors, but is as much an attitude as an architectural design or location. It is ironic that such accessibility is possible in sacred and deeply personal spaces. It is also ironic that such openness can be found at the dead end of a mountain road, in a village hemmed in on all sides by the Japanese Alps.

The connection between Isozaki's designs and the environment with its natural substances indicates the coherent character of Suzuki's practice. He has turned to sources, be they *kabuki* walks, pop songs or regional architecture, without idealising or preserving them in aspic. A two-hundred-year-old traditional farmhouse is neighbour to a concrete amphitheatre, which is a quotation of Greek ancestors. Wood is stained black in the *sanbo*, obscuring the origin while retaining both texture and functionality for the theatre. Under the thatched roofs of Toga lie sophisticated lighting rigs. There is both harmony and disjunction in the positioning and construction of the spaces. A similar tension exists between the sacred and the public. Such dualities characterise all of Suzuki's practice and carry through into his productions.

It is through human interaction with and intervention into nature, a process of juxtaposition, that we come to recognise its qualities. We are forced to remember our own beginnings as animals while acknowledging technological accomplishments. It is part of Suzuki and Isozaki's postmodern aesthetic to combine and contrast materials. The *noh*-influenced wooden stage has an aluminium surface. The Udo Theatre's grey walls and black stage give on to the soft colours of the tea bushes. In the interior of the old *sanbo*, warmed by stage lighting, we become aware of the rain outside. The doors of the Daendo Theatre open to reveal Mount Fuji. As we watch the performer sweat, so we look more closely at nature. We move through awareness of differences to deeper insights. 'The theatre can seek to absorb itself into its surroundings in order to develop an appropriate symmetry [. . .] In that relationship a new and remarkable expressivity becomes possible.'[29] For Suzuki, this symmetry values animal energy over and above electricity-dependent sources, though it does not exclude the latter as the lighting of Toga's mountainside indicates. We not only become aware of the sounds of nature but remember our own humanity and biology as we listen more concentratedly to our own and others' breathing in the surrounding silence. We enjoy and appreciate nature's spontaneity, an essential ingredient within theatre processes.

The construction of Toga Park validates a gradual approach to building such arts complexes, responding as it did organically to various ongoing demands rather than depending on pre-planning. Mito drew from this experience but with a very different imperative, not only filling a gap in the city's cultural life but also redressing some of the drawbacks with contemporary spaces facing theatre artists all across Japan. Many of these problems are familiar to Western practitioners too, though a longer history of diverse theatre building in Britain, for example, does make close comparison with Japan inappropriate. Mito recognises and values the urban context in which it is situated and avoids pandering to folksy aspirations inspired by the Toga Performing Arts Park, as might have been anticipated. It has its own qualities and atmosphere, conceptually reminiscent but certainly not derivative of Toga. As such, it could be an inspirational model for urban cultural projects throughout the country. Few prefectural governments might want to recreate the risk and singularity of the Toga complex, but many have comparable situations to Mito and could learn from it. ATM offers an influential way forward, rooted in global traditions such as the architecture of Shakespeare's day. It is only a shame that its legacy is clouded by a specific theatre design dependent on a singular theatrical vision which limits some of its future potential.

Shizuoka also posits some useful solutions to the 'fundamental problem' of space that Suzuki outlined, integrating sophisticated technologies and modern designs with a natural environment, and bringing work of international quality to the regions outside Tokyo. Despite the fact that it has only recently opened, it has so far avoided the pitfalls of tourism and educational duty which blight an institution such as the Royal Shakespeare Company in Stratford-upon-Avon. Similar to SCOT, this has three types of theatre building in its regional centre, as well as a metropolitan base in London. The RSC has sadly become a production-line theatre company, predominantly serving tourists and students with a popular but narrow selection of the Elizabethan repertoire. It is a victim of its own and certainly Shakespeare's success and renown. Much more needs to be written on such comparisons, and I hestitate to make this connection even at a superficial level, but this example does show the achievement of Suzuki in focusing on aesthetics and the performer's needs over and above economic demands.

In a preface to the 2000 *Drama Review* interview with Hijikata, Suzuki is described only as artistic director of SPAC, with no mention of SCOT. He once articulated idealistic and inspirational projections of how the performer can embody space and feel an emotional or even spiritual attachment to a place and to theatre buildings such as those in Toga. This sense of home was linked to the concept of group bonding and identity. Now Suzuki has abandoned his former empire, he and his performers no longer have a home with all the values this implies. To what extent Suzuki's theories helped or encouraged SCOT members in practice, after the enthusiastic pioneering of the 1970s and 1980s, is debatable. With only three long-term members of SCOT left (at the time of writing in 2001), new approaches are necessary. Yet the Shizuokan model is in danger of becoming merely a replica of Toga's, in the way that the new farmhouse theatre in Toga reproduced the old one only on a larger scale. Shizuoka may have personal resonances for Suzuki but this is not transferable to other people. Architecture alone is not enough to prevent the Shizuoka development from becoming a 'mini-Tokyo', as Suzuki once portrayed this area, a 'non-place' which is home for nobody. It is good that Suzuki is shifting forward and his future certainly lies in Shizuoka, but should we now discount the values described so fervently in *The Way of Acting*? What are his priorities now? It seems that the Toga Arts Park and even SCOT, a company rooted so deeply in one place, have run their course and may go the way of Mito.

FOUR

•

THE SUZUKI METHOD

Tadashi Suzuki's training method has consistently influenced the field of performer training since the late 1970s, when it began to be articulated and was first written about in English in Brandon's 1978 article for the *Drama Review*. Its impact continues to spread, led by those who have trained directly with Suzuki and SCOT, or by those who have learned the method from what might be called 'second-generation' teachers. Groups like Frank in Australia and SITI in America have helped disseminate the practice widely. As well as their regular weekly sessions, Frank have conducted training for young people in Croatia in 1999, 2000 and 2001. SITI led a two-week workshop in Aberystwyth, Wales, in 1998, in addition to their annual classes and short courses in numerous world cities. These organisations are both sanctioned by Suzuki, but there are numerous other individuals who teach the training on an informal basis, either after working with SCOT, or after participating in workshops such as Frank's or SITI's annual three-week intensive course in Saratoga Springs, New York State.

It is impossible to quantify the extent of engagement with Suzuki's training world-wide beyond noting that it surfaces in the work of practitioners across continents and countries, from Argentina through to Denmark. It was even the core of a daily training programme for the American StageWest Company when it operated as a repertory theatre under the artistic direction of Eric Hill, a former collaborator with Suzuki. The method has also been taught by Suzuki himself in America, including at the University of Wisconsin at Milwaukee (1980–4 where the training was introduced into that country), the Juilliard School, New York (1981–3), and the

University of California at San Diego. It has also been taught at many other institutions, including New York's Columbia University, where Ellen Lauren is a Faculty member. This broad engagement indicates the respect it has gained world-wide, especially in America.

Suzuki's way of shaping the actor opens up many questions about what performer training is for and how it might be conducted. His process is demanding, precise and extremely technical, but paradoxically this allows the trainee great freedom. The performer is working on himself rather than a character and can create his own fictional context for the movements if desired. The external form is fixed but the imaginative focus is not prescribed other than engagement with a presupposed audience. The Suzuki method exposes many such contradictions, all of which illuminate the process of performing and its multiple phases, and that includes workshops, rehearsals and warming-up, as well as the public event of performance itself.

Suzuki training also attempts to integrate physical and mental systems, to create a 'body-mind'. The practice is demanding corporeally and is particularly hard on the feet and legs, yet requires equal concentration and strength of will. This *gestalt* is what makes the training so beneficial and partly explains why it has been adopted in many contexts outside SCOT and Japan. Such emphasis on integration is familiar to observers of Asian performance traditions. What Suzuki's process provides is accessibility to well-established Asian practical philosophies that might otherwise be restricted to specialist groups, be they indigenous populations or students learning from the age of seven, as with *noh*. It thus acts as a functional bridge between East and West, and traditional and contemporary models.

The personal title given this training indicates Suzuki's entrepreneurial spirit but also the fact that he is the foremost articulator of its ethos. The approach linked to director Lee Strasberg is called '*the* method' or 'method acting', hiding its progenitor. The 'Suzuki method' hints at this director's autocratic style but, more concretely, it affirms his persistent research and artistic leadership. This began with his tentative quest for a training system in 1972 with the Waseda Little Theatre, and culminated later in wider recognition with SCOT, when the method was opened up regularly to non-company members and non-Japanese in the 1980s. The approach is simultaneously specific to its founding group and the cultural context of its invention, but also widely applicable. This breadth and transferability is enabled by its outward simplicity, directness and clarity of purpose. Suzuki's focused vision stems from the fact that he draws on the deeply ingrained and well-defined principles of the traditions of *noh* and in particular *kabuki*, with its muscular and vigorous *aragoto* style, but it is also the result of his own rigour and exactness. The potential for widespread application grows from the very specificity and detail of this technique.

Most Asian performance techniques are passed to students by performers themselves, for in the traditional arts there is no such role as a director. Forms like *noh* and *kabuki* have no training system as such beyond the direct transmission of knowledge from performer to performer. In *noh* theatre training, as Richard Emmert has noted, 'There are no exercises for developing the body. Instead, the body is trained and developed entirely by learning the movement patterns, the *utai* chant, or the instrumental patterns of play after play.'[1] Suzuki, however, was trying to create new exercises rather then simply perpetuate old forms. He had to regenerate established principles without adopting the specific methodologies of instruction of those practices. Devising such a performer training system could not be the solo intellectual achievement of a non-performing director. It had to grow from dialogue among performers and between performers and director. Some of the Suzuki training exercises inevitably evolved out of rehearsals for performances. 'Standing Statues' (a sequence described later) grew from choral work on stage pictures for *Dionysus* (1990). This does not undermine Suzuki's key role in the establishment of his methodology (selecting, clarifying and articulating) but remembers the collaborative stage of its development. Suzuki's process evolved out of performance creation and was initially collaborative, though it later sublimated these foundations.

The idea of a system should be treated with caution, as the misinterpretation of Konstantin Stanislavski's exercises have taught us. The existence of many groups and artists who utilise Suzuki training compounds this complexity, questioning the notion of ownership and the direct linking of Suzuki's name to the techniques.

One cannot deny Suzuki's singular role as *auteur* of the training. It is the 'Suzuki method', for he created it, yet it is now taught or used in rehearsals around the world in many contexts. Some proponents are sanctioned by him and several positively seek such approval, but many more do not. When does the assignation of the 'Suzuki method' become inaccurate, if indeed it does? Ownership of techniques and authorship in theatre are always complex, muddied by the collaborative nature of making performances. Yet there are key principles in the practice and in its intention which are specifically Suzuki's invention, centred on the methodical placing and use of the feet.

The word 'method' is as problematic as 'system', but is more appropriate in emphasising a practical philosophy rather than just a coherent set of exercises that lead to a result. Suzuki's approach is admirably precise and rarely improvisational and there is a fixed methodology (or methodologies) embodied in this practice. However, the human element should never be forgotten in the performance/training interstice. It is a mistake to believe that if you follow a method, execute it regularly and meticulously, you will become a good performer. How the individual responds to the task set and reveals him/herself through such demands is what makes any system viable. It is also the core of performance. What Suzuki's exercises offer is a physical and mental template by which to measure yourself. A template needs to be methodical or it will only ever be individual, unquantifiable, open to interpretation and therefore hopelessly unsystematic. Inevitably, the way of instruction will vary according to who is leading the training and the participants, but the potential for interpretation of prescribed exercises is extremely limited. Their function is embodied in the form itself.

Before defining this form, I should clarify my own position. I have never been directly trained by Suzuki, but did observe a brief demonstration in Toga in August 1999, which gave some indication of the fast pace at which he works. Initially I tried to ascertain the nature of the stamp (or stomp) in workshops with students holding *The Way of Acting* in one hand. My first direct experience of the method came in Vicenza, Italy, in September 1995. The course was taught by Ellen Lauren, a co-founder of SITI, whom Suzuki introduced to us as the best teacher of his method. It took place while SCOT was touring Europe performing *Dionysus* and *Electra* at Vicenza's Teatro Olimpico as part of a small festival. This followed their production of *Dionysus* there in 1994. The workshop was a two-week session for nine performers, all Italian except for myself and one German, Antje Diedrich, with whom I subsequently founded the Suzuki Training Practice and Research Group in London in 1999. Suzuki observed some of the Vicenza classes with a presence that transformed the quality of attention in us trainees, even though he did not verbally interject. The workshop taught me the hopelessness of my textbook training from *The Way of Acting* and impelled me to deter such futile attempts by writing an explanatory account of the exercises for the *Drama Review*,[2] which clarified what the practice actually is. This chapter is based loosely on that article.

I have also participated in and watched training led by several practitioners with backgrounds in SCOT, SITI or Frank, including Lauren's sessions for SITI in New York and the International Workshop Festival in Northern Ireland, both in 1996. I do not feel that my authority to write about Suzuki training is invalidated because of my lack of direct experience of Suzuki's own teaching style. This chapter has already emphasised the limitations of prescribing such authorship and highlighted the rigidity of the form. My experience is perhaps closer to that of the majority of those who have recently, or will in the future, make contact with this process, for Suzuki now rarely leads training for non-members of his companies.

During the workshop I attended in Italy, all the participants (who were experienced professional performers) found the intensity draining and demanding but enlightening. For those at the earliest stage of their careers or theatre experience, Suzuki's process may be technically difficult and may feel limiting. You will not learn how to warm up or cool down the body and voice. You are vulnerable and exposed in what is essentially a solo practice and cannot hide. The fact that you are always doing what the group does exposes personal differences of even the subtlest kind. The emphasis on technique may be frustrating, with little encouragement of individual creativity.

Novices will not learn how to devise theatre, for Suzuki's method has scant relation to compositional techniques. It does not propose a creative process but asks you to repeat codified patterns as faithfully as possible in a given format. The major exceptions are the 'freestyle' parts of the sequences. These demand independent interpretation within the tight frame of the exercises, but the freedom relates mostly to arm and head positions rather than the whole body and its movement. Yet the training's diagnostic abilities will reveal your rhythmic and bodily patterns, test your will, and expose your acceptance of or resistance to daily physical training. However you engage with this method and whatever your individual needs are, it is certain to show you the concentration, precision, physical engagement and application required to become a performer.

There have been few descriptions or analyses of the Suzuki method written in English. Suzuki's own reflections in 'The Grammar of the Feet' in *The Way of Acting* give scant indication of what actually happens in a training session. The clearest explanation is by James Brandon in 'The Training of the Waseda Little Theatre: the Suzuki Method' in the *Drama Review*. This grew out of observations made in 1976 with WLT, just before the relocation to Toga. The training was then led by Suzuki.

No account can be comprehensive or impartial. I hope to convey to you, the reader, the experience of the training and its various pressures as I have perceived them. To do so, I focus on central exercises which are fundamental to the training and which I have observed with different teachers in various situations. Some practitioners elaborate on these, develop new exercises or select only elements of the ones described here. I wish merely to touch on such additions or variations in order to clarify the intrinsic and principle qualities, intentions and experiences of the training as a relative novice might encounter and understand them. My description and analysis touch on the historical development of the training only briefly, for it is not by defining evolution in a chronological way that you can clarify such a method's practice and purpose.

Initially, I will detail the external forms which the body learns to inhabit. Essentially, these do not alter much when you become advanced in the training, as you might improvise around basic techniques in contact improvisation, for example. The pattern remains fixed, emphasising increasingly detailed and precise work on the use of space and rhythm, rather than modification or experimentation. You must dig deeper rather than wider. Beginners thus work with the same exercises as SCOT or SPAC company members, though these veterans are more likely to add ornamentations, such as arm positions, and work with greater speed. It is for the teacher primarily but also the individual to decide the level at which to work and the appropriate intensity, which inevitably depends on the duration of the training. A beginner on day one will be struggling to remember a pattern, so it is inappropriate to extend the focus out as with a more experienced participant. Time is spent initially on absorbing the flow and shape of the movements in the body and finding how to centre yourself within these.

After I have depicted mechanical textual 'diagrams' in their simplest form, I will examine the principles which make these exercises operate efficiently as separate components in a total training programme. These rules or laws cut across most of the exercises, though they are emphasised to a greater or lesser degree within specific ones. I will then explore the broader cultural issues of the transferability and application of this method, which is best articulated through examination of the voice and text. The relation of the training techniques to performance is touched on but developed further with specific reference to Suzuki's own *œuvre* in the next chapter.

With this form you can never escape the presence of the teacher, a notion written even into the training's title. My descriptions should not be relied upon as instruction. The instructor is indispensable to your understanding and achievement, which is dependent as much on what they see as what they teach you to see in yourself. Your experience of this method is built on their approach and you never reach a position where you can jettison them or rise above the training to work entirely alone (solo practice can help but is no substitute). Whether that commanding figure is Lauren or Suzuki himself, you have to accept their authority with humility. This acceptance is a lesson in itself and one which I hope you acknowledge as you attempt to bring alive these sequences in your head or in the studio.

The Basic Exercises

The 'Basics' are four short sequences that are often practised towards the beginning of the training and which are one of the first elements to be taught. An essential ABC of the 'grammar', they are usually run through one after the other and repeated many times within a session. They are physically demanding, but Suzuki training itself does not include warm-ups, relaxation or an easing-out phase. These are indispensable to avoid injury or strain but the teacher either leads this or lets the students take responsibility themselves, as they see fit. Japanese *tabi* (the white or black bifurcated socks that isolate the big toe and which are worn by *noh* performers as well as being part of traditional clothing) are the best footwear. These can help both with sliding walks and gripping the floor, as their soles are made of strengthened cloth. If *tabi* are not available, socks are fine, though they wear out much more easily from the contact with the ground. Shorts can also be worn to show the teacher an individual's leg positions and muscular effort. All exercises are executed together unless the space is too crowded and the group is out of necessity split in two. The teacher stands in front of the trainees, who are scattered around the room.

Basic Number One
(Ashi o Horu – Throwing Feet)

You start with legs and heels pressed together, pushing against each other to create light tension in the legs and an energised lower half of the body, and with the feet pointed forty-five degrees to the left and right. This is ballet's 'first position'. You must sense the contact with the floor through this aligned stance and find a feeling of stability. The gaze is fixed on a point on the horizon and the breathing is relaxed. Few specific instructions about the breath are given throughout the training, but it must be expansive and released. The arms hang by your sides, given a little attention by imagining that you are holding two poles in a light fist which are parallel and at right angles to the upright body.

With this position established, you raise the right leg slightly forward along the diagonal and then stamp directly to the right.

Rather than leading from the foot, you should feel the centre shifting rapidly to the right, extending the line of the hips. The stamp is with the whole of the foot and should be firm and energised, threatening to destabilise and challenge the centred and grounded body. The left leg simultaneously straightens, remaining so as all the weight rests on the bent right leg. This weight transfer can be tested by lifting the left foot off the floor without moving the torso further to the right. There are several such tests which are indispensable for measuring and demonstrating your attainment or lack of it. The left leg is then drawn in swiftly so that the heels just touch, while the knees remain open and slightly bent in a 'box' (trapezoid) position. Throughout this manoeuvre the head must stay at a constant height. The tendency is to drift upwards so you need to adjust by pushing the weight down towards the floor. You then squat swiftly to finish with the spine erect and the centre (the pelvic bowl) slightly lifted and projected forwards rather than sunken back, before returning to the starting position. When down, you must not sit back on to the heels.

The move down and subsequently up is practised with varying tempos over counts of fifteen, ten, eight, three and one, or other variants at the instructor's discretion. A number is spoken, followed by the signal to move in the form of an energised shout or the sudden sharp bang of a stick on the floor or a mat. The count can stop at any point and the position must be held until the sequence resumes. Once upright, the actions are then repeated to the left. Another test is done when the weight is on either the right or left leg. You must shift the centre from one side to the other over given counts, moving the hips in a straight line and at a regular pace.

Basic Number One thus introduces key principles such as centring, moving with rhythmical counts, the stamp, energised open positions, and precisely controlled use of the space. It also establishes the method of instruction, with the teacher implacably and commandingly taking the group through the drill.

Basic Number Two
(Fumikae — Stamp and Change)

This sequence develops previously taught principles, rather than introducing new elements. You stand in a line at the back of the room or in columns at evenly spaced intervals so you can progress forward. The knees are bent, with the back straight, feet and legs pressed together and the centre of gravity low. With a rapid movement, the right leg sweeps forward to show the sole of the foot to an imaginary partner opposite you and is then pulled back, bringing the bent knee in as close to the body as possible with the foot flexed upwards. This is done as a single continuous move, during which the level of the torso and head must stay constant. The fast shift of weight is destabilising and you have to fight to gain control of this one-legged 'luxury balance', to use Eugenio Barba's terminology. In two moves, you then stamp directly down and slide the foot forward along the floor until the back leg is straight, with the back foot flat. The hips must finish positioned over the front leg, which takes all the body's weight. This can be tested by lifting the back leg without moving the torso forward over the front foot, similar to the first test cited for Basic Number One. You then shift up on to tiptoes and down, as two isolated movements, taking care to centralise the suspended weight over both feet and maintain a sense of connection to the ground. You swap sides and lead with the left leg, pulling it through from behind the body. The sequence continues with alternating legs.

Arm positions can be added later. The right or left elbow is raised directly to the side at shoulder height. The arm is bent tightly to the chest, with the hand flexed away from the body and clenched to hold an imaginary pole. When you go up on tiptoes, the arm goes straight up – pressed tight against the ear – and then back down in two sharp shifts, after which you come down from tiptoes. Alternatively, the movement up and down of the torso can be combined with the extension of the arm as two moves. Both operate on the same principle of testing the balance but they segment and articulate the ascent and descent differently. You may add an actual pole which must remain both vertical and unwavering.

The sequence can also be practised to music as you proceed in a slow march across the stage in evenly spaced pairs, emphasising the stops at the end of every movement. It is vital to avoid flow and not follow the music passively but attempt to keep on top of the rhythm, almost attacking it. The stamp can also be varied so that it does not make forceful contact with the floor, but stops just short. In this instance, the impetus downwards must be the same as with the full-force stamp, but controlled and held back at the last moment. After this, the weight is transferred on to the leading foot so it can slide forward. This light stamp is harder than the full one because of this staggered rather than combined placing of the body's weight. The feet must always remain in parallel and close together rather than splayed and turned out, in order to keep the energy tightly concentrated in the centre.

The direction of the 'march' can also reverse immediately after the stamp, but only in response to the teacher's command. After stamping down, you slide the foot backwards to put all the weight on the back leg, with the front leg straight. You go up on to tiptoes and down and then pull the other leg sharply up in order to stamp again. These movements happen in the same order as the forward progression, yet they have different demands. A difficult shift of weight is needed to go up on to tiptoes, and the feet must be absolutely straight and not turned out to the sides in order for the front foot to slide past the back one. You can further test the tiptoe balance by shutting your eyes in that position.

Basic Number Three

This exercise extends the same technical elements by demanding greater energy, more complex arm movements and the use of diagonals. The feet remain turned out forty-five degrees from the forward-facing torso throughout the sequence. You start with the right foot in front of the left, right heel to the left foot's instep, and sweep the right leg out to the side before pulling the foot back to the centre with the leg raised. It is as though the leg is wrapping itself around a vertical pole positioned vertically just in front of the body. You then keep the leg turned out with the foot tucked in and held up, before stamping down. The sequence is repeated with the other leg leading and so the weight needs to shift as you stamp. This can be combined with *roppo* arms, *roppo* being a technique for dramatic entrances and exits in *kabuki* that uses exaggerated movement. One hand is held flexed at the side of the head and the other arm is stretched forward with a soft rather than taut extension. Fingers remain splayed and relaxed. The arms switch as you swap legs, with the arms moving out to the sides and then up before falling sharply to rest in their final position. The exercise demands a constant level of the torso as well as stability, which is severely challenged by the rapid arm movement. The combination of arms and stamping tests coordination and detail, with the simultaneous focus on the upper and lower body as well as the precise positioning of the fingers. The arms easily tire and droop in this exercise.

Basic Number Four

This exercise opens up your use of space, which correspondingly makes precision and speed difficult. The starting position is like a tennis player waiting for his opponent's serve. From a crouched ready position with legs apart (head held and not relaxed) and with knees partially rather than deeply bent so that the centre is slightly raised, you pivot very fast on one foot (initially the left). This move opens the body to the right to face the opposite way from the first position. You finish, standing focused ahead on a distant point, with the feet apart, back straight and knees soft, re-establishing contact with the ground after the swift upward sweep. On command you return to the crouch and then pivot on the other foot, opening the other way by turning to the left. You repeat this symmetrical pattern but alternate by stopping with the torso pointing forward and with the feet and legs tight together rather than open, but with the knees still slightly bent. You must project the same level of energy in both open and closed positions.

When this is established, arm movements are added, reminiscent of martial arts and especially kendo with its long wooden staves. Your arms swing open to the sides, pass over the head together and travel down to below the navel, as though slicing a partner with a sword down the middle from head to groin. Hands are in a loose fist, the right above the left. The speed of the turn and the precision and finality of the body stopping are key demands of the exercise. Shouted commands or the bang of a stick initiate the revolutions. In this exercise in particular, with a large shift in the body position rather than the smaller movement of a limb, the impulse-giving commands need to be quick and energised in order to create a dynamic response in you. The turning both ways also requires kinaesthetic coordination, and it can take time for the pattern to become inscribed in the body. Novices often turn on the wrong foot in the wrong direction.

Ten Ways of Walking

As the Basic exercises group into one unit, so the walks combine into a single flowing sequence. After learning them one at a time, you practise these together to music as you move diagonally across the space. There are a couple of pieces of pre-recorded music which demand different paces, but even the slowest is quick. They are reminiscent of contemporary jazz or film scores with subtle Asian influences, and are extremely rhythmical. One frequently used piece is 'Voodoo Suite' by Perez Prado. The order of walks is not always fixed but does usually begin with the stamp and end with the shuffling moves. Great concentration is needed to keep even gaps between you and the other trainees and to progress in a straight diagonal line, particularly if the body is not facing along the diagonal (see 6, 7 and 8 below). Once you reach the fixed end point, you return to cross the line with the next walk. The sequence lasts approximately ten to fifteen minutes in total. Elaborations on the basic sequence include: carrying objects; choosing and changing arm positions (for example, on tiptoes the arms might constantly alter position); walking backwards; leading off from the left rather than right leg, which means facing the opposite way on diagonal progressions. All are done at speed to the rhythm of the music, though with defined stops if required. The same principle applies as in Basic Two, that you must not follow but should 'attack' the beat.

1. Stamping or stomping. This is a central movement to the training. With the same starting position as Basic Number Two, you pull the right leg up as high as possible and stamp directly and forcefully down with the whole foot. You then do the same with the left leg. The level of the torso must remain constant and there must be no wobbling as the weight shifts rapidly from side to side. The arms are held straight at the sides, hands in a light fist. Each stamp must be as full and engaged as the first one, however tired one is towards the end of the walk. This sequence is known as *ashi-bumi* in Japanese.

2. Pigeon-toes. The arms are placed in the small of the back and the knees are slightly bent. The knees remain pressed tight together throughout, with one leg slightly forward and the toes turned sharply in. The leg that is not forward (initially the right) sweeps ahead in a semicircle, maintaining contact with the floor. It comes to rest sharply in front of the other foot. The process is repeated for the other leg, with the body moving forwards in a straight line. This sequence is known as *uchi-mata* in Japanese and recalls how women traditionally walked in kimonos as well as the *onnagata's* usual way of walking. The *onnagata* is a female character played by men in *kabuki* theatre. (One unconfirmed myth is that in *kabuki* training the *onnagata* are taught to keep their knees together by holding a piece of paper between them as they move.)

3. Outside of the feet. Knees are bent and opened outwards to form a 'box' shape and the torso is inclined forwards with a curve in the back so that the lumber area becomes almost like a ledge. The arms hang by the side and the weight is placed on the outside of the feet. The right foot circles upwards and then forwards followed by the left one in a motion like pedalling a bicycle. This sequence is known as *wani-ashi* in Japanese.

4. Inside of the feet. The knees are pressed together, the weight is placed on the inside of the feet and the hands are held in the small of the back, one on top of the other with the top hand's palm facing outwards. In turn, each foot is kicked out rapidly and directly to the side before being brought forcefully back to the centre. As the weight shifts quickly from side to side there must be minimal sway and the torso must remain as level as possible. This sequence is known as *soto-mata* in Japanese.

5. Tiptoes. With the arms straight by the sides, you progress on high tiptoes with small steps and knees slightly bent. There must be no bounce and a smooth gliding motion, even though there is a slight, brief stop on each step to counter the forward motion. Alternatively, the walk might include more defined stops with the rhythm of the music rather than continual flow. The movement must always lead from the torso's shift forwards, which the feet must then support.

Although the body is stretching upwards, you must counter this to keep contact with the ground. This sequence is known as *tsumasaki* in Japanese.

6. A sideways slide. With knees bent and feet together, directed forwards, you circumscribe semicircles with the left and then the right foot. The face, torso and hips point forwards and the feet press into the ground as they slide sideways. There must be precision in the stops and fast shifts of weight. Again, the movement begins in the centre rather than with the feet. This sequence is known as *yokoaruki No. 1* in Japanese.

7. A sideways manoeuvre with the body directed forward. With the feet together and pointing forwards you pull the knee of the left leg sharply up before stamping to the left, thereby shifting the weight. You pull the right leg up, keeping it bent, and then place it across the body, beyond, slightly in front of and close to the left foot. The movement of the left leg is repeated, always keeping the torso directed forwards and the body level. The movement of the legs tends to pull the body out of line so it is important to maintain the diagonal. The knees (as in all the stamps) must come up to maximum height when pulled up and the torso must remain level. This sequence is known as *yokoaruki No. 2* in Japanese.

8. A sideways stamp. Movement is to the left, as in the sideways stamp of Basic Number One. The head faces along the diagonal, but the torso remains pointing forwards as the body shifts fast to the side. As the left leg stamps to the side, the back leg straightens. The right leg is then pulled in next to the left leg and the move repeated.

9. Sliding walk. The torso glides quickly across the space, maintaining one level with small, rapid, shuffling steps. Maximum speed must be achieved immediately from standing with no graded build-up, as though a wind is blowing you across the space. The feet maintain contact with the floor, though the toes rise a little at the end of each small step, reminiscent of the *noh* walk *suriashi*, which means 'rubbing step'. In *noh*, *suriashi*, is generally practised much more slowly (though it can be used for rapid exits) and is often employed to represent a ghost or supernatural figure.

10. Duckwalk. The position is a low crouch with the arms stretched forwards, slightly bent and the palms turned upwards. You shuffle forwards at high speed, minimising sideways and vertical movement and keeping the centre slightly raised and back straight, rather than settling back on to the haunches. This is the most physically demanding walk, requiring particular strength in the thigh muscles. This sequence is known as *shikko* in Japanese.

Slow ten tekka ten

This exercise is in sharp contrast to the fast, exhausting walks and demands mental stamina and focus. You form two evenly spaced staggered lines opposite each other. To music, you then traverse the room at a very slow pace, passing in the middle. The torso must move at a constant tempo and remain level and controlled. The feet must not be separated into the constituent elements of heel–ball–toe, but meet the floor as a unit and also point forwards, as if following tramlines. The sensation created is that the body is being pulled across the space by a thick rope attached to your centre, while being simultaneously tugged back by a lesser tension. This opposition is known as *hippari-hai* in Japanese. It is similar (though on a different axis) to the centring achieved by the upper body pulling up and the lower half pushing down into the ground that is found in *noh* and other traditional performing arts. At a prescribed time in the ponderous music, you turn, change to another level and return across the space. This turn is always out to and never away from the imagined audience.

There are two difficult shifts of balance in the walk: first, when the foot wants to rush to take the forward-moving torso's weight; and second, when the torso wants to stop as the weight falls solely on to the back leg. You have to resist and control the forward momentum and then the lack of it in order to maintain an even speed. It is important that the focus is fixed clearly on the horizon and does not become diffused, as can be a tendency. An image that is frequently used in this exercise is the notion that you move the whole space with you as you turn back into the room. You should sustain the projection of your energy forward, imagining what you are moving towards, but with a clear sense of the space behind. Objects and arm positions are added, which are fixed after the turn in a 'freestyle' position of your choice. Another variant is that the arms move slowly and constantly at a different rhythm from the rest of the body on the return walk.

Stamping Shakuhachi

Stamping Shakuhachi is a central exercise of the Suzuki method and its stamp is commonly recognised as its central motif. This has arisen partly because it is described in *The Way of Acting*.[3] It involves repeated stomping to music (as in the first mode of walking) for approximately three minutes before a total collapse to the floor. You must move steadily and from the centre, with no sudden changes of direction. There are no fixed paths until the group comes together in a line at the back of the space facing away from the audience as the loud rhythmical brass and percussion music comes to a climax. You collapse like a marionette having its strings cut, though there is not a total release on the floor. The body faces down and is slightly contracted so that the energy built up by stamping does not dissipate in an open sprawl. You then rise very slowly to your feet and progress to the front of the space (as in Slow ten tekka ten), holding the arms and torso in a fixed position that you sustain as you walk forwards like a moving statue. The music for the second section (which is also approximately three minutes long, though the demands of the stamping make the first part seem much longer) is a gentle shakuhachi flute melody. It should appear to an observer that this causes you to rise rather than your own volition. As the music finishes, you find stillness at one end of the space, facing the 'audience', so it is important to become familiar with the melody and time any changes precisely. The ending is also the starting-point for the next exercise so it is a position of readiness as much as closure. In *The Way of Acting*, Suzuki suggests that the performer needs to control the breath and loosen the pelvis in order to execute this exercise.

Standing and Sitting Statues

Standing Statues develops and accelerates the rising up from the floor in the middle of Stamping Shakuhachi. From a standing starting-point, you move repeatedly to 'freestyle' frozen poses interspersed with low crouches. You must find and hold a statue immediately after the shouted command or the bang of the stick. The speed of the reaction demanded means that you often repeat patterns and shapes, so you should try constantly to broaden your repertoire. These poses are held on tiptoes and may be oriented ahead, to the left or right, and low or high. It is important that the whole body faces one direction or stops at one level; the arms or head should not move as separate units. The focus should be on something or someone imaginary rather than nothing. The face, neck and shoulders must all remain relaxed so that the statue is held with soft tension. You may then be asked to isolate and release the neck, an arm or the whole body, before returning to the crouch. This is one of the few exercises in the method where the work of the imagination is evident and improvisation is necessary. It thus provides openings into compositional and image-based theatre-making.

Sitting Statues is similar to Standing Statues, though with a different relationship to the floor. There are three basic positions as well as the starting-point. First, you move from a relaxed, seated tucked ball to balancing on the buttocks, with the head and body facing forwards and the arms loosely circling the legs. You must pull the spine and head up to make the back straight and keep the centre revealed. The second position is still forward-facing but with the legs stretched out straight in front, raised a few centimetres off the floor and with the feet flexed back. The third position is the same but with the legs wide apart. The upper torso must continue to face forwards and be lifted up off the floor, which demands great concentration, breath control and strength in the stomach muscles. You must not counterbalance the legs with the upper body (which is much easier) but keep the legs only just off the floor to ensure this does not happen. The arms are held bent, with the hands in a loose fist next to the thighs. You always return to the relaxed-ball position in between poses. This is also true of 'Freestyle Sitting Statues', where statues are chosen randomly.

Voice

The voice is trained initially in the three positions of Sitting Statues, but also occasionally in 'freestyle' ones. You always face forwards and towards an imagined audience rather than your co-trainees when you speak. This technique is derived from the notion that in Greek theatre the masked actors talked to the gods through the priest of Dionysus enthroned on the *prohedria,* which was usually situated at the front of the orchestra. It also reflects the very presentational style of *kabuki* on its wide, flat stage and of *noh* theatre, where the masked *shite* faces the audience for most of the performance. This focus is evidenced in the linearity and forward projection of the body in most of the exercises, which then extends into the voice. Various classical texts are used, depending on the teacher's preference, but usually derived from Suzuki's performance repertoire. They include Macbeth's speech – 'Tomorrow and tomorrow and tomorrow' – and Menelaus from *The Trojan Women:*

> O splendour of sunburst breaking forth this day, whereon
> I lay my hands once more on Helen, my wife. And yet
> It is not, so much as men think, for the woman's sake
> I came to Troy, but against that guest proved treacherous,
> Who like a robber carried the woman from my house.

Suzuki also uses popular songs, so that you have the further complication of singing and reciting simultaneously. In all recitation the text must be spoken or sung at speed as one unit while holding one of the three basic positions in Sitting Statues or in a freestyle pose. The tone is of hurried urgency and excitation, though always with immense control, flattening out any cadence or pitch implied in the text. Breathing must be together as a group at fixed points at the end of sentences. As the training progresses, the voice is added to any other difficult pose or shift of balance, such as the move up or down in Basic Number One, or at the very end of Slow ten tekka ten. Various levels are worked on: full voice, half voice and whisper, but the energy must be consistently high, whatever the volume.

The voice is thus considered primarily in terms of energy. There is no technical exploration of the voice as an organ of speech or the body as a site of resonators. as in Jerzy Grotowski's training. Rather than using the voice in a state of relaxation that is familiar to Western approaches, it is drawn out in positions of tension. The voice is added as you fight for balance when one leg is raised or when the stomach muscles are struggling to hold the upper torso off the floor. By then loosening any tension in the upper part of the body, you locate the effort and therefore the sound in the lower stomach or diaphragm. This can be likened to the recitation in *noh*, though this connection is not made overtly in training.

> the voice production style of no uses a variety of highly developed vocal techniques. The quality of this style can be described as 'earth-centred' referring to the great amount of strength which is focussed in the lower abdomen when it is sung, although delicate resonances in the chest, throat, and head also affect the sum total of what can be considered a no vocal style. In general, the strong vocal quality serves as an important energiser in making the performance space come alive for the actor-dancer.[4]

Such heightened energy can modulate but it must not flag. In Japanese, the full sense of the sentence is only revealed at the end of the line, similar to German where the verb always comes last. In training, the energy must therefore be sustained through to the last word. The student's voice work emulates the teacher's, when the strength of their commands has a direct impact on the student's response. This has similarities with martial arts, where the shout is called a *kiai* and the sound is considered a release of energy, or *ki*. In Japanese, the numbers – *ichi, ni, san, shi, go, roku* – are short and emphatic which helps this. In Italy, the softness of the sounds made minimal impact. The quality of the verbal count or command energises the response as the vocal stimuli are answered with action.

There are many other exercises which develop the basic techniques mentioned here, though they are peripheral rather than fundamental to the method. One is an arm exercise in which you move your straight arms rapidly and jerkily while maintaining a rooted position and firm centre. A 'voodoo walk' involves long striding steps with a very low centre, coming to a sharp stop with the music and maintaining a constant height. In summer 1999, Suzuki was developing a complex 'Elvis Presley walk' which involved swinging the hips and which was evident in the performance *Sayonara Toga*.

There are also several exercises mentioned in other people's accounts, be they Brandon's, where the trainee lifts an almost forty-pound iron ladder, or Goto's, where a partner sits on another's crossed legs as they lean backwards to lie on the floor while singing (*agura*). How and why these have disappeared or were not included in sessions I followed is appropriate to a more historical account. Exercises like those with the heavy ladder belong to another group and another culture that Brandon observed over twenty years ago and Goto saw in the early 1980s. The demands that they evidence are more extreme than those attainable in the comparatively brief workshops in which I have participated more recently in the West. It is sufficient here to reiterate that my selection is partial yet encompasses the core of Suzuki's method. It must also be remembered that even if the exercises have changed slightly, the principles are still the same, as the following demonstrates.

Fundamental Principles

The teaching structure and hierarchy in the training are both crystal clear. The teacher breaks exercises down into sections and demonstrates them. You then repeat these many times, with corrections given verbally and occasionally manually. You cannot rest unless told to nor refuse to do an exercise. The energy and commitment must be sustained throughout the session. Sometimes you watch half the group working, learning through observation of errors and progress. There is little talk and comments are not encouraged. You learn with the body, not through questions, conducting an internal monologue rather than a dialogue with others or the teacher. In such silence there can be a progressive heightening of concentration as you move from one exercise to the next, and it is vital to try to sustain and build the focus rather than let it dissipate between sequences. In the early stages, talking might be necessary to clarify certain techniques, but this soon becomes redundant and breath should be saved for coping with the demands of the exercises.

The exercises are startlingly diagnostic. The very strict form exposes individual tensions and patterns of movement and physicality, perhaps revealing that one side of your body is weaker and slower than the other, or that your leg muscles may not pull you up after the seventh time of squatting to the floor and coming up. You start to contemplate why and what allows you to do one thing and not another and when this is so. The legs tremble, so you try to stop them shaking, yet if you focus on the legs they shake even more. Muscular control comes from pushing the feet down into the floor, finding strength in the one point which cannot move. Control also comes from the centre and from focused breathing. Most importantly, you learn to avoid judging your feelings but instead to search ceaselessly for the exactitude of the form, the detail of the movement and the technique. It is as much a training of this mental application as it is a training of the muscles and nerves.

The relationship of your body to space is evident and precisely linear, with movements forwards, sideways, backwards, up and down. Sometimes the level of the torso and head has to remain constant, as you move your centre without bouncing through a fixed spatial plane parallel to the floor, which requires immense focus. When you stop a fast movement, you must do so instantly in time and space. This involves not coming to a generous slow resolution, but freezing in the moment of command or on the exact count. Sometimes a stamp is stopped before it hits the floor with full impact as in Basic Number Two. The downward thrust is resisted at the last moment before full contact is made with the ground. Awareness of space is also learned through the diagonal processions across the stage, as you struggle to maintain an even gap between you and the person in front, a difficulty exacerbated by differing body sizes. You never touch another person but learn through proprioception, the often subconscious ability of the body to orient itself in space.

The rhythms are extreme: very fast and then very slow, or with an unmodulated, even tempo. When stamping, you must try to be on top of the music, stamping not on the beat but a split second before it. You must attack and not feel or respond to the rhythm, keeping active and alive rather than reactive and passive. Music almost becomes a partner with whom to compete. It is as though the sound is being created by your movement, rather than by an external source. To help train this sensitivity, the timing of commands is constantly varied. As you move forwards in Basic Number Two, for example, a rhythmic pattern is established and then just as quickly broken. You move before the command if you anticipate too much. Motion must begin in the split second when the instruction is given and not before or after, when it is either too early or too late. This requires extreme readiness. The sound of the vocal command or bang of the stick acts as an instruction to progress, creating an impulse. You must allow the reflex response to happen. The action required may be small – a raised foot at knee height stamping on the floor – yet there is a specific and usually brief amount of time for this.

Lauren uses the metaphor of driving a car very fast before you slam on the brakes. These may either be external – the floor – or internal and muscular as you create the braking action through resistance. A notion which is found in *noh* theatre that is pertinent here is 'outside stop, inside no stop'. What the audience sees is balanced with what they experience, the sensory interacting with what is visually perceived. The car may have braked but the engine must still be revving fiercely. This stop is also reminiscent of the *mie* or held frozen position of *kabuki*, though this connection is never made overtly. (Brandon noted in his 1978 article that the stamp of Basic Number One also derives from *kabuki*'s *mie* and that the 'box' – a position with out-turned open legs – is a basic shape in *kabuki*.) A *mie* punctuates movement and momentarily frames a character in a heightened pose, but it is a consciously presented statue and is usually more fragmented than Suzuki's stop. *Kabuki* often separates the head and torso, with the head locking into place at the very last moment after the body, so emphasising the gaze.

Similarly, the principle of *jo-ha-kyu* is never mentioned, though this is key to a traditional Japanese performer's understanding of the way action can be divided up or measured. This tripartite phrase represents a never-ending cycle. Resistance (*jo*) gives way to a 'rupture' (*ha*) as the greater force breaks free, and this release speeds up, ending in the held suppression (*kyu*) that creates the '*jo*' of the next action sequence. This rhythmical and energetic separation of time and action into three phases can be applied as much to Suzuki training as to other techniques, but it is never spoken about. This is perhaps because Suzuki is attempting to break away from a dependency on exclusive Japanese frames of reference.

Repetition is central to Suzuki's approach, as it is to many other disciplines where mastery rather than creativity or originality is prioritised. A routine is initially necessary to learn the form but it soon provides the means to examine yourself in relation to a fixed structure, allowing a deepening of the effect of the training on the performer. Repetition also teaches precision and respect for the craft as you understand the complexity contained within small details. Suzuki calls the exercises *kunren,* which means 'disciplines' in Japanese, pointing to the need for repetition and daily practice to gain proficiency and understanding. Yet he emphasises that these are not merely gymnastic but acting disciplines that require constant imaginative and emotional involvement. This is often needed to surmount the difficulty of the physical task.

Centring is constantly re-established and tested through exercises that 'attack' the body's grounding. The destabilisation caused by the leg flicks up and stamps down of Basic Number Two or Three has to be redressed through controlled balancing of the centre. The walks are not so much about positioning the feet but about testing the centre. This is not simply imagined but has to be repeatedly found in order to hold and sustain difficult balances and modes of locomotion. You must be aware of gravitational pull on the body and resist this at your midpoint. Emphasis is also placed on always moving by leading from the hips rather than the periphery, in particular the feet. This is akin to *noh* theatre, where energy is synonymous with the word for hips (*koshi*), recognising that the body's centre is primarily responsible for the charged, heightened physical state of the *noh* performer.

Centring is also linked to the reiterated notion that you must fight with yourself in order to remain stable, as the movements throw you off-balance. This teaching strategy establishes more than a technical principle and is reminiscent of the attitude demanded in martial arts. Struggle becomes embedded in the training as a fundamental technique and law, encouraging emotional equilibrium in the face of obstacles and attack, be it from yourself or an external agent. This stability is linked to steady and calm breathing.

Breathing must be 'secret' or hidden, in part to conceal the effort required. There are no clues for helpful breath patterns, so you have to find them yourself, constrained by the strict physical form. Continued stamping for three minutes tests the breath, which must be sustained from the diaphragm to prevent hyperventilation and loss of balance. When you relax to the floor in Stamping Shakuhachi, the breath must be garnered to support the precise movement of standing up slowly. Control of breathing steadies balance and allows a powerful voice to be projected by a muscular diaphragm. Use of

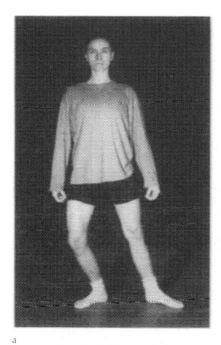

a

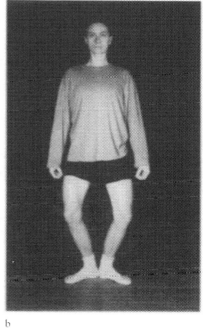

b

c

The Suzuki Method: Basic Number One

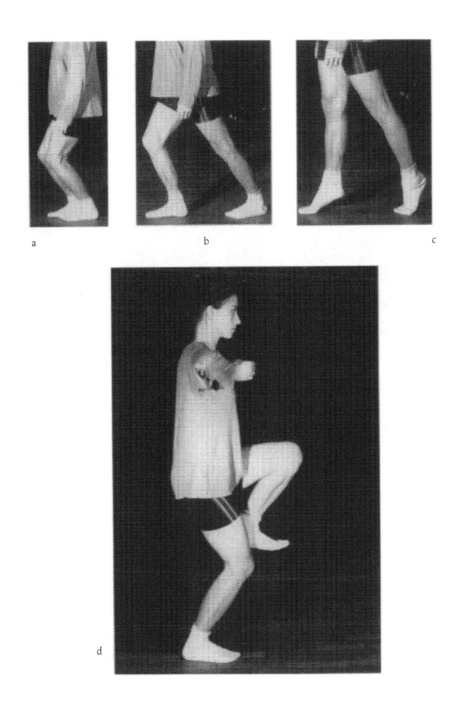

The Suzuki Method: Basic Number Two

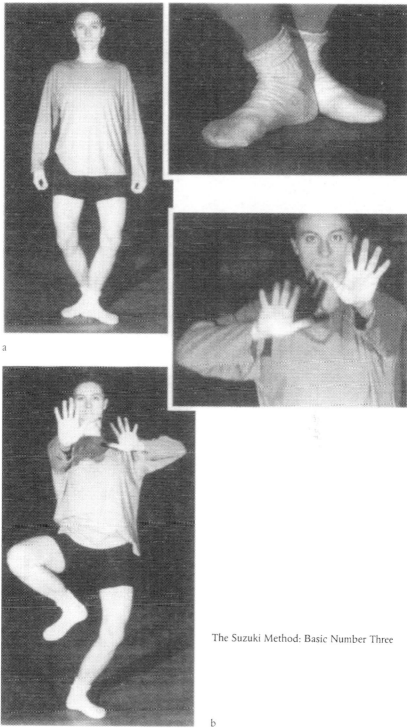

a

The Suzuki Method: Basic Number Three

b

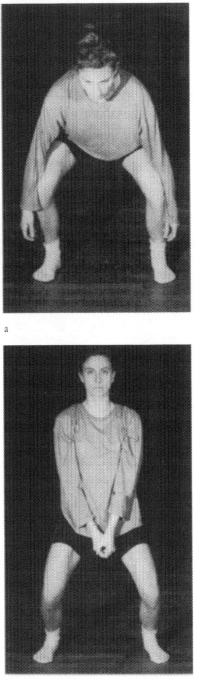

a

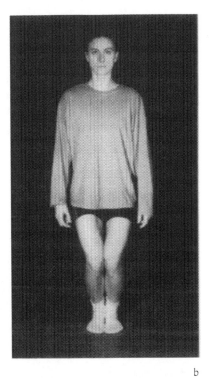

b

c

d

The Suzuki Method: Basic Number Four

The Suzuki Method: Sitting and Standing
statues

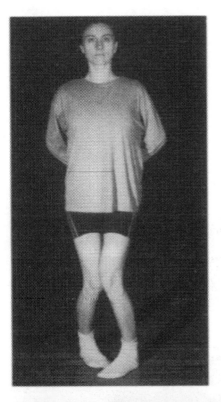 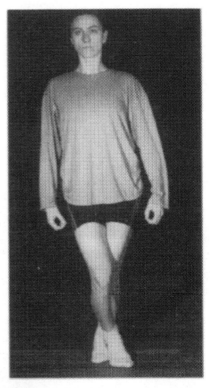

Left: Pigeon toe walk

Right: Walk Number Seven

Duck Walk

△ Toga – amphitheatre with entrance to old farmhouse theatre on the left

◁ Toga – old farmhouse theatre

▽ Toga – rehearsal for a performance of ACM's *Ashes and Bacteria* 1993

△ Shizuoka – Daendo theatre

◁ Toga amphitheatre – *hanamichi* or walkway

▽ Shizuoka Udo amphitheatre with teabushes in foreground

And you can make the obstacle insurmountable. Even in standing still. Until you have done that you have not even engaged in the technique.

Frequent conceptions of the training are that the form is punishing, the stamping hurts and the stick is as much to strike fear in you as to beat a rhythm. These may be true, but those I interviewed emphasised that the primary function and effect of the method is to develop your will and concentration. This is also its central difficulty, for how do you reconcile yourself to practise daily what you know is impossible? Suzuki training alters mental processes and is not to be simply danced. If the state of mind fostered by the training is paramount, the form is paradoxically almost irrelevant, yet it is only through the form that you can affect and change mental states. If it cannot shift them, if the performer is stubbornly unyielding, it at least makes this visible to the director, teacher or audience. As Nelis points out, you can achieve the desired effect standing still, as is evident in several of Suzuki's performances discussed in the next chapter.

Responses to the rigours of the training are dependent on the individual's desired aesthetic and their need to be changed or experience such demands. Ellen Lauren has reflected that although not every performer might *want* to do Suzuki training, they probably all *need* to do it. Yet needing is fundamentally different from wanting. Suzuki training may not revolutionise Western performance or culture, but it certainly broadens performers' and critics' perspectives of what performing can be and what it might entail. But perhaps if it is taken even more seriously, if it is understood and not dismissed as Fascistic demagogy, it could help revive flagging Western theatre culture.

If it is impossible to continue group practice, the method can just about still function without a teacher. British performer Patrick Morris discovered this approach in America, where he lived for ten years and trained under Lauren. For him, the training provides a form which can be repeated and the principles can be applied widely, as he now does in Britain. If you can create your own resistance, individual practice can be a teacher. In interview, Kameron Steele described how

The training is most useful as a tool to test your will as an actor, because it's hard to get up and do every day. That's why I still do it, even though I have thrown away Suzuki's world and his aesthetic [. . .] I still do the training because it's impossible. And as an artist you have to face the impossible and try to accomplish it every day, otherwise you don't call yourself an artist.

In spite of his personal difficulties with 'Suzuki's world', Steele aligns himself with this generic group of 'artists'. This work can provide subtle support and a sense of purpose for the individual or those outside the circles of SCOT, SPAC or SITI, or other groups using this method. The principles endure beyond the training and outside the group.

This distancing from the group can lead to other problems though. Morris has identified that performers in such cases may be too anxious to apply the training to performance. For him, what is essential is how the training affects the quality and concentration of performance rather than how it creates material. It is a vital way of keeping in touch with his body and state of mind on a regular basis, not as personal therapy, but as a performer who needs to be aware of his own body rhythms, feelings and his own physical geography. Suzuki himself frankly admits that the training is only part of the process, and rightly plays down any causal links between the training and performance. He is refreshingly pragmatic: 'It can be described as one working hypothesis for pulling off the "sham" of acting.'[16] The advantage of Suzuki's particular 'hypothesis' is that it is precise, detailed and effective, and is a tried-and-tested practical philosophy. It is not for every individual or for every culture, but it can work.

Voice and Cross-cultural Investigations

Lauren's suggestion that all performers might 'need' this training is most problematic in relation to how it serves the voice. Here lies the greatest debate about the transposition of Suzuki training to non-Japanese cultures. For Suzuki, 'Technically speaking my method consists of training to learn to speak powerfully and with clear articulation, and also to make the whole body speak even when one keeps silent.'[17] This 'speaking' is both literal and metaphorical. Yet for many non-Japanese performers, this vocal training and search for power can lead to more problems than benefits, particularly in the short term, as voices become strained and sore. The addition of the voice in the training complicates and initially weakens the energy level and the clarity of the performer's physicality, evident in postural misalignment and imbalance. When you are only tentatively familiar with the form, it is difficult to recall lines and consciously work the organs of speech. This element of the training creates further bodily tensions that exacerbate vocal stress.

This problem partly arises from a fundamental difference in technical emphasis, in that Western modes of vocal training prioritise relaxation and release as well as extensive warming-up. By contrast, Suzuki's way demands expression in moments of tension by making the diaphragm a tensed muscle that forcefully and energetically expels air. If you have too much strain, you are expected to concentrate even more on dispelling it rather than on relaxation. It is useful to consider tension as a positive rather than negative state, but without warming up or time to release the voice it can intensify vocal stress. The notion of pushing the body until you feel pain may be familiar to actors, yet the cost of losing your voice is for many too great and disempowering. Performers are reluctant to push their vocal organs as hard as they might drive the rest of their bodies. You can hobble to work with overstretched hamstrings and on bruised feet, but loss of voice cannot be hidden or massaged to comfort, leads potentially to medical complications, and has evident social and performance implications.

Suzuki's approach prioritises power and energy which lead to strong projection. It treats the voice as the action of a single muscle, which, with the movement of the diaphragm, it initially is. With time and practice, the voice shifts into the lower belly, giving great strength and allowing flexibility. Whispered recitation can be audible in a large auditorium, without the vocal strain which this normally suggests. Clear articulation is also fostered by encouraging muscularity of vocal delivery. Tom Hewitt's performance of Orestes in Suzuki's *Clytemnestra* showed such potential. However, the diaphragm is only the site of origin of the voice, a base of support on which to build, which is then mediated by the larynx and vocal chords. As Maurer described in interview with me: 'He [Suzuki] wants as straight a line with the voice as with the body.' Yet the voice does not travel directly from the diaphragm to the audience's ears but winds among the complex vocal organs before leaving the body. Suzuki's equation that voice equals energy is simplistic, or at least not yet satisfactorily articulated in theory or practice for a non-Japanese context.

The voice in Suzuki's performances is correspondingly energised, fast and loud. What he is searching for is a possession-like state and a non-daily use of language that he defines as 'utterance'. The fast delivery derives in part from a *kabuki* technique called *ippon choshi* and is energetically demanding, with phrases building up and up to a climax that requires immense breath control. The focus must be on the total physical act, emphasising the integration of processes more than mental interpretation or imaginative association. Words have a visceral, catalysing impact but little meaning. The act of speech should transform the body, almost overwhelming it. This shift of emphasis away from the meaning of the text also remembers *noh*, for as Earle Ernst points out, its 'artistry rises out of the dance rather than the words and whose chief effects are visual rather than auditory'.[18] Suzuki is not primarily concerned with conveying narratives or meaning. The danger with such total integration is, however, that words simply repeat the work that the body is doing.

It is inevitable that even those performers, such as Lauren and Maurer, who have trained as well as rehearsed with Suzuki, have less understanding of the voice than their Japanese counterparts. Body use is evident and visible, but the nuance of verbal language is discernible only to a highly trained and experienced ear. This may lead to naïve emulation or imitation. Western advocates of the Suzuki method have learned much about the physical training from observation and application, yet they are not necessarily attuned to the Japanese language.

Perhaps Suzuki himself has never found a satisfactory mode of vocal delivery in performance. His articulation of the training tends to sidestep the voice, focusing always on the 'grammar of the feet' rather than vocal grammar: 'The purpose of the method is to make the actor newly aware through experimental acting, of the physical sensibilities that have become degenerate in his or her daily life. The training also has its vocal component.'[19] For those practising without being able to observe Suzuki's performances, what are they aiming at with the voice? What creative choices does it suggest? For there are little improvisational or 'freestyle' possibilities, and yet the technique itself is slight. My impression from brief contact with the vocal training is that it is predominantly muscle-flexing, but I am not convinced that longer observation would prove otherwise. Some Western performers speaking in English in Suzuki's productions can occasionally be inaudible and the body and throat appear full of tension. Reviews cited in the next chapter also show this, though the individual can rise above such difficulties, as Hewitt demonstrated.

This limitation may be due to Westerners' simplistic imitation of Japanese ways of speaking in performance, which have long-established and various complex traditions. In *The Way of Acting*, Suzuki identified a similar reversed misunderstanding with *shingeki* actors imitating Russian gestural patterns inappropriately in their speeches when playing Chekhov.[20] He identifies how the Japanese language has specific demands, with its 'pitch accent' and long sentences. Such technical and structural differences between languages must be considered carefully in an intercultural practice like Suzuki's.

Noh expert and Japanese speaker Richard Emmert has identified that

English is not structured like Japanese, hence it is not sung like Japanese. In English, syllables often end in consonants while in Japanese they end in vowels. The use of syllable stress in English, within individual words or in combination with short articles or prepositions, also differs from the much more even sounding Japanese syllables.[21]

One Western performer who also has insight into both languages is Kameron Steele, who is fluent in Japanese and who worked with Suzuki for several years. For him, major misunderstandings arise with the application of Suzuki's training to English-language speaking. He attributes the problem in part to tension, as already discussed, though he considers this useful if it can be overcome, which he believes is rare even in SCOT's Japanese performers. Beyond this issue, Steele considers that the nature of the Japanese language has shaped the training in ways that are counteracted when the performer is working in English. In interview, he observed:

There are fewer sounds phonetically possible in the Japanese language. It's not a lyrical language. It's very rhythmical, very percussive. Suzuki was very adept at coaching his actors through how to deal with language, through how to convey meaning, through how they would use Japanese. But he has no concept of how to do that with English.

Spoken language clearly demarcates and defines cultures. We should not expect Suzuki's vocal training to be applied unproblematically to other contexts, as Steele recognises. Not surprisingly (and as Emmert's observations anticipate), one of the results of using Suzuki vocal techniques in English is a flat and monotone delivery. Most Western performers committed to the training acknowledge such difficulties and are struggling with this practical challenge of integration and adaptation. There are no solutions other than those to be worked out through diligent, self-critical and sustained application.

Reservations are not culturally specific, as the next chapter confirms. Japanese critic Tatsuji Iwabuchi, who is not in any case an enthusiast of Suzuki's work, has written about the voice in WLT and SCOT's performances in disparaging terms:

> Personally I found it disturbing that none of Suzuki's actors had good intonation or articulation apart from Shiraishi. Some did not even correct local dialects and generally speaking, the text was recited with such cramp and convulsion that it was hard to make out the content. Suzuki emphasises the element of bodily training in his theoretical writings. Why does he neglect speech training so much?[22]

Accounts of Shiraishi's voice do indeed reveal force but, more significantly, a range. British critic Michael Billington noted that 'Even without understanding her words one grasps the emotion behind them [. . .] Her voice seems to issue from the pit of her stomach and when she prays to the Buddhist god it has a dove-like quality.'[23] Others have since shown some breadth and nuance, though not to Shiraishi's level. Iwabuchi's general confusion reflects others' concerns, despite his niggling complaints about the use of dialect. Such criticisms allude to a lack of sophistication in Suzuki's process of vocal training and the voice in performance. However hard it may be for a non-Japanese speaker like myself to judge this, it is safe to say that Suzuki's training does seem to possess limited means to tackle texts in English at least. The broader difficulty of how text can be incorporated into body practices is, of course, not only Suzuki's problem but one facing all directors working with non-realistic idioms.

New Explorations

Key elements of Japanese performance techniques and principles have been made digestible and accessible by Suzuki training. It concentrates the years of tradition embedded in *noh* and *kabuki* in a transmittable plastic form. This was Suzuki's initial intention which grew from his observation of *noh* actor Hisao Kanze's performance at the Théâtre des Nations. This was not on a *noh* stage. 'I hope thereby not only to somehow modernise the traditions of *no* and Kabuki, but to study the essential beauties of these forms so as to reintroduce some of their concepts into the contemporary theatre.'[24] As Emmert's comments cited earlier showed, these practices did not possess a refined training system from which Suzuki could directly draw. Japan's National Theatre only instituted an intensive training programme in 1970, condensing approximately ten to fifteen years' learning into two years, but this was obviously still in its infancy when Suzuki began to formulate his own approach.

Suzuki was not interested in imitating traditional techniques wholesale but wanted to select, focus and create a practice for the contemporary context. Modernisation and adaptation were therefore essential to the development of the training. Suzuki considered strict replication and servility to convention a handicap and an uncreative option: 'The distance separating "art" from *kata* is enormous. Art implies the *recreation* and not the imitation of tradition. For the actor as artist, the *kata* exist to be destroyed.'[25] His language is strong, but the constraints that traditionalists can impose are stronger. As Suzuki's own inventions have now been integrated into Western theatre for over twenty years, further ongoing reconsiderations and adjustments are needed, led and driven by Western artists.

It is a delicate balance for groups like SITI and Frank to continue to respect the source while trying to find their own route. But they seem to have the will to persist and experiment, reflecting a strength which may derive from what Brandon has described as being part of the flow of tradition: 'One common practice underlying theatre training in Asia is that you enter a process that has no end. You do not enter a goal: you enter a stream or flow that began long before you joined it and will continue after you are gone.'[26] There are few alternatives in America, for example, to either the Strasberg flow of tradition which reaches back to Stanislavski, or to musical theatre with roots in the music-hall and variety shows. In Europe, the work of Jacques Lecoq lengthened the threads that began with Jacques Copeau and which were carried forward by Etienne Decroux and Michel Saint-Denis, visible now in the successful British company Theatre de Complicite. Odin Teatret, Grotowski and the Gardzienice Theatre Association have also provided a rich source of voice and body training for European and American artists. But these processes depend more on the group than Suzuki's does. His practice can and is being taken forward by individuals, which perhaps gives it a head start over the others.

Although Suzuki has pulled out of the collaborative partnership with SITI, what he espoused there seems now to be coming to fruition. The richness SITI members find in the combination of Anne Bogart's Viewpoints and the Suzuki method echoes Suzuki's aspiration for harmony when 'something stronger is made from two different things'.[27] Lauren suggested in interview with me that the SITI company uses Viewpoints 'to build shows and Suzuki training to maintain them', emphasising how these two work so effectively in tandem – Suzuki training provides a foundation of stamina, concentration and precision, and Viewpoints an improvisational creative potential. Similar harmonious mergers could now free the voice work. Other disciplines may have more to offer the voice than the Suzuki method alone. The future may lie in intercultural fusion or the interplay between different processes, rather than wholesale appropriation of Suzuki's multiculturalism.

Advocates argue that it is necessary to do Suzuki training for many years before you can begin to understand its deep effects. Those who have done it for long periods champion the benefits and the insight this allows. This is a truism of many modes of training, including Suzuki's. Any method must be authoritatively inhabited and become 'second instinct' or second nature in order for it to function. You should not simply consider the form empty *kata* or patterns of movement, as Nelis learned. However, as antithetical to the central principles as it might be, the fact remains that you can learn the form and grasp its intentions in a matter of weeks. This is a long way from the world of training for *bunraku* puppetry, for which it is commonly recognised that it takes ten years to learn to operate the feet and a total of thirty years before the trainee can take on a leading role.

Central also to Zeami's writing on *noh* and to traditional Japanese performing arts in general is the idea that duration leads to quality. The actor will only attain Zeami's 'Flower of Peerless Charm' (reach their peak) in their late fifties or sixties. Only then are they afforded the luxury of being able to experiment with the strict form. In *The Kabuki Theatre*, Ernst comments that the training of the *kabuki* actor is considered 'finished' only after he has reached fifty, even if he began as young as seven. Lauren believes that over long periods personal growth changes the experience of the training. Perception of it alters, even if it changes very little in practice. Yet how many Western performers are prepared to be so single-minded and have the patience to follow such an educational model, even if they recognise the need for it? Although Suzuki's method promotes the principle of long-term application, it also ironically allows the performer quick insights and fast results.

The training does evolve and develop and is not set in stone, as a comparison between Brandon's 1978 *Drama Review* article, Suzuki's *The Way of Acting* and my 1998 piece for the *Drama Review* indicates. Broadly, there has been a shift away from posture towards locomotion and a streamlining that has eliminated the more dangerous exercises, such as that with the heavy iron ladder which Brandon witnessed. This first shift is also evident in the account of a training lecture/demonstration given by Suzuki for the Japan Foundation, outlined in a report from March 1983. This was written by Israeli performer Zvi Serper. He describes how 'Suzuki treats the body as the combination of locomotive and stationary modes, the stationary mode being composed of standing, sitting on a chair, sitting on the floor and lying down, with the key factor being invariably the use of the feet'.[28] This dual focus is repeated in *The*

Way of Acting. Brandon notes that Suzuki gave weekly lectures on posture to the WLT performers, which they listened to attentively, as he clarified distinctions between the principle positions of *noh* and *kabuki*. The emphasis on posture and daily movement, such as sitting and standing, was then sublimated, as such principles were crystallised in the exercises and ways of moving. It is more direct to instruct the feet through various walks than through sitting. Posture and habitual movement provided foundations on which the training was laid but these became less perceptible as it focused on the extra-daily rather than the daily.

Beyond this shift of emphasis, Lauren has noted how the walks have become less smooth and graceful and more aggressive and angular. This is exemplified by the relatively recent addition of walk number 8, with its sharp lines and stamp. Differences in modes of teaching will create further adaptations and reassessment. Once the work is taken beyond the SCOT family or SPAC, its form may even alter. Lauren has invented new exercises for advanced classes with SITI which adhere to and reinforce the same principles. In Brisbane, Frank's rigorous twice-weekly four-hour sessions with their troupe have greatly extended the basic exercises. They assert that anything can be thrown at the trainee to test them inside the clearly defined guidelines and exercises, including carrying other performers while walking.

Changes to the form and different modes of teaching grow partly in response to cultural resistances. The notion of Samurai-like discipline is hard to enforce when the teaching is done by Westerners on their home ground. Suzuki's actors expect a high level of commitment, instruction and perhaps even humiliation. Teachers in a Western cultural context may try to instil discipline through the form alone, yet even this can elude them. Workshop conventions and boundaries of what is acceptable within the teacher–pupil relationship cannot be replicated according to Suzuki's model. They need to be reinvented for another context without losing essential ingredients. It should also be remembered that the foremost teacher of the Suzuki method, according to Suzuki himself, is a woman, Ellen Lauren. I do not want to imply that this makes her teaching less strict, but this has a social impact if not just on the term 'master'.

For the majority of Western performers who are trained in and who consequently work with psychological approaches which centre on originality, creativity and which use improvisation as their rehearsal tool, Suzuki training may be incomprehensible and seemingly of little direct use. Yet for those looking beyond the dominant stream, it provides an accessible, feasible alternative current. Performers with whom I have discussed the training have affirmed how the lessons it teaches can be applied to performance in general, no matter the style, period or director's process. The reader may well have seen high-quality naturalistic acting and been oblivious to the performer's debt to Suzuki training. Suzuki's method may have evolved initially to deal with the extremes demanded by classical drama, yet this is not its only application. If performers are consistently and precisely trained, directors can spend more time inventing in rehearsal, encouraging the experimentation seen in the work of Bogart. It does not then fall to them to spend rehearsal time training actors and bringing them together with a shared vocabulary, when instead they could be generating performance material.

The Suzuki method has developed a long way from what Brandon described as a 'training system that is especially Japanese',[29] with Suzuki dressed in a kendo uniform. Western actors no longer need to travel to Japan for enlightenment, for this process gives them access to distilled central principles of centuries of performance tradition. At least in relation to Suzuki, Brandon's 1989 statement seems out-of-date: 'I cannot express too strongly how significant it is that Western performers apprentice themselves to Asian masters. They learn the intrinsic values of the performing system by assimilation, directly and without the intermediacy of a Western interpreter.'[30] Of course this still has value, but it increasingly seems a luxury in these times of financial struggle for artists and the marginalisation of experimental theatre within mainstream culture. Furthermore, the relationship between masters and disciples has altered since 1989 and is continuing to evolve through the interaction of East and West. We are now in the third or fourth generation since Brandon's first encounters with Eastern practices. As such approaches as Suzuki's continue to be integrated into Western performance processes and then undergo their own revisions within that new context, we need to reconsider the limiting geographical division of West and East. This is the constructive legacy of intercultural performance practice such as Suzuki's.

FIVE

•

SUZUKI'S PERFORMANCE PRACTICE

There is no direct causal link between training and performance, as Suzuki openly admits. Mastering techniques of performing (if this is indeed possible) does not lead automatically to success in the live event, where there are so many variables. As already suggested, the training enables more understanding of performing as a process than performance as an end point. Besides, several of Suzuki's productions preceded the training, which evolved from the actors' experimentations with a range of texts in the early 1970s after over a decade of his work as a director. Yet there are undeniable connections between these two aspects of the creative process. In this chapter, key elements of Suzuki's performance repertoire through the instances of some central productions will be analysed, in order to cast light on this interrelationship.

Nine pieces which might be considered representative of the whole of Suzuki's extensive repertoire will be examined: *The Little Match Girl, On the Dramatic Passions II, The Trojan Women, The Bacchae, Dionysus, Clytemnestra, The Tale of Lear, The Chronicle of Macbeth* and *Three Sisters.* This is a selective list, but one which demonstrates major developments in his theatre practice. The analysis is based on my observations of live performances as well as reviews, critical interpretations and video recordings, taking into account the usual limitations these present. It will reveal the central stylistic, dramaturgical and aesthetic tenets of his productions, at the heart of which is the performer and his relationship with the audience. The study will not assess how Suzuki operates as a director in rehearsal but examine the results, as evidenced through the performer's contribution to the productions and the public reception of this. The focus is on the performer, for it is only by recalling the objectives of the training that one can make sense of Suzuki's diverse output. This will also help move the analysis closer to an emic approach.

There are several connections between the laws and aesthetics of the training and the performances of the WLT and SCOT in particular. The forward-facing linear positioning of the body continues through into the performances. The contact with the ground and ways of walking are conspicuously explored on stage. The use of the voice echoes that of the workshop, for training speeches are drawn directly from performances. There is a similar heightened quality of energy found in the two processes as well as common rhythmical principles: the sharp stop, rapidity and slow movement. The sudden holding of statues appears again and again, most noticeably in choral work where it creates a strong visual focus.

Repetition can also be seen within the performances, as an actor adopts a consistent way of moving, for example, or in recurring musical motifs. It is more startlingly apparent from production to production, which challenges Western expectations of originality. Directorial concepts and even sections of text or roles rematerialise in several works. As indicated in Chapter One, such reiterative reinvestigation has roots in Japanese culture. Suzuki recycles extensively and intentionally as his sequential pieces illustrate (for example, *On the Dramatic Passions I, II* and *III*). At its worst, such repetition indicates a dearth of ideas and laziness. At its best, it forces the audience to question their craving for newness, changing perceptions of both the nature of the theatre event and a director's body of work. Repetition in training helps the performer learn the necessity of facing daily challenges and encourages engagement with fine detail. In performance, it might help the audience observe more closely, as similar material is tackled from diverse angles and is dislocated to new contexts. It is a fine line that Suzuki treads, though not always perhaps with the best of intentions.

As there are connections between training and performance, so there are differences, though these are fewer. Suzuki's performances are sprinkled with humour arising from an absurd vision, but however comic some of the training movements like pigeon-toed walking are, laughter must be stifled. Seriousness is vital in the workshop as it is in rehearsal. This does not preclude light-hearted playing among actors in performance and between actors and the audience, but there is no preparation for this in the training.

There is undoubtedly a different quality of engagement and interaction between the actors in performance, as they respond not to the teacher but to each other and the audience. An audience is continually implied in the training, but with all trainees repeating the same exercise, there is no sense that you have to balance the whole stage picture or adjust yourself to others. In performance, you must work less individually and more as an ensemble, creating a total rhythmical synthesis of text and action in space. The presentation of each role and the playing of that objective entity, be it individual or choral, requires a shift of focus beyond the exploration of one's own technical and emotional resources. In performance, the audience must make sense of each element and to enable this the performer must select and modify their individual input in relation to the whole *mise-en-scène*. The characterisation or role playing has to be readable.

It is important to trace the links between the method and the performances as a way into understanding Suzuki's artistic vision, but overemphasis on this starting-point can obscure other influences. A breadth of inspiration is apparent in the range of materials that Suzuki has produced. His early work with the WLT involved the interpretation of new plays, centred on Suzuki's collaboration with Minoru Betsuyaku on productions such as *The Little Match Girl*. Later, he created condensed adaptations of Shakespeare, including *The Chronicle of Macbeth* and *The Tale of Lear*, as sort of chamber pieces. At the other end of the spectrum, extravagant outdoor festival performances like *Greetings from the Edges of the Earth* (with its spectacular lighting and fireworks) build on the huge firework displays held throughout Japan in the summer months. Suzuki has also drawn extensively on traditional indigenous texts and modes of performance, be they principles of *noh* walks or a *kabuki* play. Occasionally, he has even directed traditional *noh* pieces in their entirety. His classical Greek productions (most famously represented by *The Trojan Women*) grew out of this research into the sources of world theatre and contained a strong choral presence, with demanding solo roles. Suzuki has also created several absurdist commentaries based on the works of Anton Chekhov and Samuel Beckett, whose plays are presented either as single entities (though often heavily abridged and with interpolations such as songs) or as major contributory parts of collages that unify various textual extracts. These collages have operated almost as showcases for the WLT and then SCOT. Finally, Suzuki has also ventured into the more commercial terrain of music theatre, including productions of *Sweeney Todd* and *Cyrano de Bergerac*. The range is striking.

Suzuki's training does not begin to reflect this diversity of styles and textual materials, but works more on a pre-expressive level. Eugenio Barba has called those aspects of performing which are technical, spatial and energetic 'pre-expressive', to break down the total complex process into its constituent elements. Suzuki's training gives the performer essential tools and understanding with which to tackle any material. Rather than stretching the performer's abilities, this method opens them to a range of texts and performance demands from a solid and singular base. It gives performers a foundation and source from which to interpret, explore and respond to the director's own dramaturgical preferences and aesthetic sensibilities, be it Suzuki or any other artist.

Before evaluating specific productions, there are certain overriding characteristics that appear to greater or lesser degrees in many performances and which will be examined in more depth during the course of my analysis. First, Suzuki nearly always organises his company on stage with a chorus and central protagonists. This is essential to Suzuki's Greek dramas but it also appears in his adaptations of Chekhov, to name one example, where a chorus is not prescribed in the original text. This device derives mainly from Greek theatre, where the chorus comment on the protagonist's actions, yet it also shares similarities with the static choruses of *noh* and *kabuki*, who accompany stage action with chanting or music. The chorus gives his productions a social dimension, as individual characters interact or respond to the representative group. Second, Suzuki uses the recurring metaphor of all the world as a mental hospital. This recontextualises many texts but is particularly evident in *The Tale of Lear* where it provides a clear framing device. Suzuki's adoption of this can be traced back both to Japan's instability and social conflicts and the sensibilities these created, as well as the framing devices explored in some of Betsuyaku's and other writers' plays in the 1960s (both these influences are briefly described in Chapter One – see pages 17–18). Third is Suzuki's dramaturgical technique of collage and juxtaposition. Like the Polish director Tadeusz Kantor, who coined the term, Suzuki is a 'text-mincer' who plays eclectically with multiple texts, be they songs, plays or poems. This structuring is partly enabled by the chorus's comments on the main action, but is reinforced by the crazy world within a world of his theatre. The irrational absurdity this generates often leads to humour or pathos. A fourth recurring aspect is his use of pre-recorded music to create contrasts or shifts in mood. This is a device found in nearly all his work. It affirms the simplicity of his staging, which is reliant on the performer, lighting and sound to create a sense of mood, place and time, rather than on complex scenography.

It is not as easy to find consistency in the nature of acting in his performances. This has altered as Suzuki's relationship to text has shifted and with the demands of each production, in particular its casting which has often been bicultural. With the departure of Betsuyaku, rather than interpreting plays the performers began to explore their own history and psychophysicality as a form of self-encounter. As the training became formalised, notions such as animal energy and speaking through the gods became established. Suzuki's theories of what acting and theatre are have pragmatically shifted as external circumstances have changed and as he has made fresh discoveries. I will therefore reveal some underlying axioms and approaches to performing as I examine each piece, rather than attempt to contain him with a monolithic theory. My analysis of his training presents key principles, though this explains little about how Suzuki expects actors to apply these to a range of performance styles and texts. This chapter will tangentially show the chronological progression of his ideas and how these have been underpinned by central tenets of his method.

Two ways of seeing provide a background to Suzuki's practice. Intraculturalism has markedly shaped Suzuki's vision through the training but also through the use of dramatic texts. His work is always refracted through the prism of Japanese performance traditions and materials. This leads occasionally to quotation (as in the kimono-style costumes for *The Tale of Lear*) but more often to the direct embodiment that is central to intracultural processes. For

Suzuki, intraculturalism is not about imitating surfaces, but about engaging with deep principles and patterns. This is evident in the way that the theatres Isozaki and Suzuki created drew inspiration from ancient Greek, Elizabethan and Japanese structures. Transformation and updating might obscure original sources and authenticity might be manipulated, but the intention is reinvention rather than replication. In the training, you learn to make sharp stops without acknowledging the connection to *kabuki*'s *mie*, for such knowledge is not needed even though the principles must remain intact.

Suzuki's intraculturalism is balanced by the interculturalism engendered in the radical political climate of the 1960s and 1970s, outlined in Chapter One. His vision evolved within a period of Japan's increased openness to outside influences. As one of the principle exponents of what could be hesitatingly called postmodern performance techniques in Japan, we should approach Suzuki's 'modernist' use of indigenous source cultures, his 'primitivism', if you like, with caution. His application of deep structures and principles yields easily to pastiche and satire of his own culture and traditions. My analysis exposes such combinations and juxtapositions, which are particularly evident in Suzuki's collages.

Collage,
On the Dramatic Passions II
and Kayoko Shiraishi

Suzuki's theatrical explorations began at Waseda University where he studied Political Science and Economics between 1958 and 1964. Typical of his generation, he had no formal university education in theatre, but worked actively for the extra-curricular club Waseda Free Stage (WFS), of which he was chairman from 1960 to 1961. The WFS broadly modelled itself on *shingeki* company structures, with similar left-leaning political and artistic policies. It is no surprise, then, that Suzuki initially worked on Western naturalistic texts, though not necessarily ones with socialist ideals. Early productions included Chekhov's *The Anniversary* (also known as *Jubilee*, 1959), *Death of a Salesman* (1960), *The Three Sisters* (1961) and *A Streetcar Named Desire* (1963). The influence of *shingeki* was deeply rooted, even on someone who was to become as experimental as he did. Yet although Suzuki was using Western texts, he was sceptical about prescribed ways of working on them. When Moscow Art Theatre actors visited Waseda University, Suzuki was singularly unimpressed by his teacher's admiration for an actor who could cry at will. For Suzuki, this was not a sign of good acting.

This scepticism about *shingeki* led Suzuki to expand his repertoire beyond a familiar orthodoxy, and in 1961 he directed Jean-Paul Sartre's *The Flies* and the new play, *A and B and one Woman* by Minoru Betsuyaku. In December of that year, core members of the WFS (including Suzuki) set up their own professional company outside the university, called simply the Free Stage (*Jiyu Butai*). Their principal performer was Ono Seki (he committed suicide in 1974) and their main playwright was Betsuyaku. Betsuyaku was deeply inspired by Samuel Beckett and under his sway he crafted a stripped-back minimalist style. Many of his plays of this period depict the psychological interplay between characters who are arbitrarily brought together, with black humour or irony providing social criticism. The Free Stage's first performance was Betsuyaku's *The Elephant* (*Zo*), 3–8 April 1962, which is typical of this style. Between 1961 and 1967, Suzuki directed five of his plays in total: *A and B and one Woman, The Gate, The Elephant, The Little Match Girl* and *The Smile of Dr Maximilian*. Very little is recorded about Suzuki's work at this time, and almost nothing of note is published in English.[1] More is known about Betsuyaku because of the subsequent publication of these plays, including some in English.

The building of alternative means to go beyond *shingeki* had a troubled inception. *The Elephant* was the Free Stage's only notable production before their change of name to the Waseda Little Theatre (*Waseda Shogekijo*) in 1966. It is now considered a central text of Japanese drama from this period, but critics were then unprepared for such a radical stylistic departure. The passive world-weary acting style of Ono Seki, the minimalist décor and the gloomy atmosphere brought some life to a deliberately repetitive text where very little happened. The story of two surviving victims of Hiroshima's atom bomb was dark and despairing. Like Sartre's *Huis Clos* (*In Camera* or *No Exit*), it offered no alternatives or ways out. Such themes and misery would resurface successfully in Suzuki's later work, but the 1962 audience would not swallow such a style or material and *The*

Elephant was poorly received. Betusyaku and Suzuki's pioneering enthusiasm was dampened by this critical failure.

Suzuki's 'official' history begins with the founding of the WLT, which gave him renewed impetus. Betsuyaku's *The Gate (Mon)* was the first piece that the newly configured company produced, though this also received negative notices. (Two of the performers were Ikuko Saito and Tsutamori Kosuke, both of whom still work with Suzuki today). This was followed by *The Little Match Girl*, shown in their own 120-seat studio theatre. The play is loosely based on the narrative of Hans Christian Andersen's story. Like Andersen's, Betsuyaku's interpretation is a dark tale, his adaptation depicting the interaction of a destitute woman and two apparent strangers. She turns up unexpectedly at their house and reveals her sorry past to them. Just as it transpires that they had a daughter who 'disappeared' aged seven and it seems that the visitor might be her, the girl's brother also enters. The play alternates between the narration of Andersen's tale and the painstaking dialogue of the passive house owners and the interrogative intruders. The piece ends without reconciliation, as the narrator turns the audience's attention back to the pitiful death of Andersen's frozen match girl.

The production was a success, for critics had become more accustomed to the new experimental idiom of Japanese minimalism. The piece also artfully captured a combined mood of national self-examination and censure, recalling the years of poverty in Japan after the Second World War. The actions of the young girl, who lifts her skirt to the light of a struck match in order to make a meagre living, were contrasted with the comfort and safe rituals of the middle-aged couple. They do not wish to take any responsibility for the past, however desperate the visitors' needs. The production also indicated the artistic standard that the company could achieve, given time and space.

As today, space was at a premium in Tokyo and most groups survived by renting rehearsal and performance rooms on a short-term basis. The studio which the WLT opened on 10 November 1966 was a small space (30 by 40 foot) with a tiny stage. It had an end-on seating arrangement with an entrance/exit to the dressing-room/office through the centre of the audience. It was built above a coffee shop in the Shinjuku area of Tokyo (not far from Waseda

University) entirely with private funds raised by the company. Most significantly, it permitted them unlimited access to work in the venue where they would also show their performances, a rarity among the city's groups.

Suzuki's programming with the Free Stage and the WLT shows his commitment to the three major playwrights to emerge from the *angura* movement – Betsuyaku, Sato Makoto and Juro Kara. *The Little Match Girl* won the Kishida Prize for Playwriting in February 1968. Suzuki produced Makoto's *My Beatles or the Funeral* (later rewritten and retitled simply *My Beatles*) in 1967 and Kara's *Virgin Mask* (known also as *A Girl's Mask* or *A Girl with A Mask*) in 1969, which was likewise awarded the Kishida Prize. In spite of his allegiance to these emerging and successful writers, Suzuki began to become interested in the potential of directing more as a creative than interpretive role.

The technical and spatial limitations of the coffee-shop studio stimulated a shift in emphasis on to the actor's body. For Suzuki, 'It was a great discovery for me that the energy of the actor alone enabled the actor to be accessible to so many people.'[2] Initially this repositioning accorded with Betsuyaku's minimalist vision. But as the actors spent time in the evenings after their day jobs developing new exercises and techniques, the notion of devising their own performance texts under Suzuki's watchful eye dominated.

This change was also fuelled by an encounter that transformed Suzuki's artistic vision. In 1967 he met Kayoko Shiraishi, starting a collaboration that lasted until 1990. Shiraishi had no training and her emphatic and energised performance style was entirely unsuited to the quiet measure needed for Betsuyaku's texts. She struggled with such parts (she played the wife in *The Little Match Girl*) and kept forgetting her lines in rehearsal. But with Betsuyaku's departure from the company in August 1969 Shiraishi came into her own. The decision to create collage pieces allowed Suzuki a much more interactive and controlling relationship with the performer. As importantly, it also let him cultivate appropriate artistic vehicles for what he already saw as Shiraishi's considerable skill. Her involvement in the WLT was a turning point, not only for Suzuki personally, but for the company as a whole: 'What Shiraishi did when she came to our theater was bring back memories deeply rooted in our body, memories which the modern theater had extinguished. I was struck dumb. Then I decided to change myself. To tell the truth, I've been changed ever since Shiraishi came to our theater.'[3]

So transformed, Suzuki turned towards *kabuki*. He had been watching *kabuki* closely and reading about it avidly while at university, particularly fascinated by the *onnagata* (female impersonator) role.[4] Later, he would explore *kabuki's* acting principles, but for now he wanted simply to reinstate premodern texts. Along with groups like Black Tent Theatre, he saw the necessity of counteracting the textual dominance of *shingeki* plays, reversing the losses that followed *shingeki's* rejection of premodern theatre. To move his performers' range and abilities beyond the low-key, stripped-back acting style obligated by contemporary Japanese writers like Betsuyaku, he sought new materials and creative processes.

Suzuki believed that Shiraishi embodied techniques essential to premodern Japanese forms. Some Japanese critics even described her as the reincarnation of the priestess Okuni, the shamanistic founder of *kabuki,* whom legend has described as first dancing in a dry river bed in Kyoto. As such, it was hardly surprising that she could not adapt to Betsuyaku's style. Suzuki's first collage piece, *And Then, And Then, What Then* (based on a *kabuki* play), enabled Shiraishi's full integration into the WLT. The textual collage *On the Dramatic Passions I* (1969) furthered the move into new areas of physical and vocal expression. With its collection of texts (from sources as diverse as *Waiting for Godot,* Edmond Rostand's *Cyrano de Bergerac* and *kabuki* scenarios), *On the Dramatic Passions I* began life as a demonstration of acting études rather than a self-contained performance. Along with *On the Dramatic Passions II* (1970, subtitled 'The Shiraishi Kayoko Show') and *On the Dramatic Passions III* (also 1970) these pieces showed off Shiraishi's extensive talents, blatantly presenting her virtuosity, as the subtitle of the second in the series demonstrates.

Collage encouraged the placing of traditional texts alongside modern ones in a range of styles. Suzuki's directing progressed through exploration of this diversity. Collage became his hallmark, a form which he still practises today, more than thirty years after he first developed the technique. Suzuki stepped beyond textual interpretation, redefining his role as architect of the dramaturgy.

Inevitably, the empowerment of the performer and the opportunity for individual development that collage provided was contiguous with Suzuki's firmer jurisdiction, as he shaped the material. This increased authority led to the departure of six of the main actors in 1971, who wanted a return to what they saw as more democratic processes. This breach left the WLT emasculated and inactive for almost a year.[5] The rupture grew out of a power struggle but also indicated the company's move in a radically different direction. For the WLT, Takahashi's 'revolution' (discussed in Chapter One) did not just require the contravention of *shingeki* but also implicated revision of the group's own practices. This was bound to have considerable and destructive impact on their internal structure. New sensibilities were being aroused and side effects were inevitable.

The collage technique centred on the juxtaposition of texts knitted together with simple framing devices. *On the Dramatic Passions I* operated around the naïve notion of 'an acting teacher showing his female student several dramatic scenes as part of her acting lessons'.[6] The second in the sequence portrayed Shiraishi as a madwoman. This device was more sophisticated, allowing not only a distorting prism through which to view the separate scenes and a complex questioning of reality, but also a passionately engaged and unpredictable acting style. The location of events in an individual's interior universe has endured until today and is particularly evident in *The Tale of Lear,* as the title suggests.

Suzuki's theatrical collage is not so much about the arrangement of images (pictorial collage is a familiar visual art technique); rather, it is concerned more with the cohesive organisation of several disparate elements. Regarding *On the Dramatic Passions II,* Suzuki explained: 'What I did is connect what my company members had done. My piece did not intend to connect words of different plays but to connect the body. To my surprise, people say this piece is a collage or connects parts. But it is not. Making a collage is not the idea but the result.'[7] His approach was more about the clash of underlying principles, rhythms and texts, unified through a consistent use of the body and a frame, than a bricolage of scenographic elements. Collage reflected the process of a director attempting to unite the individual propositions put forward by his actors.

·Suzuki also exploited the surrealist technique of *depaysement*.[8]
Depaysement is a structural approach of alogical juxtaposition,
whereby two or more separate elements are placed side by side,
creating new meanings and unusual connections which are often
surreal. This fragmentation meant that Suzuki's bleak vision of
'wretchedness' was more tolerable, for it was not too dominant. A
fantasy framework enabled the performers to escape imaginatively
and find moments of release, however much their bodies were
bound in an existential prison, as Akihiko Senda's description of *On
the Dramatic Passions II* shows. He presages much of Suzuki's later
work and gives a strong sense of Shiraishi's performance:

> The play was set in a confinement room, where a solitary
> madwoman recalled fragments of numerous plays from the past,
> performing them one by one. Through the fiction of the drama, the
> passions which she was never able to satisfy in real life exploded
> with dreadful force. The dramatic effect of this play, at once
> pathetic and grotesque, was achieved by means of the sharp
> contrast between the classical splendour of the language and the
> abject misery of the woman's condition [. . .] It resurrected the
> traditional emotional motifs of vengeance and mad passion, evoked
> the sentimental old ballads and fanatical military songs long
> considered taboo by the postwar intellectual establishment, and put
> the spotlight on such vulgar realities as bodily functions.[9]

On the Dramatic Passions II was based on Shiraishi's portrayal of
Princess Hanako-no-mae from a classical *kabuki* tragedy by Tsuruya
Namboku IV. This was layered further by framing the whole as the
projections of a madwoman, who, in her forced isolation, was
transforming herself into other characters. Shiraishi was also clearly
herself playing the madwoman who in turn was enacting classical
roles from *kabuki* and *shimpa* as the Princess (*shimpa* is the
melodramatic, sentimental style of Japanese theatre from the end of
the nineteenth century). Potential confusion was allayed by
Shiraishi's acting style and her clarity. At times the roles fused but for
the most part the audience was always aware of the process of
Shiraishi's transformation. As the title indicates, the piece dealt with
the nature of emotion within the theatre and did not attempt a
faithful rendition of the texts themselves. The characters and words

were merely vehicles for Shiraishi's public demonstration of her transformations and transportations, and her stage persona. Similarly, the supporting actors did just that – supported and focused Shiraishi's metamorphoses.

French critic 'L. D.' reviewed a performance at the Théâtre Récamier for *Le Monde* in May 1973:

> By the movement and control of each of her muscles, she composes multiple masks with her cheeks, her mouth and her forehead, even with the skin itself, which are stranger and more powerful than make-up. Her voice, pulled from the depths of her chest, rolls in her throat, slides up and up, bursts and breaks out into sudden whispering. The musical and physical game recalls the drunkenness of violence and murder.[10]

There was detail and immense technical control within her apparent absorption and trance-like state. Yet however much possessed and on another level of consciousness, this physicality was not abstract or detached. It was rooted not just by the feet but also by a textual and social context that had wide ramifications. Shiraishi was playing roles from the traditional theatre usually exclusively played by men – the *onnagata* questioning centuries of sexual bias within the performing arts. Her various portrayals of Japanese women furthered the social critique. Madness allowed such taboos to be performed on stage. The overwhelming impact and skill of Shiraishi's performance permitted such transgressions and gave a clear physical centre to the excesses.

The conviction with which Suzuki exposed social taboos was central to the piece's huge critical success. Artistically, it attracted interest not only for Shiraishi's wild stage persona, but also for the mix of materials from so many sources. This range veered from popular forms, such as pop songs, to classical elements such as the *noh* mask worn in the opening scene or *kabuki* texts. Authenticity and tradition were plundered, corrupted and reformulated, distilled through Shiraishi's body, presence and voice. Critics commented that she was depicting an archetypal Japanese woman, but her scatological physicality undermined any tendencies towards nostalgic romanticising as the Princess wet herself uncontrollably.

On the Dramatic Passions II marked Suzuki's incarnation as an international figure. The metatheatrical nature of Suzuki's pieces (with their collage technique and framing devices) lent itself to all contexts. At this time, around the world, theatre was investigating itself, pushing at its own parameters, be it in Jerzy Grotowski's paratheatre in Poland or Peter Brook's tour in Africa. In France, the public identified with the imprisoned woman, however rooted in Japanese soil such frustrations and roles were. When the piece toured there in 1972 (Théâtre des Nations, Paris) and 1973 (Nancy Festival), French critics admired the fact that it avoided exoticism and worked on what Claude Baigneres called a 'universal' level.[11] Suzuki exploited and interrogated the culturally specific to open his theatre to a wider audience. Through the personal, he addressed common human concerns. In the first visit to France, the seeds of the Toga complex were sown, as outlined in Chapter Three. Suzuki's understanding of *noh* practice shifted exponentially forward as he witnessed Hisao Kanze's *noh* performance in a non-*noh* space.[12] This search for the universal through the combination of traditional and modern, the local and the global, has motivated Suzuki ever since.

Yasunari Takahashi has written that 'many critics agree to consider [*On the Dramatic Passions II*] one of the milestones in the history of post-war Japanese theater'.[13] This status was accorded for several reasons: its provocative investigation of cultural givens, including the position of women in Japanese society; its reconfiguration of Japan's traditional performing arts; its provision of an alternative to *shingeki*; and the innovative style of performance and mode of acting, personified by Shiraishi. Such material made Suzuki an artist of national and international renown. In a 1973 review of the World Theatre Festival, Victoria Nes Kirby wrote of Shiraishi: 'Her acting was one of the most talked-about subjects at the festival this year.'[14] Grotowski invited the piece to the Théâtre des Nations in Warsaw in 1975, which was a large gathering of influential theatre artists from around the world that included Joseph Chaikin, André Gregory, Eugenio Barba and Peter Brook. Polish critics compared Shiraishi's abilities to Ryszard Cieslak's, Grotowski's own acclaimed central actor.

Domestically, this performance assured Suzuki's position as a leading avant-garde artist. In 1974, he was appointed artistic director of Iwanami Hall in Tokyo, a huge performance space owned by the

Iwanami Publishing House, who have translated many Western classics into Japanese. This was not 'selling out' or joining the establishment, but financial and material support from a renowned intellectual family that was indispensable in Japan's minimally subsidised performing arts sector. This patronage allowed Suzuki to experiment further and reinforced his position at home. It also allowed him to think on a larger scale and open himself to wider influences.

From this position of strength, Suzuki could move on to other processes. Beyond the intertextuality of collage lay a more challenging project – the recontextualisation of classical European drama within Japanese performance traditions. Since his first visit to France and following Hisao's presentation, Suzuki had been alive to new possibilities, questioning whether historical forms like *noh* and *kabuki* bear any relation to ancient Greek drama. Was there any sense in seeking such cross-cultural connections, with works separated by tens of centuries and geography? Could principles from Suzuki's indigenous sources revivify the Greek plays?

The answer lay in the adaptation of singular texts rather than the juxtaposition of many. A rapidly evolving acting method could enable stylistic departures from more orthodox modes of presentation, holding on to the discoveries found in the collages while applying these to different materials. The emerging training could also support the physical, emotional and verbal demands of the classics. Premiered in December 1974, *The Trojan Women* (*Toroio no Onna*) began a long relationship with Greek drama that led not only to the construction of amphitheatres in a tiny Japanese village and in the mountains outside Shizuoka, but a sustained interrogation of Greek plays throughout Suzuki's career. This has centred on *The Bacchae* (1978), *The Tragedy The Fall of the House of Atreus* and *Clytemnestra* (both 1983), *Dionysus* (1990), *Electra* (1995) and *Oedipus Rex* (2000).

The Trojan Women and Greek Adaptations

The Trojan Women is Suzuki's most celebrated production and the piece by which all his work is measured. First performed in 1974, it is recognised mostly in its 1977 reincarnation, which toured the world from then until 1990. This was seen in London in 1985 at the Riverside Studios, fresh from its success at the Los Angeles Olympics Arts Festival the year before. Its acclaim means that more has been written about this production than any other. I will not therefore dwell at great length on its content. (Goto's thesis gives a clear synopsis of the action and Marianne McDonald extensively discusses issues of textual adaptation and interpretation in *Ancient Sun, Modern Light*, unpicking the notion of a 'classic' in a postmodern context.) Rather, I shall consider the implications of *The Trojan Women*'s style of acting and its relationship to actor training. I shall connect this to the broader development of Suzuki's practice and his artistic vision.

It can be argued that this production demonstrates the most coherent integration of directorial technique and concept with actor training method, and that its international success depended on this symbiosis. Reviews commented extensively on the performers' techniques, for the material foregrounded these without making them seem superfluous. *The Trojan Women* was conceived simultaneously with the method. Brandon's article on the training (the first solid evidence in English of its existence) was published in 1978, based on workshop observation in winter 1976. The two processes (the making of a performance and the establishment of a training method) were integrated, as this analysis will show. For Suzuki, the contemporary presentation of Greek drama relies less on the interpretation and contextualisation of the text, and more on finding an appropriate mode of acting: 'The problem doesn't lie in whether or not there is a god, but in the fact that unless Greek texts are performed with the same kind of energy as in the age when they were originally performed, it becomes difficult to revive them successfully.'[15]

Suzuki continued his explorations with collage – including *Don Hamlet* (1973) after Chekhov and Shakespeare, and *Night and Clock* (1975), based loosely on *Macbeth* – but his engagement with classical drama necessitated more focus on 'dramatic passions'. The drama in classical texts went beyond the sensibilities that had stimulated Suzuki's earliest work with Betsuyaku and other writers linked to the minimalist absurd. In these, frustrations and fears were internalised and the characters were often driven by helplessness or an inability to articulate their malaise. Externally, this was embodied in bleak, symbolic staging: Betsuyaku's hallmark lamppost (reminiscent of *Waiting for Godot*'s tree) or the simple domestic table that is a focus for the match girl's intrusion. Such symbols provided an object around which the characters could centre their existential introspection. Greek texts (with their chorus, tragedy and the grand social scale of their drama) necessitated the ability to play a broader emotional range with great intensity in vast auditoria on an empty stage. Characters and stories from the epic myths replaced the smaller symbolic actions (or absence of action) of the absurdists and the chaotic clashes of collages. Rather than being Shiraishi's construct, madness was ingrained in these ancient texts, ensuing from impulsive actions, guilt or the desire for revenge. Correspondingly, the notion evolved that Suzuki's training could equip the actor to perform classical roles in large spaces. Resurrected by Suzuki, Greek protagonists walked alongside the ghosts of *noh*.

Euripides is the Greek dramatist most utilised by Suzuki. His *Trojan Women* is an almost plotless treatise against the horrors of war, where narrative tension is replaced by emotional anxiety. Euripides' play follows the fate of the Trojan women survivors of the war, refugee prisoners waiting to be shipped off as spoils for the Greeks. The Trojan War has raged in order to return Helen to Menelaus, after her kidnapping by Paris. Troy has been destroyed and the women's lives are all behind them, their fate undecided. Dramatic tension derives conversely not from what happens but from the anticipation of what might take place – a *Waiting for Godot* full of threatened violence and fear, on a level akin to the heightened state Suzuki expects in his training and performance. The play then maps out the women's futures: Helen is to be given back to Menelaus, Hecuba to Odysseus, Cassandra to Agamemnon, and Andromache to Achilles' son. It is announced that Polyxena (another of Hecuba's daughters) is to be killed as an offering to Achilles, which happens later offstage. Astyanax (Andromache's son) is also killed – thrown from a high battlement to his death in order to stop the bloodline. Euripides' drama ends as Helen returns home with her husband Menelaus, the threat of death hanging over her, and as Astyanax is buried by his grandmother Hecuba.

In Suzuki's production, the majority of the words were Euripides' but he supplemented these with contemporary texts: Japanese poetry by Ooka Makoto and the sentimental love song 'The Crossways of Love', which he tacked distastefully but ironically on to the end. He reinvented Euripides' play (essentially by boiling it down further to heighten the characters' stark emotional outpourings) and brought it up-to-date. The cemetery in which Suzuki located the play was Japan in 1945 as much as it was any burial ground in the world at any time. Towards the end of the adaptation and before her own death, Hecuba described Troy's destruction: 'Troy now burns scarlet in the sky . . . Our nation sinks and dies.' Through the specific depiction of Japan and its post-war identity crisis, he symbolised the general, without making it banal. He suggested both the timelessness and geographical indiscrimination of war, while also depicting the recent fate of Japan and the country's own wartime atrocities.

Suzuki wrote explicitly in the programme about his social motivation for performing this play: 'I do not think any other work has so successfully expressed one aspect of universal man. Nor is this just because war itself remains a present reality for us. The fundamental drama of our time is anxiety in the face of impending disaster.' Thematically, he showed the futility of people's attempts to resist man's most destructive instincts and to command fate, located in the particular experience of women. He explained further: 'I intended to express the disastrous fate of women caused by war, which was initiated by men, and the complete powerlessness of religion to aid the women or the war itself.' This universalism was historical as well as global. The past mixed with the present, the local with the international, sometimes seamlessly coexisting, sometimes with a rupture, as in the final pop song which was sung in English and Japanese.

Artistically, the original production of *The Trojan Women* was a vehicle to demonstrate and combine the skills of three renowned performers. *Noh* actor Hisao Kanze (Old Man and Menelaus), *shingeki* actress Etsuko Ichihara (Cassandra and Andromache) and Shiraishi (Hecuba), who all acted alongside the chorus. It was a deliberate fusion of styles from diverse performance traditions. The intermingling critiqued these forms and exposed the hermeticism in which they usually operated. In order to contain this stylistic melding, the play kept only segments of Euripides' source, framing them as the recollections of an Old Man. In the second, streamlined version, this function was given to Shiraishi as an Old Woman[16] (both these archetypes are found in *noh*). What began as an experiment with Japanese theatre forms developed into a world-class piece of theatre, realised through Shiraishi's metamorphoses.

Illuminating light is cast on the processual development of the piece by Patricia Marton's report from 1975,[17] which focuses on the work in its earlier phase. It then had a different frame, beginning with the nonchalant entrance of a contemporary 'Everyman', who sat still on stage throughout. In the second version he became a silent Beckettian 'Tramp', who entered later and then sat silently, operating as a disruptive, alienating device. The original ended as three tourists with flashing cameras were shown around ruins (Hiroshima/Troy) by the god Jizo (the Buddhist god of Mercy and Childhood), who had transformed into a tourist guide. In the second piece Jizo remained still almost throughout. The Greek army was symbolised by 'four white-faced men on stilts', who in the 1977 scenario appeared merely as enigmatic 'Figures' in black. This lifting of the army off the ground seems to go against one of Suzuki's principal tenets and indeed, the later piece omitted the stilts, showing the ongoing formulation of Suzuki's acting principles. The method was evolving and crystallising and transforming content, as images were converted into a body practice. The technical support and precision the training gave the performers allowed Suzuki to simplify the action, as the case of Jizo indicates. Peripherals were gradually stripped away until *The Trojan Women* focused almost exclusively on the role of Shiraishi alone and the whole group's much stiller physicality.

The production had a moving and powerful anti-war message that stunned critics throughout the world and transcended national specifics. It was constructed around the shell-shocked Old Man/Woman who wanders with a few possessions through a ruined cemetery just after World War II. Shiraishi created an emotional tempest with this role in the second version. Like the little match girl, this figure unearthed sentiments about post-war Japan and its destruction at the hands of America and 'Little Boy', the inappropriately named atom bomb that fell on Hiroshima. At the eye of this storm was Jizo, who was the first to enter the space with a slow *noh*-like sliding walk. He stood motionless and statue-like throughout the hundred-minute performance, passive and seemingly powerless. Only at the end of the play, when a young girl threw flowers at his chest, did he flinch and double up before regaining his poise. His stillness amplified Shiraishi's violent torment and passion.

The performance was built around the flow between tension and release, as in the stillness of Jizo and the excitation of the Old Woman. The slowness of many movements was such that transformations appeared to have happened almost imperceptibly, like the shedding of Shiraishi's darker kimono-style cloak for a white one, as she evolved from Hecuba to Cassandra (a transformative costuming device known as *hikinuki*, adapted from *kabuki*). Such transitions were juxtaposed with moments of alarming rapidity and therefore surprise. The suspense of waiting was undercut by the sharpness of quickly executed actions.

Violence expressed itself in diverse ways, the most notable being the murder of Astyanax, who was not thrown from an offstage battlement as in the original. British critic Michael Billington wrote: 'The three top-knotted samurai [Greek soldiers] (one in modern specs) tear the clothes off Andromache's body, seize her muslin-doll child, sever its limbs and then casually toss the dismembered baby at the feet of the bent-double Hecuba.'[18] Suzuki ritualised and then underplayed the violence, avoiding the pitfall of presenting unspeakable acts in a literal or generalising way. These condensed actions had great impact. The careful use of symbols indicated Suzuki's skill in selecting, honing and making the socially unacceptable palatable for the stage. He forced the spectator to witness what they would rather not see and aroused horror by showing the complexity of violence, in this example through the combined precision and casualness of the act. The dramatic effect of such moments depended on razor-sharp timing and the use of extended and then suddenly compressed rhythms.

The second version also suggested the notion that the Old Woman was possessed by various spirits (primarily Hecuba's) as she reenacted the Trojan women's story. As in *On the Dramatic Passions II*, this permitted Shiraishi to attain a heightened emotional level. But even though the Old Woman exorcised her own ghosts through these multiple possessions and incantations, dramaturgical devices such as the glaring intervention of contemporary life in the final song did not allow the audience to empathise or resolve the problem of 'man's inhumanity to man'. The ghosts continued to haunt the public after they left the auditorium, since there was no opportunity for communal grief. For the spectator, the emotion and the overwhelming sense of the characters' wretched fate was repressed and thereby sustained beyond the performance, rather than liberated within it. This perhaps explains the shock of the emotional impact expressed by the majority of critics in their reviews. Metaphorically, Shiraishi was still in the chains of *On the Dramatic Passions II* and the audience was similarly ensnared.

Performance techniques derived from *noh* may have helped this containment, as this statement by Hideo Kanze (Hisao Kanze's younger brother) suggests:

Take Greek tragedy. It's difficult to maintain emotional tension when an actor is just standing silently, listening to the other actors speaking their lines. It's impossible to maintain psychological tension just standing there, so you have to stop your emotional and psychological flow. This technique is just one of the many that might be learned from Noh.[19]

Eugenio Barba has frequently reiterated the fundamental axiom of *noh* that seven-tenths of the action happens in time rather than space and that most of the action is thus internalised, a process which he categorises as 'omission'.[20] Shiraishi was explosive at times but with immense control, creating great psychological tension. Omission was a technique used by all the actors, but the performer playing Jizo took it to the extreme.

Barba usefully reminds us of the energy and concentration needed to sustain such poise as Jizo demonstrated. This is comparable to the *noh* theatre's sitting *iguse*, or motionless 'dance', performed by the *shite*. The exterior belies the performer's busy interior 'dance' or internal action, and the concentration and focus needed to sustain such absence of movement. This absence is known within the Japanese performing arts as *ma*. The discipline of stopping the flow, of resistance, fundamentally affected the audience's reception of the drama. The aesthetic arose from techniques practised within the training, influenced by one of the primary laws of *noh* acting (also found in *kabuki*) of suppressing and then releasing energy with formidable control. The collaboration with Hisao Kanze was vital for the development of Suzuki's training method and his performance aesthetic. It was also a two-way process, for Kanze was himself exploring potential connections between traditional and contemporary performance not only to keep *noh* alive but keep it progressing. Hideo Kanze was banished from *noh* because of such transgressions into experimental theatre.

This repression and precise focusing of the performer's attention was supported by a specific use of posture, which overwhelmed Senda. In his 1974 review, 'The Crouch as a Critique of the Modern', he emphasises the significance of the crouch, which he defined as a 'basic bodily stance not only for the Japanese but for all Asians, including the Chinese'.[21] For Senda, this corporeality was a defiant criticism of Western-derived Japanese performance like *shingeki*. But the real value lay not in Suzuki's critique but in his proposal of an alternative, intracultural approach.

The feet and the relationship of the body to the ground invoked the mood of the performance, generating its visceral impact. Jizo's entrance was a teasingly slow walk, rooted and centred. The chorus of Elders shuffled in with a sort of duckwalk and then remained in a low open crouch for long periods. Several critics (Western as well as Japanese) described them moving sideways like 'crabs'. They called the Greek guards' entrance a hip-dislocating 'goosestep'. In her transformation from Hecuba to Cassandra, Shiraishi 'rises from the ground as if on some invisible string'.[22] There were also several moments when the actors formed sharply defined statues. All these modes of locomotion and postures are embodied and repeatedly practised within the training. This difficult stylised physicality was inhabited by the performers with great commitment, creating the charged atmosphere in which the performance unfolded. The dark mood was enhanced by the shadowy impressions made by cloths and rags draped from the ceiling. With minimal scenographic support, the piece's impact was primarily attributable to the performers' use of their feet, which was a revelation to Senda.

Central to Shiraishi's performance and noted admiringly by all critics was her voice, capable of great range and power. This has already been alluded to in the French critic L. D.'s response to *On the*

Dramatic Passions II. Similar forces were at work here, for again there was no attempt to create conversational speech. The text was uttered in long monologues and choral incantations with minimal dialogue, facing the audience rather than each other. Vocal energy and concentration were sustained by controlling the diaphragm. Suzuki's confidence with simpler staging and a focus on the interior concentration of the performer projecting outwards, rather than external demonstration, was now apparent. This use of the voice and the whole body 'speaking', as well as an emphasis on dynamic stillness, are fundamental to the training. Suzuki was deftly translating training techniques into performance, benefiting from the consolidation of his method and the mutual enhancement that the synchronous development of a training approach and performance style brought.

The discoveries Suzuki made in this production were developed further. His subsequent repertoire of productions derived from Greek drama is extensive, though it appears to be greater than closer inspection shows. Many pieces reworked previous versions or synthesised them, making it almost impossible to classify any production as definitive. He added and subtracted characters and continually reordered bits of the textual and dramaturgical jigsaws. This complexity confounds the observer even before considering the range of casts or venues he has used and the effect these have on production. Such evolutions make analysis of his process of adaptation or rewriting complicated. Interpretative evaluations also become self-defeating, for Suzuki is deliberately defying closure and secure readings. I cannot avoid some interpretation but will focus more on central artistic developments within his relationship to Greek drama with reference to three more productions. Again, the emphasis will be on what these indicate about Suzuki's practice and the training rather than his literary explorations and techniques.

The next major production was Suzuki's *The Bacchae*, based on Euripides' version. Like *The Trojan Women*, the piece is remembered outside Japan in its second bilingual version from 1981, rather than that of the 1978 Tokyo première. This first production had Hisao Kanze playing Dionysus and Shiraishi as Agave, though they also took other roles. Hisao, however, soon had to stand down and he died of cancer at the end of 1978.

Samuel L. Leiter has described *The Bacchae*'s content 'as a conflict between freedom and totalitarianism as dreamed by political prisoners'.[23] The prisoners acted out Euripides' play, revealing the ideological clash between Dionysus and Pentheus. The piece showed that those who collectively seek the hedonism of Dionysian pleasure cannot ignore the consequences, exemplified by Agave. She entered towards the end of the piece, clasping the head of her son and still in a trance. Cadmus 'woke' her to reveal the awful truth that in a Dionysian frenzy she and other followers of the god had torn his body apart. Pentheus then returned to slay Cadmus and Agave at the very end, positing that reality (and in particular the shackles of totalitarianism) cannot be escaped. The liminal is by its nature transitory and artistic creation fleeting, as the prisoners' short-lived escapist re-enactment of *The Bacchae* suggested. The lesson for Japan and for all societies was that history is cyclical. Hiroshima was perhaps not such an exceptional incident and lessons still had to be learned.

Dramatically, the piece extended ideas and techniques from *The Trojan Women*: the clash of old and new, and East and West; the casting and large chorus; a complex framing of an interior world within another; and the mix of classical material with a pop song. All these elements were becoming hallmarks of Suzuki's work, as the training provided repeatable rehearsal methodologies. He was building on the success and techniques of *The Trojan Women*, still centred on Shiraishi but with more active input from the chorus, as performers draped in a giant red and white flag of the Japanese navy danced across the space at one point. Whereas in *The Trojan Women* Shiraishi alone embodied the fate of the women, here there was more focus on the nature of communities. The chorus critiqued both conformity and passivity within groups.

Rhythmically, the whole shifted between stillness and rapid action. Held moments of *mie* (of which Tom Hewitt as Pentheus was an admired American exponent) alternated with quick exits. Violence was symbolically enacted. Shiraishi displayed her 'vocal pyrotechnics' (as one critic described her technique), leading Roderick Mason Faber to declare that 'Shiraishi should be declared a national treasure of Japan',[24] a role normally attributed to *noh* or *kabuki* actors in their later years. Marianne McDonald conjectured that 'One might guess that *The Bacchae* had to be performed without Agave when she left the company. She is impossible to replace.'[25] After her departure, the role remained but was perhaps never again played with such combined gusto and control.

For Senda, *The Bacchae* was as forceful as *The Trojan Women*, if not more so. Although he has described himself generally as a 'doubter', this piece was 'rarely for him [Suzuki], a handsomely restrained and mature production [. . .] scrupulously woven together [. . .] a sense of theatrical mastery was evident'.[26] The performers' physicality made less impact than in *The Trojan Women* (it was not new) but Senda found it more sophisticated and integrated with the material. The dramaturgy held the disparate elements together. Senda also considered Kanze's acting unequalled, though his portrayal was cut short by his illness and death. He used the praise of this review to air more general doubts and signal his discontent with much of Suzuki's other work (though not *The Trojan Women*), which he had found uncontrolled, contrived and generalised.

We should take Senda's impartial judgement more seriously than the more biased views of Iwabuchi. He scorned the 'concept behind the performance', baffled by its lack of meaning and incongruities, especially the intrusion of the pop hit 'The Headland of Erimo' at the end. He qualified his judgement by openly declaring himself a 'Brechtian' and thus 'not a good spectator of Suzuki's theatre'.[27] It seems that whatever Suzuki did, Iwabuchi would not respond favourably. In spite of such a mixed reception and reservations (perhaps attributable to the difficulty and sophistication of what Suzuki was attempting), the performance was successful enough to encourage Suzuki to turn his attention to international and intercultural projects, using his intracultural understanding of Japanese forms as a foundation.

The second version of *The Bacchae* began life at the University of Wisconsin, Milwaukee, in 1981, with twelve American actors whom Suzuki had taught as students there, as well as SCOT members. All were trained in the method by Suzuki, albeit some for only a matter of months. This American/Japanese collaboration was possibly enabled by the security Suzuki felt with his base in the Japanese mountains. Hindsight shows that this potentially isolating move from Tokyo opened up more, not fewer, international possibilities, as

Suzuki had predicted. After performances in America, the piece toured to Toga and Tokyo.

As Iwabuchi stated, *The Bacchae's* exact meaning is hard to pinpoint, but both versions suggest that a constructive pathway lies in the middle ground between the rational and the impulsive. The casting itself emphatically underlined the importance of such negotiations, with its mixed-race company. So too did the 'dialogue' in Japanese and English, though the two languages never translated each other, operating autonomously in their own linguistic worlds, united only by their mode of delivery. Suzuki was demonstrating that cooperation is not only vital but also possible and that the 'other' can approach nearer to the self, without losing its identity or becoming merely a 'translator'. For him, such a production process was fundamental to his search to make theatre universal. A performance like this puts into sharp relief the potential tokenism of cross-cultural practice. With such a difficult project, it was understandable that meaning might become peripheral.

In 1990, *The Bacchae* spawned *Dionysus*, which was initially staged by the Acting Company of Mito as their première production. Suzuki has written briefly about the production's social dimension. He exploited source texts from Greek drama to critique man's need for stories and narrative. Stories (of which histories are a central component) can be used for good or bad ends, but are frequently manipulated by religious or totalitarian organisations:

> Euripides' *The Bacchae* shows the process by which individuals are 'scapegoated out' of the narrative world [. . .] *Dionysus* focuses on how both the passionate belief in the group values of story, and the doubting of those values, are contained within *The Bacchae.* Both sides of this dichotomy are presented on stage simultaneously.[28]

The scapegoat Agave (played by Ellen Lauren) crossed the threshold between the two sets of values when she became aware of the murder of her son Pentheus, which she believed she had done. In fact, Suzuki showed Dionysus's priests ritualistically killing him, but Agave was implicated in his sacrifice. In a trance, she cannot remember what happened anyway, thinking she had killed a lion in the mountains. Awakened and informed of what happened, she then joined the dispossessed 'wheelchair people' or 'Believers of the Farewell Cult' whom Suzuki described as 'people who have dropped out of "story", wandering aimlessly in wheelchairs'.

Suzuki was timely in revealing the mechanisms of cults, considering the sarin gas release on Tokyo's subway by the Aum Shinrikyo cult in 1995. This group was highly active in the 1980s and 1990s in Japan, and came to international recognition with their 1995 attack, which killed twelve and left almost 4,000 injured. Two perpetrators were sentenced to death for this in July 2000. Suzuki was addressing local and topical issues, but these were not confined to Japan alone. He was seeking ways to make the Greek plays contemporary while maintaining their contact with the gods, their metaphysical dimension. The content had to resonate as much with a present-day audience as it did for the ancient Greeks. Mixed-race casting and topicality were techniques used to this end. The gods symbolised earthly narratives or sect leaders as much as mythical deities.

The word 'goodbye' was a repeated motif in the performance, often combined with the wheelchair doom-mongers' chanting of Macbeth's 'Tomorrow and tomorrow' speech. For Eelke Lampe, Suzuki 'embraced a postmodern "goodbye" to the concepts of story and history as they have been operating under modernity'.[9] The piece indicated not only the deep schisms that can separate groups but also reinforced how one set of ideologies are merely replaced by another when communities subdivide. There is no refuge or escape from stories (as Agave's scapegoating and personal tragedy indicated), but stories can also no longer provide the grand narratives we desire or even need. 'Passion' and 'doubt' coexist simultaneously in a postmodern age.

This version of *The Bacchae* presented the role of Dionysus as choral. The presence of Dionysus's priests added a social dimension, moving away from an analysis of individual ideologies and the historical mythological figure of Dionysus himself. Suzuki could thereby address issues globally, focusing on religion and communities more generically. Lampe has noted that in the bilingual version, which launched SITI in 1992 and toured to American cities, the actors playing individual roles were seven

Americans while the chorus was Japanese. Through highly suggestive casting and other devices, the production responded sharply to its regional context.

The energetic physicality and complex use of rhythms supported the classical material. The Believers' rapid scurrying as they perched on the edge of wheelchairs shattered the otherwise vibrant stillness, contrasting with the slow, elegantly robed white-faced priests of Dionysus. The image of the wheelchair men was absurd and comic, a vision from Beckett's *Endgame* multiplied. With their feet barely touching the floor but sweeping themselves swiftly along, the physicality was demanding, however at ease the performers seemed. Suzuki's constantly reiterated metaphor of man's sickness and the world as a hospital were embodied in the wheelchair-bound performers/characters. This is an idea he has since used repeatedly.

The image relied on sharp contradiction – strong grown men without apparent physical disabilities unified by a restraining homogeneous physicality. Man's psychological 'imprisonment' (according to Suzuki's existential perspective) was made visually explicit. It also specifically embodied *Dionysus's* thematic debates, showing how the blind acceptance of narrative hooks can handicap us. The wheelchair men looked back to the central character of *The Elephant*, trapped inside his irradiated body, as well as the imprisoned Princess of *On the Dramatic Passions II*. It seems perverse that these highly trained actors were so radically confined, yet this reminds us that the training is merely an aid to acting rather than a vehicle for demonstrating 'physical feats', as suggested in the title of Marie Myerscough's *American Theatre* piece, 'East meets West in the Art of Tadashi Suzuki'.[30] Shiraishi's virtuosity (that was initially foregrounded) had become integrated into Suzuki's practice through the training. The lesson of Jizo in *The Trojan Women* was that the heightened energy and demands of the method must be internalised. You should not show the struggle or breath but should 'kill' the daily body and its tendencies, just as a Beijing Opera acrobat aims to somersault repeatedly without sweating. Suzuki's training is a lesson in restraint and control of the will or instinctive inclinations. He continued this into performance with visual and physical choices such as the wheelchairs, which then attract social significance.

* * *

Suzuki's *Clytemnestra* (1983) also had a strong social dimension, exploring and updating the breakdown of the modern family and its values, which leaves man isolated and living in 'spiritual chaos', as Suzuki sees it. This clearly pertains to Japan with its *salarymen*, but not Japan alone, for the erosion of these beliefs and systems is not so localised. As Orestes, American Tom Hewitt was the only non-Japanese performer in the original version, giving a wider context to this predicament. The play ended with Electra and Orestes in an incestuous sexual clinch as he foolishly suggested that 'This embrace can take the place of marriage, of children'. The next moment they were both murdered by the ghost of their mother Clytemnestra, played by Shiraishi. The last word of the performance and of Orestes as he died was his shouted 'Mother'.

First shown in the amphitheatre at the 1983 Toga Festival, *Clytemnestra* was based on six tragedies that all concern the House of Atreus. The playtext (which Suzuki describes as 'requotation' rather than adaptation) is published in *The Way of Acting*, but this indicates little about how it might have been performed. Occasional stage directions indicate violence, as characters stab each other or drag on a dead body, represented by a small rag doll. Most actions were integral to the plot, such as Orestes' matricide, and there was little extraneous movement. There are intriguing references to the framing in this text, which Suzuki's notion of 'requoting' indicates. One scene 'is from the memories of Orestes and Electra' and another is what passes through Orestes' consciousness. How this metaphysical complexity might be suggested can only be understood through recognising Suzuki's stylistic approach and the heightened state he demands in performance. Words acted as curses, pleas, judgements, confessions, plots and occasionally choric commentary. They drove the piece to its inexorable end, underlining the decisive actions that could not be forgotten or undone.

The dominant mode of performance was energised vocal delivery from fixed positions, but a video recording shows that some walks from the training were used in entrances and exits: Clytemnestra's slow final appearance that recalled the entrance of a ghost from *noh*; the serving women's grotesque scurry on stage; and Tyndareos' exaggerated and comic stepping exit underneath an open umbrella after he has passed damning judgement on the children. This

THE ART OF STILLNESS

accompanied the popular sentimental love song 'River of Fate' and Electra's wails.

Beyond the entrances and exits, concentrated moments of action, and the mix of lavish kimono-style robes and modern functional clothes (Orestes wore rags), there were few evident points of orientation for the spectator. It was as if the characters were lost. Motionless, they stared into the emptiness that surrounded them, isolated by spotlights and scattered across the stage in vivid tableaux. Performers were rooted to the ground but otherwise in a void, identifiable as mythological figures only by their names and deeds. The minimal props included a symbolic doll, a knife, Tyndareos' umbrella, and metal waste-paper bins with Marlboro logos. As Electra chopped off her mother's lover (the rag doll) Aegisthus' penis, Orestes hugged a bin tightly. Out of place, these objects iconically suggested the present without denying the timelessness of the issues Suzuki was examining.

In his summing-up, Tyndareos called Electra and Orestes 'human trash'. Suzuki was hinting that Western commercial values are perhaps one of the causes of the breakdown in social and family values, a point supported by the casting. In such a consumer culture as America possessed and Japan was championing in 1983, even the heinous violence of matricide had become throwaway, not sanctioned by Apollo as in the original myth. With his carefully selected symbolism and casting, Suzuki was in part remonstrating against American imperialism and the unquestioning import of new values. Yet the blind pursuit of tradition was shown to be equally questionable, justifying awful revenge and perpetuating violence. Suzuki intentionally exposed such dualities without supplying answers, for they perhaps reflected the complex reality which had pervaded his childhood.

Other design elements cultivated the piece's stark minimalism. As well as the isolating overhead lights, Sylvie Drake noted how sound was a 'major component of the piece'. 'Enveloping the nightmare vision is Suzuki's sound track – score is not an adequate word – part modern music, part traditional Japanese clappers, part sheer noise, but chilling on all counts.'[31] The serving women rushed on with 'pieces of naked flesh piled on trays' to the spartan music of Public Image Limited's 'Four Enclosed Walls', with Johnny Lydon's (aka

Johnny Rotten of the Sex Pistols) eerie moan over pounding drums. This was stopped abruptly by Orestes' impassioned growl: 'What is our action now towards Mother?' With the actors predominantly still, sound created the transitions between moods and scenes and underscored them. This was a development from *The Trojan Women*, where music underlined rather than operated autonomously. Here, it added another overwhelming and overtly functional layer.

John Flynn recognised the alacrity that the training can give the performer. He described the whole piece as a 'relentless flood of worlds, times, and realities. *Queen Clytemnestra* takes place with the speed and illogic of emotionally charged thought.'[32] Electricity-dependent technology added to and heightened the human energy. Sound and light are perfect vehicles for creating a rushing vortex of moods and impressions on stage, depicting a world gone mad. Suzuki utilised them fully in this production. When the performance was shown outdoors, McDonald describes how Clytemnestra's shadow at the end was 'projected against the backdrop of a tall tree in the Toga presentation (and against Parnassus when the play is performed in Delphi)'.[33] Man and nature and past and present merged, each commenting on the other.

Clytemnestra was then reworked to create *The Tragedy* (subtitled *The Fall of the House of Atreus*, also 1983), with Shiraishi still in the starring role and a cast of seventy in total. This revision is most interesting in relation to Suzuki's whole career, rather than in its own right. Its proximity in time to his 1981 production of the musical *Sweeney Todd* shows Suzuki's ability to move swiftly between his own alternative, rural structures and those of the larger commercial world, which is predominantly urban. Elaborately staged at Tokyo's 1,900-seat Imperial Theatre (this was built in 1911 and was based on a typical European opera house), performances of *The Tragedy* were attended by at least 45,000 people. The income this generated helped raise money to develop the Toga complex. Yet however necessary this urban event was in economic terms, its artistic failure showed the value of the rural context and of nature (in its broadest sense) in Suzuki's work.

James Brandon condemned the piece's ambition: 'terrible miking, theatre too large, speeches too long, movie stars in lead roles'.[34] In the programme notes Suzuki stated that 'what draws him to Greek drama is the similarity between Japanese society today and Greece two thousand years ago', a connection that McDonald also makes. However valid such comparisons might be and however precisely Suzuki explicated this, *The Tragedy* demonstrated that artful contextualisation did not necessarily make Suzuki's theatre work. What this piece lacked were principles derived from the training – focus on the performer's practice rather than the director's concept. It also lacked a supportive environment, though this was not always essential to the success of his productions. Suzuki's Greek adaptations made such an impact on world audiences because of the performers' techniques rather than the concept or interpretation *per se*.

Framing was adopted for all the Greek productions as a unifying mechanism, demonstrating that this device was not only useful for knitting the disparate elements of the collages. *Clytemnestra* and *The Tragedy* pulled together numerous characters as part of the memories of an Orestes-like figure. *The Bacchae* employed at one time a group of political prisoners enacting Euripides' story and at another the reminiscences of Cadmus. Possession was at the core of these frameworks, nowhere more evident than in the liminal antics of the Bacchantes and Agave in *The Bacchae*. Reality was constantly questioned and unstable and the audience were disorientated by the deliberate multi-layering, as they had been with Shiraishi's Princess Hanako-no-mae. As with that role, the actors' techniques enabled such complexity without clouding it.

Through Suzuki's adaptations or 'requotations', the audience entered into fantastical worlds. This allowed the director to focus on more visceral aspects of the performance. Words became energy and their meaning secondary, obfuscated anyway by their unreliable origin in the imagination or in warped fantasy. The framing devices enabled a particular style of acting, though they also helped bring the subject matter up-to-date. By the time he created *Clytemnestra*, Suzuki had found a way for the body to 'speak' the drama of the classics. Increased stillness and longer monologues evidenced his confidence with this, as did the international collaborations. These showed Suzuki's desire to test these notions of an integrated word and body and universalism more cogently, by taking away from the audience the luxury of understanding all the dialogue. They were often only given half the story, but 'stories' are unreliable anyway, as Suzuki's productions had suggested. After *The Tragedy*, he continued these explorations (recycling and reinventing) with other Greek productions. These included *Electra* (1995) and *Oedipus Rex* (2000) for the Spring Arts Festival in Shizuoka. Nothing since, however, has surpassed the international impact of *The Trojan Women*.

Suzuki has described the progress of the three most significant pieces (from *The Trojan Women* through *The Bacchae* to *Clytemnestra*) as a shift from a 'traditional style', to a 'Western style', and finally to a 'contemporary style'.[35] Perhaps the first two explorations were necessary in order for Suzuki to create his own personal 'contemporary' synthesis in *Clytemnestra*. This third position is where he really wanted to be, transcending sources and original, with a theatre that is neither Western, intercultural nor even Japanese, if one can be so reductive. This would be Suzuki's theatre using the 'Suzuki style', in the way that the method is Suzuki's. Artistically, he occasionally stepped too far outside his own parameters, as in *The Tragedy*, losing the orientation that a precise use of the body gives. But, like all theatre directors, Suzuki is driven by the desire to find his own theatrical idiom which can be transferred to any text, as his productions of Shakespeare and Chekhov show.

Shakespeare

Suzuki's many interpretations of Shakespeare's plays demonstrate that his approach and style are not limited only to Greek drama. His process of adaptation may vary from piece to piece and from author to author, but has consistent hallmarks. He imposes a transformative stamp and vision to create a metatextual commentary on the original. The notion that the training prepares the performer for classical roles refers as much to Shakespeare as it does to Euripides' plays, though the complexity of Shakespeare's language makes questions of translation and the use of the voice more problematic, as suggested in the previous chapter.

The Tale of Lear, which is considered Suzuki's most successful adaptation of Shakespeare, will be analysed first. *The Chronicle of Macbeth*, which was a more troubled international project, will then be examined. *The Tale of Lear* attracted extensive critical responses and *The Chronicle of Macbeth* aroused controversy. These pieces are useful for gauging the public reception of Suzuki's work, revealing some of the potential provocations inflamed by cross-cultural collaborations, as well as investigating his ongoing application of certain techniques and mechanisms.

Suzuki used framing devices to adapt both playtexts, relying on drastic cutting rather than rewriting as his key operating principle. He kept Shakespeare's lines at the core of his extensively abridged versions, though in *The Chronicle of Macbeth* he supplemented the play with other short textual extracts. This cutting fuelled critical remonstrations. When Suzuki presented *The Tale of Lear* in London, he received scathing attacks in the British press. Ownership and protectiveness of the Bard still pervade British culture, linked to the narrow-mindedness of 'bardolatry'. (This is the suspension of critical judgement and overestimation with which some critics have invested Shakespeare for centuries.) Suzuki was toying with Shakespeare's structure as well as his language and the reviews implied that as a linguistic and cultural outsider he had no right to do this.

What the British critics' veiled nationalism and prejudice exposed was the value of Suzuki's mission to create cross-cultural projects. He is not working in an ideological vacuum without purpose or foundation and is admirably pragmatic in his attempt to challenge foreign perceptions of the Japanese. This is still marred by ignorance and misunderstanding, as critical reception of his work in Britain and to a lesser extent in Australia showed. Edward Said has argued that 'orientalism' arises from narrow etic perspectives that distort other cultures, thereby further moulding and constraining them. Said first articulated such notions in *Orientalism* in 1976, but this does not mean that such tendencies have since been vanquished. We should not accept without question current depictions of a harmonious 'global village', which is led more by the desire to create world markets than by the search for cultural cooperation and understanding. Said's pioneering book kindled many more critiques that also depicted false or biased visions of other cultures. 'Orientalism' in itself has not gone away and Suzuki is attempting to counter such persistent misrepresentations of Japan.

Before examining the perils of cross-cultural transferability and reception further, the work that Suzuki actually created should be clarified. *The Tale of Lear*'s genesis was in 1984, when it was called *King Lear* and was performed by an all-male Japanese cast from SCOT for the Toga Festival. In a now familiar pattern, in 1988 *King Lear* was renamed and revised with twelve American male performers. *The Tale of Lear* was an American bilingual production coordinated by four repertory companies: Milwaukee Repertory Theater, StageWest, Arena Stage and Berkeley Repertory Theater. This travelled around America for 147 performances, playing to approximately 80,000 people, before embarking on several international tours with Japanese actors, that took in London several years later.

The piece was framed by the decrepit figure of Lear (Tom Hewitt in the American version) in a nursing home, being read the story of King Lear by a 'female' nurse. Lear's muddled memories turned into the 'tale' into which he was drawn as a participant/observer. As well as being Lear's own fantasy of this story, it is also an enactment of the real story, as the two frames merge. The performance ended with the king's death, after which the other characters instantly exited, leaving the nurse alone with the dead body. To close the play, s/he uttered a grotesque cackle and looked up from the book as Lear rose up and sat by her/his side. Suzuki excised the loyal character of Kent from the text in order to emphasise human evil and the negative effects of ambition. He wanted to focus closely on our destructive impulses, using Shakespeare's play as a vehicle.

The all-male casting remembered both Elizabethan and Greek traditions, as well as those of *noh* and *kabuki*. It created stylistic cohesion and thematic consistency, suggesting that delusions of power and plotting are principally male domains. Marie Myerscough has noted that Suzuki holds the belief 'that males can give a better portrayal of evil',[36] though she does not qualify his statement. The dominance of men on stage did create a threatening and intense dark mood, but whether this is the exclusive domain of male performers is debatable. The emphasis on masculinity was also complicated by the fact that some of them played women. In the best tradition of Asian performing arts, they did this subtly but convincingly, with no attempt to imitate them totally as an *onnagata* might. The gender dynamics of *King Lear* were thus distilled to focus generally on the group and their interrelationships (a recurring concern of Suzuki's) as distinct from the specific interplay between men and women.

In his interpretation, Suzuki wanted to depict the behaviour as universal and break the play out of its established gender conventions. He could obviously draw on his own experience with WLT, SCOT, ACM and SPAC for the production (though this is not to suggest that Lear in his dotage represents Suzuki!). The casting reflected his own company structures (which have predominantly comprised men) and even Japanese society, where power is traditionally under male control. It allowed a focused critique of authority within social groups by narrowing the audience's attention down on to key issues, while subordinating discussions about gender.

Controlled focus was as evident in the performances as it was in the piece's thematic considerations. The characters' fierce battling energy and rivalry was muted, curbed by courtly laws and outward obedience with only occasional but progressively increasing outbursts. Whereas Shiraishi as an actress repeatedly exploded and boiled over, in this all-male piece the lid was kept firmly on. It was such latent energy that hit audiences so forcibly. Suzuki used this resistance expertly (we should remember Hideo Kanze's comments on the stopping of flow in *noh* theatre, noted in the analysis of *The Trojan Women*). Pent-up emotions were sometimes undercut by the lolling nurse in modern uniform, casually reading and laughing intermittently at the story about Lear, which reminded the audience of the frame. This was returned to partly so that the power contests did not become all-absorbing, but also to keep a dual focus on the tale of an individual's demise and descent into madness as well as on the analysis of the group.

The piece continually used such shifts of focus and rhythm. Fast entrances ended in abrupt stops, with the actors poised, like Gloucester, on the edge of a cliff. The performers' feet, wrapped in white *tabi*, were almost hidden by lavish floor-length kimono-like gowns, allowing them to glide or sidle silently into place. These positions were reserved rather than extravagant like *kabuki*'s *mie*. From their energised wide and low stances, they spat out Shakespeare's lines with speed. Subtraction and restraint provided *The Tale of Lear*'s force, interjected by moments of violence and dark, almost carnivalesque, humour that allowed only minimal release.

Economy was also apparent in the *mise-en-scène*, which again remembered the simplicity of both Elizabethan and *noh* staging. The few props included the story book, a sword, a bedpan that Lear wore as a crown, a laundry cart in which he was transported by the nurse like dirty linen, and a blank scroll that depicted agreements, maps and, at its most generalised, authority. After the opening frame with Lear and the nurse alone, the twelve actors appeared suddenly at the back of the stage as black screens slid sharply back to reveal what looked like top-lit statues. The moment was fast, thrilling and simple, contributing to what Herbert Blau described as 'moments of brilliance in the staging'.[37] Later, these screens allowed other instant entrances and exits, fostering a sense of conspiracy and deception.

Side lights swept across the empty space to delineate the statuesque poses and highlight the stillness with strong silhouettes. This is a lighting choice that Suzuki frequently utilises. It is enabled in this and other productions by the fact that the actors rarely make eye contact with each other. If they did, they would be blinded by the lights, which can make moving on stage difficult without precise choreography. As in all his work, the performers' focus was mostly projected forward, but it was always made clear, by subtle shifts in posture and by the staging, who was talking to whom. There was also scarce physical contact unless it was to blind, make a blood pact, or when Lear stumbled on with Cordelia lying across his arms at the end of the piece. Such poignant moments were supported by Handel's string orchestration of the Largo from *Xerxes* that repeatedly and loudly swept over the held images.

Dramatically, *The Tale of Lear* departed from the Greek adaptations in one major way. The piece had a sense of stylistic cohesion rather than disjunction and juxtaposition, evidenced by various directorial choices: the all-male casting; the use of Western classical music (Tchaikovsky's 'Dance Espagnol' from *Swan Lake* was amusingly played at times) rather than Japanese pop or military songs; the uniformity of kimono-like costumes, designed by Suzuki; and most of all, in the use of a single text. There was still a mixture of Eastern and Western influences but this range was limited, and such elements were integrated rather than exposed for their dissimilarities.

There was another important difference between this and the Greek productions, which the delivery of Shakespeare's text accentuated. A reiterated criticism of *The Tale of Lear* was the use of the voice, the weakest area of the company's technique. With Greek drama, there is little concurrence about how it was originally performed and in particular how the text was or should be recited. Shakespeare's verse, however, has attracted many more formulations about proper modes of vocal delivery. *The Tale of Lear* therefore invited comparison with Western approaches to verse-speaking. Mohammed Kowsar offers one such perspective: 'The full-speed roaring and ranting adopted for almost every speech was anathema to the complex and fully orchestrated verses of *Lear* [. . .] the unbearable heaviness of speech in Mr Suzuki's production, which tended to cancel the exquisite lightness of the stage movements.'[38] While its rhythmical, visual and spatial dimensions received unanimous praise, the aural aspect was considered too overbearing. It is important to note that this arose in Shiraishi's absence, for her vocal work had always been so acclaimed.

Shades of opinion on how the contemporary actor should speak Shakespeare's verse (which is often tainted by 'bardolatory') were exacerbated by inconsistencies mentioned in the chapter on training. Suzuki has not provided a coherent, pragmatic and transferable way of tackling the delivery of such complex texts in English. It is with Shakespeare that this becomes most apparent. In Greek drama, possessed performing conjures the presence of the gods, for that is whom the characters are speaking to and through. The ancient Greek language in translation is also not as dense as Shakespeare's and closer to contemporary everyday speech, even if the mythical content of such dramas is more removed from our experience. Shakespeare's words can easily be obscured in performance if spoken in a state of possession, if 'uttered'. Recitation of the text needs to appear to be spontaneous, but it also needs to be conscious and decided, such is its linguistic complexity. As well as their stories, Shakespeare's plays are brought alive by the richness of metaphor, rhythm and numerous other verbal devices, which can be masked by excessive speed or incantation. The perpetuity of Shakespeare's *œuvre* partly depends on the actor's ability to convey a complexity that Suzuki's vocal training has been unable to capture, as far as can be surmised from reception of his plays in their English-language versions. Alastair Macaulay made a similar criticism of director Yukio

Ninagawa's voice work (noted in Chapter Two). Such objections are expressed frequently with regard to Suzuki's productions, but the difficulty of verse-speaking is a problem that many English-speaking directors have not fully resolved, so can we expect so much of Suzuki?

It was the body work and staging which made this piece rise above such challenges. Senda characterises *The Tale of Lear*'s strength as stemming from the training even in its bilingual version where the guest performers were inevitably trained for shorter periods than SCOT's more permanent cast:

> The quality that Suzuki strives for is born of a dynamic tension of excess internal energy that is at war with the actor's impulse to restrain and control. The American actors performing *Lear*, possessing stronger individual presences than the average Japanese actor, seemed to burn with this tension, releasing bursts of energy that resisted structure. In this performance, I was witnessing the Suzuki Method moving beyond national borders and in new creative directions.[39]

In the American production, the training held a potentially difficult collaboration together, but it simultaneously unified and separated. In a preview article before the Barbican Festival, Suzuki was quoted as saying: '[*The Tale of Lear*] is about a society where man has ceased to believe in other men. There is no binding morality. Perhaps America is the country where we see this most clearly.'[40] While all plot around him, Lear is thrown on the rubbish heap (or in the laundry basket). This role model proffers no escape from man's biological destiny. We all age and our biology eventually takes over. Only the method of dealing with sickness and 'raging storms' is culturally specific and in this regard, Suzuki suggests, America is perhaps most remiss.

Suzuki is not afraid to take such critiques to where they hurt most, provocatively asking questions without suggesting answers. Many would recognise the social sickness that Suzuki is depicting through Lear's representative plight. But to use Shakespeare to do this is doubly provocative, as his reception in England demonstrated. The negative sentiments of the piece also conflicted with the political sensibilities of British critics Michael Billington and Benedict

Nightingale, who have often publicly admitted their preference for polemical or Brechtian theatre. (Tatsuji Iwabuchi openly described himself as such to explain the reservations he has with Suzuki's work – see his comments on *The Bacchae* earlier in this chapter.) They want to see the potential for change articulated in their drama.

The politics of the piece were just one small element which led to fierce attacks by critics at its British première. This was part of the Barbican's 'Everybody's Shakespeare International Festival', which ran from 25 October to 19 November 1994. This was a festival that invited foreign companies to show their responses to Shakespeare and it aroused deep feelings and sharp debate. The whole event drew fire and was deemed a critical failure in many newspapers, leading to its artistic consultant Michael Kustow employing a national daily (*Independent*, 19 November) to mount a rigorous defence on the day the festival finished. In this, he picked up comments from the critics, questioned them, and defended his judgement against these 'low-grade taunts'. The panning of *The Tale of Lear* reveals less about the quality of the piece itself and more about the context in which it was shown in Britain. This brought out overprotectiveness of the 'national' (rather than what might rightly be considered the international) figure of Shakespeare.

Admittedly, there were problems with the production in the vast main theatre space that sits in the predominantly concrete Barbican Centre. The scale of the auditorium reduced the performance to a flat and visual rather than experiential field. Digital translation (relayed on a wide screen low down on the proscenium arch) accentuated this flatness, encouraging the audience to look rather than listen and feel, and to peer awkwardly at an adjacent rather than central space. For many in the audience beyond the first few rows, the actors were reduced to indistinguishable figures shouting streams of unintelligible Japanese that was somehow related to a heavily abridged translation. The nuance of variation in their costumes was also obscured by distance. The performers' voices seemed forced in the large auditorium, detached from their source by the subtitling. Music attempted to fill the vacuum but was isolated from the action and transformed by the dominance of the architecture into a sentimental device. J. R. Mulryne concurs that the Barbican offered a 'wide shallow stage that construed action as instance rather than experience'.[41] Although it is unclear exactly what he means by 'instance', it is evident that the space flattened the experience into image and shortened the duration and effect of the action's emotional impact.

The British critics' appraisal of *The Tale of Lear* was based only on these Barbican performances, so some of their misapprehensions are justified. Yet problems with the space and technical devices like the subtitling only opened more unpleasant sluice gates. One of the main prongs of the multi-barbed attack lay with the adaptation, or rather the very notion of adaptation. This was *The Tale of Lear* rather than *King Lear*, reframed, reduced to one hundred minutes, and with central characters like Kent and interactions such as Lear and Cordelia's reconciliation cut. This did not 'disturb' Billington, though. Rather 'it is that very consistency that worries me: it leaves no room for the emotional ambiguity and moral paradox that lies at the very heart of Shakespeare'.[42] But adaptation and radical cuts are inevitably bound to both reduce and simplify. Critics should assess not what is lost but what is added in revision and reinterpretation. Perhaps they still consider it taboo to tamper with Shakespeare's plays.

Michael Kustow selected sections of Benedict Nightingale's 11 November *Times* review to demonstrate the 'resistance to foreign innovations in Shakespeare production' that Poet Laureate Ted Hughes identified when he read *The Tale of Lear*'s critiques. Nightingale reduced the production to 'Finely attired actors moving very slowly, standing very still and speaking in very loud, abrupt Japanese'. What Hughes enjoyed, though, were 'some essentially Shakespearean qualities that our English ritualised convention too often lacks'. For him, it was a 'Noh play – not an interpretation of Shakespeare's *King Lear* using Japanese stage conventions and styles'.[43] He saw it as quintessentially Japanese rather than 'British Shakespeare', which is what Ninagawa created unsuccessfully with his *King Lear* in 1999. In *New Sites for Shakespeare: Theatre, the Audience and Shakespeare*, John Russell Brown describes how he researched Asian performances in order to find ways to recreate the ceremonial and ritualistic aspects of Shakespeare's plays. It is for this achievement that many appreciated Suzuki's approach and deemed it a success. What Nightingale (and to a lesser extent Billington) seem to prefer is culturally exclusive and narrow-minded. Why shouldn't the stillness of *noh* be applied to Shakespeare? It is another matter if this application does not work, but this did not really seem to be the issue. In this case, the critics' judgements seemed to stem from prejudice as much as evaluation of the event itself.

My own understanding of *The Tale of Lear* is based on viewings in the old Toga *sanbo* in 1993 and at the Barbican, where I watched two performances, from the front and the back. Seeing the piece in both spaces was revealing, but even the change of seat at the Barbican made me feel like I had watched two different plays. In Toga, the piece was overwhelming: in the energetic intensity of the performances; the subtlety of expression underneath the forceful utterance of text; and the slow, nuanced choreography that drove the piece forward with a choking relentlessness. Events were unstoppable, and, helpless, the audience watched the tragedy unfold. The music swelled repeatedly to its many crescendos, resonating in the wood of the farmhouse which was already vibrating with the actors' voices. Its consistency was its virtue, as the piece surrounded the audience and image was subsumed by experience. The production epitomised Suzuki's notion that the theatre event is principally about the audience sensing the actor's 'physiological tension'. The intention of every word was clear and nothing was lost in abstraction. Viewing the performance at the front of the Barbican auditorium only partially recreated such sensibilities.

Comparisons between the presentation in Toga and London validate Suzuki's decision to create his own 'ritual space' in the remote mountains of Japan. The problem comes with touring, though this obviously has financial imperatives and is integral to the artistic survival of Suzuki's work. In some cases, the relocation of a performance from its home space works. Yet the downside can be the negation of a piece's inherent qualities, as happened at the Barbican. This poor reception has undoubtedly prevented Suzuki from showing his work in Britain for several years. He should have been represented in Britain's Japan 2001 festival, but did not appear.

Frustrations with British critical responses to this influential aspect of world theatre are not mine alone. In his 'Japanese Shakespeare and English Reviewers' in *Shakespeare and the Japanese Stage*,[44] Tetsuo Kishi analyses the desire for exoticism of critics like Billington, with specific reference to Ninagawa's work and his *Peer Gynt*. The overriding irony of the plaints against Suzuki is that he was attempting to universalise Lear's condition and open it to world audiences by detaching it from its specific gender, historical and regional context. Intercultural, universalising projects are fraught in practice, but one lesson that can be learned is how spaces affect the theatre event and must be chosen carefully. *The Tale of Lear* might have worked in the Barbican's smaller Pit theatre.

Another major initiative by Suzuki with which to examine the international reception of his work was his Australian version of *Macbeth*. This has been written about in detail by Ian Carruthers, so my analysis is brief. *The Chronicle of Macbeth* further illuminates the relationship of training to performance, developing Senda's assertion that *The Tale of Lear* derived its strength from the performers' techniques. It had an all-Australian male cast of twelve (including, as Banquo, John Nobbs, the co-artistic director of Frank) with the exception of American Ellen Lauren as Lady Macbeth. The project was instigated by Carrillo Gantner of Melbourne's Playbox Theatre to examine the potential integration of Asian performance techniques into contemporary Australian theatre. After a two-week casting and short rehearsal period, the piece toured to Australian cities as well as Tokyo for the 1992 Mitsui Festival, of which Suzuki was then artistic director.

Suzuki's exploration of *Macbeth* began with the WLT in 1975. *Night and Clock* was a collage framed as a mental patients' game of attempting to become Macbeth. Like *King Lear*, Suzuki was attracted to *Macbeth* for its themes, its framework and the title character's questioning of his sanity. His 'all the world is a hospital' metaphor naturally suited this text. Conceptually reminiscent of Peter Weiss's *Marat/Sade*, *Night and Clock* typified Suzuki's concerns and techniques of this period and was so successful it won the Kinokuniya Prize for an original work. *The Chronicle of Macbeth* continued his process of re-examination of previous works, but was based loosely on a quite different version that Suzuki had directed with the Acting Company of Mito in 1991. Like *The Tale of Lear*, it received a mixed reception, with critics and audiences confused and puzzled, though the latter were more positive. Leonard Pronko's

Theatre Journal review from the Mitsui Festival summarises the combination of successes and failures, the losses and gains, which Suzuki's production contained.

The main problem, which was identified by Lauren, was the actors' lack of Suzuki training (surprisingly, Pronko does not refer to this). Lauren has described how the vocal delivery may have seemed flat or tense: 'you can hardly breathe and at first everything that comes out is strangulated. The point is that they [the Australian actors] have not gained sufficient physical control to stop that from occurring.'[45] There had been too little time for the training to become second nature. Gantner's intention was confounded by the fact that most Asian training approaches are long-term processes, which to some extent also applies to the Suzuki method. It was too much to expect techniques to be used intuitively while the actors were still trying to grasp Suzuki's aesthetics (in particular his emphasis on action, energy and utterance rather than text and meaning) and while they were reformulating their own physical and vocal practices. The project was perhaps flawed before it even began, using performers who were for the large part, with the exception of Lauren, comparative beginners in the Suzuki method. This had not proved a problem for the American actors in *The Tale of Lear*, but then several of them had worked with Suzuki before.

The other problem that both Lauren and Carruthers have touched on recalls the reception of *The Tale of Lear* in London and relates to Suzuki's adaptation. *The Chronicle of Macbeth* stirred up less prejudices but led many to question the reason for Suzuki's artistic choices. He constructed the play as the fervent and diseased imaginative ramblings of an aspiring Macbeth, within a further framework of a story about a Reverend Father and his Believers. This piece was the second part of the 'Farewell Cult' trilogy, of which *The Bacchae* was part one and *Ivanov* was part three. It therefore progressed and contributed to a discourse on the nature of individuals and their communities, a complexity which only followers of Suzuki's previous works could enjoy. Audiences were puzzled why Suzuki added so much – the frame, his interpretation, even sections of text from Beckett's *Endgame* – to Shakespeare's core text.

The actors' struggles on both a conceptual and physical level heightened the audiences' own difficulty with Suzuki's sometimes inexplicable directorial practices. He demanded great concentration and flexibility of performers and spectators. The cast may have been familiar to the Australian audiences, but this did not help surmount the distance many felt from this interpretation. The text was spoken in English and the piece was clearly an adaptation or 'chronicle', but the unusual nature of the Suzuki style proved overwhelming. Surprise and artistic provocation are fundamental to a stimulating theatre experience, but this must be balanced with clarity. The essence of Suzuki's acting technique is struggle, but there is a point when obstacles become insurmountable. The audiences were confused and the visceral impact of the piece (so integral to Suzuki's theatre, as Shiraishi demonstrated) became obscured. This is confirmed by an unpublished collection of papers by artists and academics (including Lauren and Gantner), one of whom had done a survey of audience responses.

It is possible that the Suzuki vocal style in English made the audience's connection to the piece more difficult, taking their focus away from his forte – the staging and physicality. The lack of training Lauren identified impacts most visibly (or rather audibly) on the vocal delivery. Leonard Pronko's comparatively positive review of the performance in Japan – where the language would have been less of an issue – supports this. Whatever the reasons, this collaboration passed off with much debate but little public enthusiasm. As well as the perils of intercultural practice, it proved the central role Suzuki's acting method plays in knitting his complex multi-referential pieces together. This recalls his statement on the collages that attempted to 'connect the body' rather than texts.

The training supports a classical style as the performer works with the heightened states and extreme levels of tension enshrined within Greek or Elizabethan playtexts. Suzuki has drawn on *Macbeth* and *King Lear* to the greatest extent and *Romeo and Juliet* and *Hamlet* to a lesser degree, but he has not touched the comedies. Writing about *The Tragedy* in 1985, James Brandon suggested that 'One thing Suzuki and Ota share is their disinterest in comedy [. . .] Suzuki and Ota both have a sense of humour; I wish it showed more in their work.'[46] But Suzuki's theatre does possess humour, though it is often personal to the director or specific to the Japanese audience, leaving the Western observer mystified. In themselves, these comic aspects are often successful with refreshing immediacy, but their positioning and function within the productions can be baffling. Humour sometimes derives from absurd visual incongruities, such as men in red high heels shuffling along in their wheelchairs. At other times it depends on pure silliness, like a comic expression or the hip-wrenching walks of a chorus of nurses in his 1999 collage *Sayonara Toga*. Suzuki exploits physical or visual juxtaposition and the contrasts of collage to show characters outside familiar parameters. Lear in a laundry trolley is one example, as are Chekhov's characters in baskets. We can look not only to the absurdism of Beckett and Betsuyaku but also to Anton Chekhov for the sources of comedy in Suzuki's performances.

Chekhov

Almost nothing has been written in English about Suzuki's connection to Chekhov, with the exception of Erika Fischer-Lichte's 'Intercultural Aspects in Post-modern Theatre: a Japanese version of Chekhov's *Three Sisters*'. Humour translates awkwardly across cultural borders, though this is less so with physical comedy. The idiosyncrasy of Suzuki's comedy may also explain why this is an uncharted area. Yet Suzuki's exploration of Chekhov is well established, beginning with the farce *The Anniversary*, which he directed as early as 1959. Since then, he has directed *Three Sisters* (in 1961 and in 1984 with Kayoko Shiraishi as Masha), as well as *Uncle Vanya* and *The Cherry Orchard*. He combined these three major works into *The Chekhov* in 1989 in Toga, which also toured to New York and Massachusetts. In the 1990s he produced *Ivanov* with Tsutamori Kosuke in the title role and with the other characters in baskets (except a wheelchair-bound Anna). Even the tightly woven and self-contained worlds that Chekhov created were appropriate for adaptation.

Faithful to Chekhov's texts, Suzuki's humour is often dark as well as farcical. We laugh at the characters' misfortune, despair and inertia. Over this, he layers an absurd visual field and physicality, with Groucho Marx false glasses and noses, tattered umbrellas and characters stuck in baskets supping noodles. The basket-men in *Ivanov* are like comic *Snow White* dwarves. These people lack the epic scale or status of those in Shakespeare or the Greek dramas, but their lives are just as poignant. Suzuki is emphasising that the same human conditions apply in everyday life for all people, be they regal, a servant, a matricide, or a lonely Russian teacher.

It is not only humour which Suzuki drew out from Chekhov's plays, but also a bleak Beckettian existential world view of characters in limbo, waiting without knowing for what. The sisters' cry 'To Moscow' is as representative of humanity's refuge in illusion as *Waiting for Godot*'s tree is a symbol of futile expectations. Whereas in *Dionysus* characters were confined in wheelchairs to show their alienation, in the Chekhov deconstructions they were trapped in large baskets. Their masked heads peered over the rim and holes cut in the bottom allowed them to shuffle along amusingly but awkwardly. This osmosis into basket-men was stimulated by social breakdown, as the fantasy of escape faded and the domestic group imploded in internal wranglings. Ivanov watches the basket-men surround him from the safety of his desk before he joins them in a basket with a gun at the end of the play. Suzuki boils down and reduces Chekhov's masterpieces to such symbolic motifs and refrains. Chekhov can be manipulated to present the same world view as Shakespeare or Euripides, to focus on issues of fantasy and reality, the nature of communities and man's destiny, as Suzuki explains:

> All of Chekhov's characters are incapable of looking at reality and their lives with any degree of objectivity. They speak constantly of an illusory world that is somewhere other and better than where they are. In the course of conversation, the characters see the state of their misery.[47]

This remembers the darkness of Suzuki's vision of the 'human scale' and necessary wretchedness, articulated in the mid-1960s at the beginning of his career.

Adaptation of Chekhov continued and extended Suzuki's interest in Beckett and the Theatre of the Absurd that arose in the 1960s. Chekhov's plays were germane for highlighting the problem of man's isolation and solitude in a rapidly transforming society. The world of *The Cherry Orchard* has parallels with post-Second World War Japan, portraying a society on the verge of deep change. In performance, Shiraishi as Madame Ranevskaya leafed through the tens of telegrams sent to her from Paris, before she erupted into a set piece of a Japanese sentimental popular song to taped music. The crouching chorus applauded her mid-tune as she grimaced. Traditional Chekhov yielded to absurd, grotesque parody. White dust sheets were draped across furniture on the black *sanbo* stage, but to contrast with this Chekhovian design cliché, Shiraishi wore a black evening dress and black hat with a frilly hem that comically exaggerated her facial contortions. Like *Ivanov*, the piece shifted between intense emotional outpouring and comic routines, between tension and release.

Suzuki used Chekhov to investigate East/West cultural and political dynamics. Chekhov is situated midway between Japan and Europe (if one considers Europe in its Cold War political form rather than its geographical one that stretches to the Urals). As he exploited Japanese performance aesthetics and principles to revivify Greek dramas that he then toured to Western audiences, so he 'succeeded in responding to the current [1985] situation in Japan by staging a European play'.[48] The dominant issue then was Westernisation and its potential destructive impact on traditional practices, which Suzuki exemplified in *Three Sisters*. By making Andrei and Natasha Japanese and other characters more European in their dress and manners, he made the clash of values at the heart of the play pan-cultural. Without eulogising the past or demonising the future, the *Three Sisters* that Fischer-Lichte saw in Frankfurt in 1985 became a harsh critique of Japan's post-Second World War embrace of Western ideas and materials. The collision of worlds was emphasised by a simple design at the core of which were both armchairs and tatami mats.

By so radically altering these texts, Suzuki not only challenged entrenched assumptions about staging these plays that are central to *shingeki*, but he also provided a self-reflexive commentary on Japanese theatre and culture. Fischer-Lichte proposes that Suzuki was attempting to forge what might be called 'world theatre', part of the intercultural impulse which she considers to underlie much postmodern theatre. Chekhov is suited for Suzuki's own game-playing of abridgement and adaptation because of the immense baggage and tradition the Russian's plays carry and embody. Design for Chekhov's dramas implies plank flooring, bare walls, trees and dust sheets, emulating Viktor Simov's original scenography for

Konstantin Stanislavski. Suzuki is attempting to wrench Chekhov out of context, break his work out of the stranglehold of naturalism, and bring him up-to-date for a Japanese audience:

> In my production of *The Three Sisters*, when the actors say *we must live*, they curl up in chairs, and are force-fed rice. Or three old ladies sit on toilets, standing on top of them at the end to declare *we must live!* I can defend such a staging because humans, no matter how confused their inner life may be, cannot very well do without continually eating, excreting and babbling every day.[49]

Suzuki focuses on the exterior rather than the psychological interior of the characters. He reminds us that naturalism was itself a stylisation before it became the orthodoxy, and develops this notion along an artistic spectrum into the realms of the absurd.

Nothing within the training indicates how Suzuki's use of humour might evolve in rehearsal or appear in performance, nor does it give the performer an inkling of this aspect of Suzuki's vision. Mostly it is the director's intervention, his interpolation of objects or other design elements, for example, which creates the comedy, rather than the actors' playing skills or rhythmical interaction. The same acting principles that inform the tragedies carry over into the more comic pieces, the humour reliant on deadpan delivery and the performer's insouciant innocence of their effect. The incongruous moments of absurd surrealism that are interjected, even into a sombre piece like *The Tale of Lear*, allow the audience to change gear briefly, though the performers must sustain concentration and seriousness. It is their total physical commitment to each second of performance, their rooted justification for their presence on stage, which gives the humour something to work against. But this very seriousness can in the next minute expose a puzzling or irritating intrusion and incongruity.

We can find reasons for Suzuki's choice of texts by looking for thematic parallels with the contemporary situation in Japan, as I have done with *The Cherry Orchard* and as Erika Fischer-Lichte did. There is also value in comparing Greek drama and *noh* to evidence why Suzuki was drawn to a writer like Euripides. Mae Smethurst develops Arthur Waley's early research into this subject in his 1921 *The Noh*

Plays of Japan. She explores in detail these forms' structure and style in *The Artistry of Aeschylus and Zeami: A Comparative Study of Greek Drama and Noh* (though she does not refer to Suzuki). Shinto (with its celebration of nature and ritual practices) and *noh* have connections to the rural Dionysian rites that are reformulated in the playtexts of ancient Greece. There are also thematic links between the content of Elizabethan and traditional Japanese performance, with their focus on the supernatural, violence, power, the fall of great figures and heroic deeds, familial bonds and feudalism. Akira Kurosawa's film version of *Macbeth, The Throne of Blood* (1957), which recontextualised Shakespeare's characters as samurai warriors, adeptly conjoined the two ages and cultures. Intracultural connections can also be discerned. Goto has noted how Suzuki's framing devices are 'virtually identical to the double structure of a classic Japanese no play'.[50] I have mentioned other associations in passing, but is it ultimately wise to ask why this Japanese artist has drawn on so many European texts, a question which Suzuki admits he is frequently asked? For Suzuki, the dramas of Chekhov, Shakespeare, Beckett and Euripides are part of world drama, the legacy of the human race. He is as likely to work with such texts as Peter Brook is, for they offer the contemporary director challenging and familiar material for reworking and interpreting in a range of styles and periods. Besides, the question reveals a worryingly etic perspective.

It is harder to discern why Suzuki has gravitated to lesser-known texts such as *Cyrano de Bergerac* in 1999 at the SPAC Udo theatre, or *Sweeney Todd* for his 1981 production at Tokyo's Imperial Theatre. These show Suzuki's ability to be flexible with his directorial abilities, to be a commercially minded manager encouraging new audiences for his work in unfamiliar contexts, as much as an innovative experimental artist. Yasunari Takahashi considers the production of *Sweeney Todd* a 'symbolical' act, not only of the capacity of those in the avant-garde to cross over successfully into (and thus capitalise on) commercial theatre, thereby opening up a potential diversity of activity, but also as the end of the 'little' theatre movement of the 1960s and 1970s. *Sweeney Todd* was not performed by the WLT but Senda still considered it groundbreaking, with 'precise, tense and exciting' direction and mostly 'very good central performances'.[51] Its scale in the vast theatre was perhaps useful preparation for Suzuki for the Toga amphitheatre, though the piece differed in numerous ways from his usual material. He included a scene in a mental hospital in Act Two and added a framing device, but unlike anything before. The choice of this musical reminds us rather of the spartan economic conditions in which Japanese directors operate.

Suzuki's collage approach has allowed him to ecologically and economically recycle previous materials. The 1999 Toga Festival included *Sayonara Toga* in the new farmhouse theatre. This performance integrated, *inter alia,* selected scenes from Chekhov, Beckett, Juro Kara's *Long John Silver,* musical comedies and *Electra,* alternating between static dialogues, a chorus of dancing nurses and Chekhovian women dressed elegantly in white, shuffling on in baskets. It was presented as a new piece, although essentially it glued together sections from earlier performances as a way of saying goodbye to Toga or at least the festival. The recycling that those familiar with Suzuki's work over a number of years can identify might fuel criticism that he has nothing new to say. What it ensures, though, is the time and money to develop new pieces slowly, without the pressure to make three or four productions from scratch every year, as is the case in Britain. Collages need to be thought through and finely structured, but they also contain the 'ready-made', the playful, and the rough and ready. The training prevents these collages from slipping into chaos and validates the possibility of keeping old pieces honed in order to resurrect them (or sections of them) swiftly and with a sensibility akin to that with which they were initially created.

What is striking about Suzuki's many productions and the range of material he has explored is not what he has used and the cultural implications of this. The broader question remains as to how Western and Asian drama can interact, for Suzuki has only found *his* answer, positing one model rather than a prescription. The Suzuki method provides a tangible methodology for this by creating a unifying physicality and coherent acting process. Armed with this practice, the WLT, then SCOT and now SPAC could and can avoid the pitfalls of syncretism and imitation. Cross-cultural experimentation and quotation are validated by a unified group and a single-minded vision that is communicated clearly between director and performers through a daily body practice, over which are layered textual and interpretative choices.

More interesting is how Suzuki has utilised processes (and in particular the training) to achieve harmonisation of dislocations and contradictions within what might be considered the stylistic constraints of a range of texts. His eclecticism has been enabled by a specialised use of the body, which is consistent from performance to performance and maintained through regular practice. He makes his company into a cohesive unit or ensemble through such techniques. This allows them to explore world texts in the broadest sense, from different periods, cultures and geographies, without creating a syncretic muddy soup. This does not mean his productions always work – the usual principles of engagement with the spectator still apply – but he at least avoids the fundamental trap that might appear with such diversity. The fragmentation of his postmodern interculturalism and quotation, and the bleakness of his existential despair, are counterpointed with and uplifted by a rigorous physical practice and heightened energy. Occasionally, the audience lose contact with the performer, overwhelmed by context and interpretation. There are also exceptions to the rule, like *Sweeney Todd*, which did not use Suzuki-trained actors but which nevertheless succeeded in its own terms. But it is Suzuki's focused, disciplined deployment of the performer within a tumultuous *mise-en-scène* loaded with surprising self-reflexivity and cross-cultural commentary that has turned ideas and imaginings into credible and internationally acclaimed performances.

AFTERWORD

•

Suzuki's interculturalism has been consistently moderated by his intraculturalism which unite to create a singular and dynamic fusion – a practice that is both inside and outside Japan, that is of the world. His integrating mission has brought the West closer to understanding what once seemed distant and impenetrable through the most instructive tool there is: practical example. Suzuki has helped reclaim the best aspects of globalisation – collaboration and understanding – thereby sidelining commercial gain and exploitation. We can now no longer define East and West as oppositions.

Suzuki's training method has been instrumental in the dismantling of cultural barriers, providing access to what Westerners could once only observe from some distance as exotic. It no longer seems romantic idealism to consider performing as a long-term process that requires struggle, dedication, repetition and mastery of technique, leading to emotional strength or *seishin*. Such characteristics are typical of any 'way' or '*do*', as it is called in Japanese, and are concepts familiar to all martial arts. Just as these fighting forms have become popular and integrated in the West, so have principles and practices of Asian performing arts become increasingly commonplace and accepted. As long as these are understood for their combination of technical and metaphysical principles, rather than just as *kata*, we can be optimistic. Suzuki looked backwards to go forwards, as Yasunari Takahashi observed.[1] We must not ignore the lessons and values of such apparent contradictions and dualities in the search for quick results.

Academic scholarship at the end of the twentieth century made conceptual strides away from Eurocentrism, to which Suzuki made a central but provocative contribution. The ethics of Peter Brook's representation of Indian culture in his *Mahabharata* have been discussed repeatedly in the world's seminar rooms. However tired some aspects of these debates, interculturalism as a practice at least still has much to explore, as it continues to challenge the dominance of realism in Western theatre. Disharmony and disjunction can now be considered positively. This was certainly not true when Suzuki first began his cross-cultural experiments, as revealed in the Japanese critics' cautious and sometimes scathing reviews of his early work. The prejudices observed in British reviewers of Japanese theatre have surfaced as much among Japan's own critics, as they have faced the demanding challenges of their country's avant-garde. Hybridity has usurped concerns about plagiarism and misrepresentation and broadened horizons. It has been frequently reiterated that cultures are not fixed, existing in a constant state of flux. Interculturalism can help effect this flow and ebb, supporting appropriation and cross-fertilisation. Through such means, theatre might maintain its role as 'a place for thinking culturally and not for performing culture'.[2] If the performer is empowered, and through them the other collaborators in the performance process, culture can be what we make it rather than what is prescribed from above.

Suzuki has come a long way from being one of the pioneers of Japan's underground theatre movement. Certainly his work now lacks a political and social edge, reflecting the disenfranchisement and apathy that is as evident in Japan as it is in the West. His creations of public rituals have shifted along a continuum towards entertainment that now possesses few transgressive qualities. But are his feet no longer on the ground? I am hesitant about making further generalisations or predicting where his artistic practice is heading. His work is too broad-ranging and unpredictable for sweeping statements. 'Suzuki Now' is already Suzuki then. But it is not his metaphor of 'all the world is a hospital' with us as mad players sitting wheelchair-bound on the wards that has always been acclaimed, bringing followers and students to his door. Rather it is his practice that will endure, encouraging further reappraisals of the director's extensive achievements.

Where can Suzuki's project propel us? He, like many before, has shown that there can be alternatives to realism and that it is possible to make theatre of high artistic value in an underfunded capitalist 'dystopia', as Japan's present social climate has been described by Tadashi Uchino.[3] Suzuki's explorations usefully turn the question back on to us, asking what our sources are in a comparable society? His encounter with Anne Bogart helped crystallise her questioning of what (as an American) the roots of her theatre are, leading her to music-hall and variety. How we feed off Suzuki's practice and ideas is ultimately our responsibility. It is for us to find training approaches and even systems that endure beyond the far too brief three years of training we might encounter at drama school or at university.

This book has made no attempt to be comprehensive. The analysis of his performances circumscribed a very selective band of his total output. Hopefully, others will write more about the historical development of Suzuki's work and the detail of his company life, perhaps pursuing the wealth of information available in Japanese sources. Scholars who have worked or will work more closely with Suzuki might present a more 'authorised' version of his history, theories and practice. The potential constraint of needing Suzuki's 'approval' for my writing kept me well away from any notion of collaboration, with whatever losses or gains that have ensued from such distance.

To close, I want briefly to instance three practical examples of the ongoing application of Suzuki's training and approach in Britain: one theatrical, one paratheatrical and one both academic and creative. I hope that these speak for themselves. The first example is that of Scott Handy, a British actor who played Ariel in *The Tempest* at the Royal Shakespeare Company in the 1998–9 season. In order to create a sense of Ariel's lightness and his ethereal nature, Handy paradoxically used the Suzuki training to ground himself, a device which has parallels to techniques used to present the ghosts in *noh*. The paratheatrical work is co-ordinated by Roy Leighton, who trains student actors at LAMDA (the London Academy of Music and Dance), but also teaches barristers and Sotheby's staff in presentation skills for court appearances and auctions respectively, as part of LAMDA's commercial arm. This is based partly on Leighton's experience of training with Suzuki in Japan. The last project was led at the University of Kent by Frances Barbe, a choreographer/ performer who trained initially with Frank. In 2001, she began a three-year investigation of the impact of Suzuki's technique and *butoh* on British practice, through her own creative work. She explores potential collaborations with music, new circus and dance, centred on responses to classical texts. Judging by the present, Suzuki's approach to performing does have a future, however surprising the actual outcomes might be. If it endures, it will be thanks to the diverse range of applications that its fine-tuned specificity allows.

SELECTED BIBLIOGRAPHY
OF WORKS IN ENGLISH

•

WRITINGS ON OR BY SUZUKI

Carruthers, Ian, '*The Chronicle of Macbeth*: Suzuki Tadashi's Transformation of Shakespeare's *Macbeth*' in *Shakespeare – World Views*, Heather Kerr, Robin Eaden and Madge Mitton (eds), Associated University Press, Cranbury, New Jersey, 1996.

——'What Actors and Directors Do to "Legitimate" Shakespeare: Suzuki's *Chronicle of Macbeth* and Ellen Lauren's Lady Macbeth' in *Shakespeare's Books: Contemporary Cultural Politics*, Philip Mead and Marion Campbell (eds), University of Melbourne, 1993.

Dixon Bigelow, Michael and Joel A. Smith (eds), *Anne Bogart Viewpoints*, Smith and Kraus Inc., Lyme, NH, 1995.

Engeki to wa nani ka (*What is theatre?*) in an unpublished translation by Kameron Steele and others, originally Iwanami Shoten, Tokyo, 1988.

Fischer-Lichte, Erika, 'Intercultural Aspects in Post-modern Theatre: a Japanese version of Chekhov's *Three Sisters*' in *The Play out of Context: Transforming Plays from Culture to Culture*, Hanna Scolnicov and Peter Holland (eds), CUP, 1989.

Flynn, John J., 'A dramaturgy of madness: Suzuki and the *Oresteia*' in *Madness in Drama*, James Redmond (ed.), CUP, 1993.

Goodman, David, 'The Post-Shingeki Theatre Movement in Japan' in *Theatre Companies of the World: Africa, Asia, Australia and New Zealand, Canada, Eastern Europe, Latin America, The Middle East, Scandinavia*, Colby H. Kullman and William C. Young (eds), Westport, CT, Greenwood, 1986.

Iwabuchi, Tatsuji, 'The Reception of Western Drama in Japan' in *The Dramatic Touch of Difference*, Erika Fischer-Lichte, Josephine Riley and Michael Gissenwehrer (eds), Gunter Narr Verlag, Tubingen, 1990.

McDonald, Marianne on *The Trojan Women*, *The Bacchae* and *Clytemnestra* in *Ancient Sun, Modern Light: Greek Drama on the Modern Stage*, Columbia University Press, New York, 1992.

Mulryne, J. R., 'The perils and profits of interculturalism and the theatre art of Tadashi Suzuki' in *Shakespeare and the Japanese Stage*, Takashi Sasayama, J. R. Mulryne and Margaret Shewring (eds), CUP, 1998.

SCOT: Suzuki Company of Toga, no date, no publisher. Referred to throughout as the SCOT book.

Senda, Akihiko, reviews of *The Trojan Women, The Bacchae, Sweeney Todd* and others in *The Voyage of Contemporary Japanese Theatre*, University of Hawaii Press, Honolulu, 1997.

Suzuki, Tadashi, *The Way of Acting – The Theatre Writings of Tadashi Suzuki*, translated by J. Thomas Rimer, Theatre Communications Group, New York, 1986. Originally published in 1984 in Japanese by Parco, Tokyo, as *Ekkyo suru chikara* (The Power of Transgression).

——'Culture is the Body' in *Interculturalism and Performance – writings from PAJ*, Bonnie Marranca and Gautam Dasgupta (eds), PAJ Publications, New York, 1991. Also reproduced in Phillip Zarrilli (ed), *Acting (Re)considered*, Routledge, London, 1995.

Related Background Reading

Barba, Eugenio, *The Paper Canoe*, Routledge, London, 1995.

Barba, Eugenio and Nicola Savarese (eds), *The Secret Art of the Performer: Dictionary of Theatre Anthropology*, Routledge, London, 1991.

Barthes, Roland, *Empire of Signs*, translated by Richard Howard, Hill and Wang, New York, 1982.

Blau, Herbert, *To All Appearances: Ideology and Performance*, Routledge, London, 1992.

Bowers, Faubion, *Japanese Theatre*, Charles E. Tuttle Company, Tokyo, 1974 (first edition, Hermitage House, New York, 1952).

Brandon, James, 'Contemporary Japanese Theatre: Intraculturalism and Interculturalism' in *The Dramatic Touch of Difference*, Erika Fischer-Lichte, Josephine Riley and Michael Gissenwehrer (eds), Gunter Narr Verlag, Tubingen, 1990.

Cameron, Neil, *The Running and Stamping Book*, Currency Press, Sydney, 1995.

Ernst, Earle, *The Kabuki Theatre*, University of Hawaii Press, Honolulu, 1974 (first published OUP, 1956).

Fensham, Rachel and Peter Eckersall (eds), *Dis/Orientations – Cultural Praxis in Theatre: Asia, Pacific, Australia*, Monash Theatre Papers 1, Monash University, 1999.

Goodman, David, *Japanese Drama and Culture in the 1960s: The Return of the Gods*, an East Gate Book, M. E. Sharpe, London, 1988.

——*After Apocalypse: Four Japanese Plays of Hiroshima and Nagasaki* (ed and trans), Columbia University Press, New York, 1986 (includes *The Elephant* by Betsuyaku Minoru).

Havens, Thomas H., *Artist and Patron in Postwar Japan: Dance, Music, Theater, and the Visual Arts, 1955–1980*, Princeton University Press, New Jersey, 1982.

Isozaki, Arata, 'Of City, Nation and Style' in *Postmodernism and Japan*, Masao Miyoshi and H. D. Harootunian (eds), Duke University Press, Durham, 1989.

Kennedy, Dennis (ed), *Foreign Shakespeare*, Cambridge University Press, 1993.

Leiter, Samuel L., *The Great Stage Directors: 100 Distinguished Careers of the Theatre*, Facts on File, New York, 1994.

Merleau-Ponty, Maurice, *Phenomenology of Perception*, Routledge and Kegan Paul, London, 1962.

Minami, Ryuta, Ian Carruthers and John Gillies (eds), *Performing Shakespeare in Japan*, Cambridge University Press, 2001.

On the Art of the No Drama – The Major Treatises of Zeami, translated by J. Thomas Rimer and Yamazaki Masakazu, University of Princeton Press, New Jersey, 1984.

Ortolani, Benito, *The Japanese Theatre: From Shamanistic Ritual to Contemporary Pluralism*, originally E. J. Brill, Leiden, Netherlands, 1990, revised edition with new preface, Princeton University Press, New Jersey, 1995.

Pavis, Patrice, *The Intercultural Performance Reader*, Routledge, 1996.

Rolf, Robert T. and John K. Gillespie (eds) *Alternative Japanese Drama*, including a foreword by J. Thomas Rimer, 'A Brief Overview' by Yasunari Takahashi and *The Little Match Girl* by Betsuyaku Minoru, University of Hawaii Press, Honolulu, 1992.

Russell Brown, John, *New Sites for Shakespeare: Theatre, the audience and Shakespeare*, Routledge, London, 1999.

Said, Edward W., *Culture and Imperialism*, Chatto & Windus, London, 1993.

Smethurst, Mae, *The Artistry of Aeschylus and Zeami*, Princeton University Press, New Jersey, 1989.

Takaya, Ted T. (ed and trans) *Modern Japanese Drama: An Anthology*, Columbia University Press, New York, 1979.

Waley, Arthur, *The Noh Plays of Japan*, Allen & Unwin, London, 1921.

Newspapers, Journals, Reports, Theses and Others

Allain, Paul, 'Coming Home: The New Ecology of the Gardzienice Theatre Association of Poland', *Drama Review,* Vol. 39, No. 1, T145, Spring 1995.

——'Suzuki Training', *Drama Review*, Vol. 42, No. 1, T157, Spring 1998.

——'Suzuki training – an introductory file', CD-ROM and Video, Arts Archives – the Fifth Series, Exeter, December 2000.

Beeman, William O., 'Tadashi Suzuki's Universal Vision', *Performing Arts Journal*, Vol. 5, No. 2, 1982.

Billington, Michael, 'High Performance Suzuki', *Guardian*, London, April 1985.

——'King of Rages', *Guardian*, 11 November 1994.

Brandon, James, 'A New World: Asian Theatre in the West Today', *Drama Review*, Vol. 33, No. 2, T122, Summer 1989.

——'Time and Tradition in Modern Japanese Theatre', *Asian Theatre Journal*, Vol. 2, No. 1, Spring 1985.

——'Training at the Waseda Little Theatre: The Suzuki Method', *Drama Review*, Vol. 22, No. 4, T80, Workshop Issue, December 1978.

Coen, Stephanie, 'The Body is the Source: four actors explore the rigors of working with Master Teachers Anne Bogart and Tadashi Suzuki', *American Theatre*, January 1995.

Emmert, Richard, 'Training of the No Performer', *Theatre Research International*, Vol. 12, No. 2, Summer 1987.

——'No: Its non-Japanese Possibilities' in A. Horie-Webber (ed), *Contemporary Theatre Review: An Independent Journal*, Vol. 1, Part 2, Harwood Academic Publishers, 1994.

'Fragments of Glass: A Conversation between Hijikata Tatsumi and Suzuki Tadashi', moderated by Akihiko Senda, originally from 1977, *Drama Review*, Vol. 44, No. 1, T165, Spring 2000. This issue contains several other pieces on contemporary Japanese theatre.

Goodman, David, 'New Japanese Theatre', *Drama Review*, Vol. 15, No. 3, T50, Spring 1971. This issue includes Suzuki on *kabuki*.

Goto, Yukihiro, 'The Theatrical Fusion of Suzuki Tadashi', *Asian Theatre Journal*, Vol. 6, No. 2, 1989.

——'Suzuki Tadashi: Innovator of Japanese Theatre', Ph.D. Dissertation, University of Hawaii, Honolulu, 1988.

Hironori, Terasaki, 'Trends in the Japanese Theatrical World', *Asian Theatre Journal*, Vol. 1, No. 1, Spring 1984.

Hoff, Frank, 'Suzuki Tadashi Directs *The Trojan Women*', *Theatre*, Vol. 11, No. 3, 1980.

——'Killing the Self: How the Narrator Acts', *Asian Theatre Journal*, Vol. 2, No. 1, Spring 1985.

Hoff, Frank and David Goodman, 'Suzuki Tadashi – The Sum of Interior Angles', (translation of part of *Naikaku no wa*, Jiritsu Shobo, Tokyo, 1973), *Canadian Theatre Review*, Fall 1978.

Holmberg, Arthur, 'The Liberation of Lear', *American Theatre*, Vol. 5, July/August 1988.

Kanze, Hideo, 'Noh: Business and Art – An Interview with Kanze Hideo', *Drama Review*, Vol. 15, No. 3, T50, Spring 1971.

Kawamura, Takeshi, 'New Ideas, in/for Japanese Theatre' in an interview by Carol Martin, *Drama Review*, Vol. 44, No. 1, T165, Spring 2000.

Kirby, Victoria Nes, 'World Theatre Festival – Nancy' including a review of *On the Dramatic Passions II, Drama Review*, Vol. 17, No. 4, T60, 1973.

Kitazawa, Masakuni, 'The Twilight of a Tradition', *Drama Review*, Vol. 39, No. 2, T146, Summer 1995.

Koto, Shizuko, 'Tadashi Suzuki: His Theory of Theater and Method of Training Actors', Masters Thesis, University of California, Los Angeles, 1985.

Kowsar, Mohammed, '*The Tale of Lear*', Theatre Review in *Theatre Journal*, Vol. 41, No. 1, 1989.

Kustow, Michael, 'Shakespeare's Little England', *Independent*, 19 November 1994.

Lampe, Eelke, 'Collaboration and Cultural Clashing: Anne Bogart and Tadashi Suzuki's Saratoga International Theatre Institute', *Drama Review*, Vol. 37, No. 1, T137, Spring 1993.

Marton, Patricia, '*The Trojan Women* in Japan,' Theatre Review in *Drama Review*, Vol. 19, No. 1, T65, March 1975.

McDonald, Marianne, 'The Madness that Makes Sane: Mania in Tadashi Suzuki's *Dionysus*', *Theatre Forum*, Vol. 4, No. 1, 1994.

Myerscough, Marie, 'East Meets West in the Art of Tadashi Suzuki', *American Theatre*, Vol. 2, No. 10, 1986.

Nightingale, Benedict, 'Pretension in slow motion', *The Times*, 11 November 1994.

'Plays to catch the conscience', Adrian Noble in conversation with Alan Franks, *The Times*, 25 October 1994.

Popham, Peter, 'The Hills are Alive: How Experimental Theatre Gave a Dying Village Back its Hope', WINDS, August 1985.

Pronko, Leonard, '*The Chronicle of Macbeth*', Theatre Review in *Theatre Journal*, Vol. 45, No. 1, March 1993.

Rolf, Robert T., 'Tokyo Theatre 1990', *Asian Theatre Journal*, Vol. 9, No. 1, Spring 1992.

Senda, Akihiko, 'Metamorphoses in Contemporary Japanese Theatre: Life-size and More-than-life-size' (Orientation Seminars on Japan: No. 22 for The Japan Foundation, Tokyo, a report with no date).

——'The Wider World for Japanese Theatre: The Art of Tadashi Suzuki', translated by Jordan Sand, Japan Society Newsletter, June 1991 (no page numbers), reproduced in the SCOT book.

Serper, Zvi, 'JSC Lecture-Demonstration Reports – The Waseda Sho-gekijo', unknown publisher of internal report, March 1983.

Takahashi, Yasunari, 'Tradition and Experiment in Contemporary Japanese Theatre' in A. Horie-Webber (ed), *Contemporary Theatre Review: An Independent Journal*, Vol. 1, Part 2, Harwood Academic Publishers, 1994.

Thornbury, Barbara, 'From Festival Setting to Center Stage: Preserving Japan's Folk Performing Arts', *Asian Theatre Journal*, Vol. 10, No. 2, 1993.

Uchino, Tadashi, 'Images of Armageddon: Japan's 1980s Theatre Culture', *Drama Review*, Vol. 44, No. 1, T165, Spring 2000.

Webography

http://members.optusnet.com.au/~zenzenzo/
http://ozfrank.com/Frank_flash.htm
http://www.arttowermito.or.jp/
http://www.nsknet.or.jp/togapk/
http://www.shizuoka.ntt.co.jp/wnn-c/saihakken/suzukiE/suzuki2.html
http://www.siti.org/
http://www.spac.or.jp/

Videos

Asian Theatre Series, produced by Instructional Media Center, Michigan State University, Michigan:

—*Kabuki Acting Techniques 1: The Body*, presented by Leonard Pronko, 1980.

—*Kabuki for Western Actors and Directors*, presented by Leonard Pronko, 1980.

—*Acting Techniques of the Noh Theatre of Japan*, presented by Akira Matsui, 1980.

Japan Live Performance, produced by Koninek Projects for Channel Four, including brief section on Suzuki (date not known).

Japan – The Land and its People: The Tradition of Performing Arts in Japan, The artistry of *Kabuki, Noh and Bunraku*, produced by Shin-Ei Inc., Japan, 1989.

Personal copies of Tadashi Suzuki's *Clytemnestra, Dionysus, Electra, Greetings from the Edges of the Earth, Ivanov, The Tale of Lear, The Trojan Women*.

Further visual material on the training appears in the CD-ROM and video package 'Suzuki training – an introductory file' produced by Peter Hulton of Arts Archives, Exeter, December 2000.

NOTES

•

ONE. INTRODUCING SUZUKI

1 Masao Miyoshi and H.D. Harootunian (eds), *Postmodernism and Japan*, Duke University Press, Durham, 1989, p. 148.

2 From an unpublished interview with Adrian Noble at the Barbican, recorded by the author as part of the 'Everybody's Shakespeare International Festival', 10 November 1994.

3 Thomas H. Havens, *Artist and Patron in Postwar Japan: Dance, Music, Theater, and the Visual Arts, 1955–1980*, Princeton University Press, 1982, p. 16.

4 Yasunari Takahashi in Robert T. Rolf and John K. Gillespie (eds), *Alternative Japanese Drama*, University of Hawaii Press, Honolulu, 1992, p. 5.

5 *Osanai Kaoru zenshu*, Vol. 6, Rinsen shoten, Kyoto, 1975, pp. 459–60. This is quoted in David Goodman, 'The Post-Shingeki Theatre Movement in Japan' in Colby H. Kullman and William C. Young (eds), *Theatre Companies of the World: Africa, Asia, Australia and New Zealand, Canada, Eastern Europe, Latin America, The Middle East, Scandinavia*, Westport, CT, Greenwood, 1986, p. 111.

6 Yasunari Takahashi, 'Suzuki's work in the Context of Japanese Theater' in the SCOT book, pp. 20–21.

7 David Goodman gives an excellent account of the implications of *shingeki*'s fight for survival in his 'The Post-Shingeki Theatre Movement in Japan' in Colby H. Kullman and William C. Young (eds), *Theatre Companies of the World: Africa, Asia, Australia and New Zealand, Canada, Eastern Europe, Latin America, The Middle East, Scandinavia*, Westport, CT, Greenwood, 1986, pp. 111–4.

8 Cited in Akihiko Senda, *The Voyage of Contemporary Japanese Theatre*, University of Hawaii Press, Honululu, 1997, p. 4.

9 Cited in 'The Wider World for Japanese Theatre: The Art of Tadashi Suzuki' by Akihiko Senda, translated by Jordan Sand, Japan Society Newsletter, June 1991, in the SCOT book, pp. 58–9.

10 Samuel L. Leiter, *The Great Stage Directors: 100 Distinguished Careers of the Theatre*, Facts on File, New York, 1994, p. 284.

11 Yukihiro Goto, 'The Theatrical Fusion of Suzuki Tadashi', *Asian Theatre Journal*, Vol. 6, No. 2, 1989, p. 106. Originally from Akihiko Senda's '*Shogekijo no zohansha-tachi*' ('The Rebels of the Little Theatre'), *Bijutsu Techo*, May 1970.

12 Akihiko Senda, *The Voyage of Contemporary Japanese Theatre*, University of Hawaii Press, Honululu, 1997, p. 4.

13 Cited in James Brandon, 'Training at the Waseda Little Theatre: The Suzuki Method', *Drama Review*, Vol. 22, No. 4, T80, Workshop Issue, December 1978, p. 34.

14 James Brandon, 'Time and Tradition in Modern Japanese Theatre', *Asian Theatre Journal*, Vol. 2, No. 1, Spring 1985, p. 74.

15 Thomas H. Havens, *Artist and Patron in Postwar Japan: Dance, Music, Theater, and the Visual Arts, 1955-1980*, Princeton University Press, New Jersey, 1982, p. 10.

16 Ibid., p. 8.

17 *Engeki to wa nani ka (What is theatre?)* in an unpublished translation by Kameron Steele and others, Iwanami Shoten, Tokyo, 1988, no page numbers.

18 Cited in Yukihiro Goto, 'Suzuki Tadashi: Innovator of Japanese Theatre', Ph.D. Dissertation, University of Hawaii, Honolulu, 1988, pp. 121–2. Originally from a discussion between Suzuki and Betsuyaku in Takahashi Hidemoto, Matsumoto Yoshiko and Saito Ikuko (eds), *On the Dramatic Passions: Suzuki and his World*, Kosakusha, Tokyo, 1977, p. 48.

19 Cited in Yukihiro Goto, 'Suzuki Tadashi: Innovator of Japanese Theatre', Ph.D. Dissertation, University of Hawaii, Honolulu, 1988, p. 121. Originally from Tsuka Kohei, 'Plays and Players: Nostalgic Feeling for Tadashi Suzuki', *Shingeki*, October 1972, p. 41.

20 *Engeki to wa nani ka (What is theatre?)* in an unpublished translation by Kameron Steele and others, Iwanami Shoten, Tokyo, 1988, no page numbers.

21 To learn more about Suzuki's specific borrowings from traditional Japanese performance, see especially Frank Hoff, 'Killing the Self: How the Narrator Acts', *Asian Theatre Journal*, Vol. 2, No. 1, Spring 1985, and Yukihiro Goto, 'The Theatrical Fusion of Suzuki Tadashi', *Asian Theatre Journal*, Vol. 6, No. 2, 1989.

22 Thomas H. Havens, *Artist and Patron in Postwar Japan: Dance, Music, Theater, and the Visual Arts, 1955–1980*, Princeton University Press, 1982, p. 70–71.

23 Earle Ernst, *The Kabuki Theatre*, University of Hawaii Press, Honolulu, 1974 (first published OUP, 1956), p. 75.

TWO: SUZUKI NOW

1 Tadashi Suzuki, *The Way of Acting – The Theatre Writings of Tadashi Suzuki*, Theatre Communications Group, New York, 1986, p. 97.

2 Carol Martin, 'Japanese Theatre 1960s–Present', *Drama Review*, Vol. 44, No. 1, T165, Spring 2000, p. 84.

3 James Brandon, 'Training at the Waseda Little Theatre: The Suzuki Method', *Drama Review*, Vol. 22, No. 4, T80, Workshop Issue, December 1978, p. 33.

4 Eelke Lampe, 'Collaboration and Cultural Clashing: Anne Bogart and Tadashi Suzuki's Saratoga International Theatre Institute', *Drama Review*, Vol. 37, No. 1, T137, Spring 1993, p. 151.

5 Tadashi Uchino, 'Images of Armageddon: Japan's 1980s Theatre Culture', *Drama Review*, Vol. 44, No. 1, T165, Spring 2000.

6 Peter Eckersall, 'Japan as Dystopia: Kawamura Takeshi's Daisan Erotica', *Drama Review*, Vol. 44, No. 1, T165, Spring 2000, p. 97. Senda's comment is from *The Voyage of the Contemporary Japanese Theatre*, University of Hawaii Press, Honolulu, 1997, p. 10.

7 See Masakuni Kitazawa, 'The Twilight of a Tradition', *Drama Review*, Vol. 39, No. 2, T146, Summer 1995, pp. 112–3, for such a disparaging analysis.

8 Carol Fisher Sorgenfrei, 'Deadly Love', *Contemporary Theatre Review: An Independent Journal*, Vol. 1, Part 2, Harwood Academic Publishers, 1994, p. 78. See also Misako Koike, 'Breaking the Mold: Women in Japanese Theatre', *American Theatre*, April 1997.

9 Suzuki, cited in *Anne Bogart Viewpoints*, Smith and Kraus Inc., Lyme, NH, 1995, p. 85.

10 For such a definition, see, for example, Michael Billington in 'Heirs of Pirandello' in the *Guardian*, 10 March 1999.

11 Earle Ernst, *The Kabuki Theatre*, University of Hawaii Press, Honolulu, 1974 (first published OUP, 1956), p. 194.

12 Janet Goodridge, *Rhythm and Timing of Movement in Performance*, Jessica Kingsley Publishers, London, 1999, p. 38.

13 Brian Logan in the *Guardian*, 7 September 1996.

14 Alastair Macaulay in the *Financial Times*, 6 September 1996.

15 Tadashi Suzuki, *The Way of Acting – The Theatre Writings of Tadashi Suzuki*, Theatre Communications Group, New York, 1986, p. 7.

16 'Kawamura Takeshi: New Ideas in/for Japanese Theatre – an interview by Carol Martin', *Drama Review*, Vol. 44, No. 1, T165, Spring 2000, p. 110.

THREE: SUZUKI'S SPACES

1 Tadashi Suzuki, *The Way of Acting – The Theatre Writings of Tadashi Suzuki*, Theatre Communications Group, New York, 1986, p. 73.

2 Ibid.

3 This performance is reviewed by Senda in a piece titled 'The No Stage, Newly Activated' in *The Voyage of Contemporary Japanese Theatre*, University of Hawaii Press, Honolulu, 1997.

4 Tadashi Suzuki, *The Way of Acting – The Theatre Writings of Tadashi Suzuki*, Theatre Communications Group, New York, 1986, p. 36.

5 Barbara Thornbury, 'From Festival Setting to Center Stage: Preserving Japan's Folk Performing Arts', *Asian Theatre Journal*, Vol. 10, No. 2, 1993.

6 Suzuki, cited in David Tracey, 'The Theater of Suzuki', *The Imperial*, Spring 1989, in the SCOT book, p. 70.

7 Akihiko Senda, 'A First Trip to a Distant Village' in *The Voyage of Contemporary Japanese Theatre*, University of Hawaii Press, Honolulu, 1997.

8 Ibid., p. 65.

9 Tadashi Suzuki, *The Way of Acting – The Theatre Writings of Tadashi Suzuki*, Theatre Communications Group, New York, 1986, p. 70.

10 Ibid., p. 73.

11 Marianne McDonald, *Ancient Sun, Modern Light: Greek Drama on the Modern Stage*, Columbia University Press, New York, 1992, p. 26.

12 Yukihiro Goto, 'Suzuki Tadashi: Innovator of Japanese Theatre', Ph.D.

Dissertation, University of Hawaii, Honolulu, 1988, p. 291.

13 Suzuki, cited in David Tracey 'The Theater of Suzuki', *The Imperial*, Spring 1989, in the SCOT book, pp. 69–70.

14 Tadashi Suzuki, *The Way of Acting – The Theatre Writings of Tadashi Suzuki*, Theatre Communications Group, New York, 1986, pp. 100–1.

15 Ibid., p.99.

16 Art Tower Mito promotional leaflet. No page numbers.

17 Isozaki cited in http://www.arttowermito.or.jp/Tower/

18 Tadashi Suzuki, *The Way of Acting – The Theatre Writings of Tadashi Suzuki*, Theatre Communications Group, New York, 1986, p. 116.

19 Thomas R. Havens, *Artist and Patron in Postwar Japan: Dance, Music, Theater, and the Visual Arts, 1955–1980*, Princeton University Press, Princeton, 1982, p. 85.

20 SPAC facilities booklet, no page numbers.

21 Ibid.

22 Suzuki, cited in Shizuoka's web site http://www.shizuoka.ntt.co.jp/wnn-c/saihakken/suzukiE/suzuki2.html.

23 Tadashi Suzuki, *The Way of Acting – The Theatre Writings of Tadashi Suzuki*, Theatre Communications Group, New York, 1986, p. 87.

24 Marc Augé, *Non-Places: Introduction to an Anthropology of Supermodernity*, translated by John Howe, Verso, London, 1995.

25 Tadashi Suzuki, *The Way of Acting – The Theatre Writings of Tadashi Suzuki*, Theatre Communications Group, New York, 1986, pp. 40–1.

26 Ibid., p. 12.

27 Ibid., p. 80.

28 Ibid., p. 85.

29 Ibid., p. 91.

FOUR: THE SUZUKI METHOD

1 Richard Emmert, 'Training of the No Performer', *Theatre Research International*, Vol. 12, No. 2, Summer 1987, p. 132.

2 See my article 'Suzuki Training', *Drama Review*, T157, Spring 1998.

3 See Tadashi Suzuki, *The Way of Acting – The Theatre Writings of Tadashi Suzuki*, Theatre Communications Group, New York, 1986, pp. 8–9.

4 Richard Emmert, 'No: Its Non-Japanese Possibilities' in *Contemporary Theatre Review: An Independent Journal*, Vol. 1, Part 2, Harwood Academic Publishers, 1994, p. 139.

5 Suzuki, cited in Shizuko Koto, 'Tadashi Suzuki: His Theory of Theater and Method of Training Actors', Masters Thesis, University of California, Los Angeles, 1985, p. 91. Originally from Tadashi Suzuki and Yujiro Nakamura, *The Dramatic Language*, Hakusui-Sha, Tokyo, 1981, p. 131.

6 Zvi Serper, unpublished 'JSC Lecture-Demonstration Reports – The Waseda Sho-gekijo', March 1983, p. 5.

7 *Engeki to wa nani ka* (*What is theatre?*) in an unpublished translation by Kameron

Steele and others, Iwanami Shoten, Tokyo, 1988, no page numbers.

8 Suzuki in the SCOT book, p. 56.

9 Suzuki, cited in Shizuko Koto, 'Tadashi Suzuki: His Theory of Theater and Method of Training Actors', Masters Thesis, University of California, Los Angeles, 1985, p. 62. Originally from Tadashi Suzuki, *The Cozening Horizon*, Hakusuki-Sha, Tokyo, 1981, p. 230.

10 Tadashi Suzuki, *The Way of Acting – The Theatre Writings of Tadashi Suzuki*, Theatre Communications Group, New York, 1986, p. 45.

11 Suzuki, cited in Shizuko Koto, 'Tadashi Suzuki: His Theory of Theater and Method of Training Actors', Masters Thesis, University of California, Los Angeles, 1985, p. 53. Originally from Tadashi Suzuki, '*The Sum of The Interior Angles*' translation of part of *Naikaku no wa*, Jiritsu Shobo, Tokyo, 1973, p. 62.

12 Tadashi Suzuki, *The Way of Acting – The Theatre Writings of Tadashi Suzuki*, Theatre Communications Group, New York, 1986, p. 50.

13 Suzuki, cited in 'The Art of Tadashi Suzuki' by Akihiko Senda in the SCOT book, p. 58. Originally from Suzuki, *The Sum of the Interior Angles*, Jiritsu Shobo, 1973.

14 Kelly Maurer, cited in Stephanie Coen, 'The Body is the Source: Four actors explore the rigors of working with Master Teachers Anne Bogart and Tadashi Suzuki', *American Theatre*, January, 1995, p. 33.

15 Eelke Lampe, 'Collaboration and Cultural Clashing: Anne Bogart and Tadashi Suzuki's Saratoga International Theatre Institute', *Drama Review*, Vol. 37, T137, Spring 1993, p. 155.

16 *Engeki to wa nani ka* (*What is theatre?*) in an unpublished translation by Kameron Steele and others, Iwanami Shoten, Tokyo, 1988, no page numbers.

17 Suzuki in the SCOT book, p. 56.

18 Earle Ernst, *The Kabuki Theatre*, University of Hawaii Press, Honolulu, 1974, p. 165.

19 *Engeki to wa nani ka* (*What is theatre?*) in an unpublished translation by Kameron Steele and others, Iwanami Shoten, Tokyo, 1988, no page numbers.

20 Tadashi Suzuki, *The Way of Acting – The Theatre Writings of Tadashi Suzuki*, Theatre Communications Group, New York, 1986, p. 5.

21 Richard Emmert, 'No: Its non-Japanese Possibilities' in *Contemporary Theatre Review: An Independent Journal*, Vol. 1, Part 2, Harwood Academic Publishers, 1994, p. 139.

22 Tatsuji Iwabuchi, 'The Reception of Western Drama in Japan' in *The Dramatic Touch of Difference*, Erika Fischer-Lichte, Josephine Riley and Michael Gissenwehrer (eds), Gunter Narr Verlag, Tubingen, 1990, p. 127.

23 Michael Billington, 'High Performance Suzuki', *Guardian*, London, April 1985.

24 Tadashi Suzuki, *The Way of Acting – The Theatre Writings of Tadashi Suzuki*, Theatre Communications Group, New York, 1986, pp. 75–6.

25 Frank Hoff and David Goodman, 'Suzuki Tadashi – The Sum of Interior Angles', (translation of part of *Naikaku no wa*, Jiritsu Shobo, Tokyo, 1973), *Canadian Theatre Review*, Fall 1978, p. 24.

26 James Brandon, 'A New World: Asian Theatre in the West Today', *Drama Review*,

Vol. 33, No. 2, T122, Summer 1989, p. 44.

27 Suzuki, in Eelke Lampe, 'Collaboration and Cultural Clashing: Anne Bogart and Tadashi Suzuki's Saratoga International Theatre Institute', *Drama Review,* Vol. 37, T137, Spring 1993, p. 152.

28 Zvi Serper, unpublished 'JSC Lecture-Demonstration Reports – The Waseda Sho-gekijo', March 1983, p. 5.

29 James Brandon, 'Training at the Waseda Little Theatre; The Suzuki Method', *Drama Review,* T80, Workshop Issue, 1978, p. 30.

30 James Brandon, 'A New World: Asian Theatre in the West Today', *Drama Review,* Vol. 33, No. 2, T122, Summer 1989, p. 36.

FIVE: SUZUKI'S PERFORMANCE PRACTICE

1 Yukihiro Goto's doctoral thesis is an indispensable archive for the first half of Suzuki's theatrical career, which I have used gratefully. See 'Suzuki Tadashi: Innovator of Japanese Theatre', Ph.D. Dissertation from the University of Hawaii, Honolulu, 1988. There is also some detail in a short synopsis in David Goodman's 'The Post-Shingeki Theatre Movement in Japan' in Colby H. Kullman and William C. Young (eds), *Theatre Companies of the World: Africa, Asia, Australia and New Zealand, Canada, Eastern Europe, Latin America, The Middle East, Scandinavia,* Westport, CT, Greenwood, 1986.

2 Suzuki, cited in Yukihiro Goto, 'Suzuki Tadashi: Innovator of Japanese Theatre', Ph.D. Dissertation, University of Hawaii, Honolulu, 1988, p. 52.

3 Suzuki, cited in Shizuko Koto, 'Tadashi Suzuki: His Theory of Theater and Method of Training Actors', Masters Thesis, University of California, Los Angeles, 1985, p. 37. Originally from Akihiko Senda (ed), *The Dramatic Renaissance,* Liverpoto, Tokyo, 1983, p. 160.

4 For more on Suzuki and *kabuki,* see *Drama Review,* Vol. 15, No. 3, T50, Spring 1971, pp. 183–4.

5 Akihiko Senda in 'Metamorphoses in Contemporary Japanese Theatre: Life-size and More-than-life-size' (Orientation Seminars on Japan: No. 22 for The Japan Foundation, Tokyo, a report with no date, p. 10) has noted that 'there is very little cooperation among the contemporary theatre groups in Japan. There is, unfortunately, a great deal of jealousy and petty quarrelling.' He locates this struggle in the pioneering 'passion' of the 'first generation' groups like WLT.

6 Yukihiro Goto, 'Suzuki Tadashi: Innovator of Japanese Theatre', Ph.D. Dissertation, University of Hawaii, Honolulu, 1988, p. 76.

7 Suzuki, cited in Shizuko Koto, 'Tadashi Suzuki: His Theory of Theater and Method of Training Actors', Masters Thesis, University of California, Los Angeles, 1985, p. 36. Originally from Masashi Miura, 'Mental Abnormality as a Method', *The World of Tadashi Suzuki,* No. 60, Shinsho-Sha, Tokyo, 1968, p. 82.

8 Surrealism was a key inspiration for Suzuki in the late 1960s and informed his collage-making process. See Chapter One for more detail, as well as Yukihiro

Goto, 'Suzuki Tadashi: Innovator of Japanese Theatre', Ph.D. Dissertation, University of Hawaii, Honolulu, 1988.

9 Akihiko Senda, 'The Wider World for Japanese Theatre: The Art of Tadashi Suzuki', translated by Jordan Sand, Japan Society Newsletter, June 1991 (no page numbers), in the SCOT book, p. 59.

10 L. D., 'Un Japonais à Paris – Les passions dramatiques de Suzuki', originally from Le Monde, May 1973, in the SCOT book, p. 24. My translation.

11 Claude Baigneres, 'Des Promoteurs pour un "théâtre de recherche"', originally from Le Figaro, May 1973, in the SCOT book, p. 23.

12 Tadashi Suzuki, The Way of Acting – The Theatre Writings of Tadashi Suzuki, Theatre Communications Group, New York, 1986, pp. 71–2.

13 Yasunari Takahashi, 'Suzuki's work in the Context of Japanese Theater' in the SCOT book, p. 21.

14 Victoria Nes Kirby, 'World Theatre Festival', Drama Review, Vol. 17, No. 4, 1973, p. 22.

15 Engeki to wa nani ka (What is theatre?) in an unpublished translation by Kameron Steele and others, Iwanami Shoten, Tokyo, 1988, no page numbers.

16 Almost nothing has been written (in English) about why Suzuki replaced Kanze with Shiraishi, although Yasunari Takahashi suggests it was to streamline the piece and therefore make it suitable for touring, while creating a stronger vehicle for Shiraishi's talents. See Yasunari Takahashi, 'Tradition and Experiment in Contemporary Japanese Theatre' in Contemporary Theatre Review: An Independent Journal, Vol. 1, Part 2, Harwood Academic Publishers, 1994.

17 Patricia Marton, 'The Trojan Women in Japan', Drama Review, Vol. 19, No. 1, T65, March 1975.

18 Michael Billington, 'High Performance Suzuki', Guardian, April 1985, in the SCOT book, p. 33.

19 Hideo Kanze, 'Noh: Business and Art – An Interview with Kanze Hideo', Drama Review, Vol. 15, No. 3, T50, Spring 1971, p. 189.

20 See, for example, pages 29–30 of The Paper Canoe by Eugenio Barba, Routledge, London, 1995, where he quotes Hideo Kanze.

21 Akihiko Senda, The Voyage of Contemporary Japanese Theatre, University of Hawaii Press, Honolulu, 1997, p. 50.

22 Michael Billington, 'High Performance Suzuki', Guardian, April 1985, in the SCOT book, p. 33.

23 Samuel L. Leiter, The Great Stage Directors: 100 Distinguished Careers of the Theatre, Facts on File, New York, 1994, p. 287.

24 Roderick Mason Faber, 'Bacchae in New York', Village Voice, June 1982, in the SCOT book, p. 30.

25 Marianne McDonald, Ancient Sun, Modern Light: Greek Drama on the Modern Stage, Columbia University Press, New York, 1992, p. 6.

26 Akihiko Senda, The Voyage of Contemporary Japanese Theatre, University of Hawaii Press, Honolulu, 1997, p. 85.

27 Tatsuji Iwabuchi, 'The Reception of Western Drama in Japan' in The Dramatic Touch of Difference, Erika Fischer-Lichte, Josephine Riley and Michael

Gissenwehrer (eds), Gunter Narr Verlag, Tubingen, 1990, p. 128.

28 Tadashi Suzuki, '*Dionysus*', SCOT book, p. 89.

29 Eelke Lampe, 'Collaboration and Cultural Clashing: Anne Bogart and Tadashi Suzuki's Saratoga International Theatre Institute', *Drama Review*, Vol. 37, T137, Spring 1993, p. 149.

30 Marie Myerscough, 'East Meets West in the Art of Tadashi Suzuki', *American Theatre*, Vol. 2, No. 10, 1986, p. 10. This reads: 'Suzuki's training is geared to push the body to its limits, and his actors are capable of remarkable feats.'

31 Sylvie Drake, 'Power and Elegance in Suzuki's *Clytemnestra*', *Los Angeles Times*, May 1986, in the SCOT book, p. 31.

32 John Flynn, 'A dramaturgy of madness: Suzuki and the *Oresteia*' in *Madness in Drama*, James Redmond (ed), CUP, 1993, p. 167.

33 Marianne McDonald, *Ancient Sun, Modern Light: Greek Drama on the Modern Stage*, Columbia University Press, New York, 1992, p. 48.

34 James Brandon, 'Time and Tradition in Modern Japanese Theatre', *Asian Theatre Journal*, Vol. 2, No. 1, Spring 1985, p. 76.

35 Tadashi Suzuki, *The Way of Acting – The Theatre Writings of Tadashi Suzuki*, Theatre Communications Group, New York, 1986, pp. 122–3.

36 Marie Myerscough, 'East Meets West in the Art of Tadashi Suzuki', *American Theatre*, Vol. 2, No. 10, 1986, p. 10.

37 Herbert Blau, *To All Appearances: Ideology and Performance*, Routledge, London, 1992, p. 180.

38 Mohammed Kowsar, *Theatre Journal*, Vol. 41, No. 1, 1989, p. 110.

39 Akihiko Senda, 'The Art of Tadashi Suzuki' in the SCOT book, p. 59.

40 Tadashi Suzuki in Kate Bassett, 'Finding Will by various ways', *The Times*, 25 October 1994.

41 J.R. Mulryne, 'The perils and profits of interculturalism and the theatre art of Tadashi Suzuki' in *Shakespeare and the Japanese Stage*, Takashi Sasayama, J.R. Mulryne and Margaret Shewring (eds), CUP, 1998, p. 85.

42 Michael Billington, 'King of Rages', *Guardian*, 11 November 1994.

43 Ted Hughes, quoted in Michael Kustow, 'Shakespeare's Little England', *Independent*, 19 November 1994.

44 Tetsuo Kishi, 'Japanese Shakespeare and English Reviewers' in *Shakespeare and the Japanese Stage*, Takashi Sasayama, J.R. Mulryne and Margaret Shewring (eds), CUP, 1998, pp. 110–23.

45 Ellen Lauren in Ian Carruthers, '*The Chronicle of Macbeth*: Suzuki Tadashi's Transformation of Shakespeare's *Macbeth*' in *Shakespeare – World Views*, Heather Kerr, Robin Eaden and Madge Mitton (eds), Associated University Press, Cranbury, New Jersey, 1996, p. 187.

46 James Brandon, 'Time and Tradition in Modern Japanese Theatre', *Asian Theatre Journal*, Vol. 2, No. 1, Spring 1985, p. 78.

47 Suzuki on Chekhov in the SCOT book, p. 42.

48 Erika Fischer-Lichte, 'Intercultural Aspects in Post-modern Theatre: a Japanese

NOTES

version of Chekhov's *Three Sisters'* in *The Play out of Context: Transforming Plays from Culture to Culture*, Hanna Scolnicov and Peter Holland (eds), CUP, 1989, p. 180.

49 *Engeki to wa nani ka* (*What is theatre?*) in an unpublished translation by Kameron Steele and others, Iwanami Shoten, Tokyo, 1988, no page numbers.

50 Yukihiro Goto, 'The Theatrical Fusion of Suzuki Tadashi', *Asian Theatre Journal*, Vol. 6, No. 2, 1989, p. 113. Regarding *noh* structures, Goto adds: 'In the first half an event takes place in the present with a wandering priest meeting an unfamiliar person. In the second half, this person reenacts a past event; the stranger whom the priest has met reveals his true identity to be that of a ghost or spirit, relives his past before the priest, and then disappears. Left alone, the priest wonders if what he has witnessed is a dream or reality.'

51 Akihiko Senda, *The Voyage of Contemporary Japanese Theatre*, University of Hawaii Press, Honolulu, 1997, p. 171.

AFTERWORD

1 Yasunari Takahashi, 'Suzuki's work in the Context of Japanese Theater' in the SCOT book, p. 21.

2 Rachel Fensham and Peter Eckersall (eds), *Dis/Orientations – Cultural Praxis in Theatre: Asia, Pacific, Australia*, Monash Theatre Papers 1, Monash University, 1999, p. 8

3 Tadashi Uchino, 'Images of Armageddon: Japan's 1980s Theatre Culture', *Drama Review*, Vol. 44, No. 1, T165, Spring 2000.

INDEX

•

INDEX

INDEX